Think, Care, Act

Teaching for a Peaceful Future

A volume in
Peace Education

Series Editors:
Ian Harris, *University of Wisconsin-Milwaukee*
Edward J. Brantmeier, *Colorado State University*
Jing Lin, *University of Maryland*

Peace Education

Ian Harris, Edward J. Brantmeier, and Jing Lin, Editors

Educating Toward a Culture of Peace (2006)
by Yaacov Iram

*Education of Minorities and
Peace Education in Pluralistic Societies* (2006)
by Yaacov Iram

Encyclopedia of Peace Education (2008)
edited by Monisha Bajaj

*Peace Education:
Exploring Ethical and Philosophical Foundations* (2008)
by James Page

Transforming Education for Peace (2008)
edited by Jing Lin, Edward J. Brantmeier, and Christa Bruhn

*For the People: A Documentary History of the Struggle for Peace and
Justice in the United States* (2009)
by Charles Howlett and Robbie Lieberman

*Books, Not Bombs:
Teaching Peace Since the Dawn of the Republic* (2010)
by Charles Howlett and Ian Harris

Spirituality, Religion, and Peace Education (2010)
edited by Edward J. Brantmeier, Jing Lin, and John P. Miller

Think, Care, Act: Teaching for a Peaceful Future (2011)
by Susan Gelber Cannon

Think, Care, Act

Teaching for a Peaceful Future

by

Susan Gelber Cannon
Episcopal Academy

Information Age Publishing, Inc.
Charlotte, North Carolina • www.infoagepub.com

Library of Congress Cataloging-in-Publication Data

Cannon, Susan Gelber.
Think, care, act : teaching for a peaceful future / Susan Gelber Cannon.
p. cm. -- (Peace Education series)
Includes bibliographical references and index.
ISBN 978-1-61735-426-7 (pbk.) -- ISBN 978-1-61735-427-4 (hc) --
ISBN 978-1-61735-428-1 (e-book)
1. Peace--Study and teaching. 2. Multicultural education. 3.
Education--Social aspects. I. Title.
JZ5534.C36 2011
303.6'6071--dc23

2011020336

CONTENTS

FOREWORD

Ian Harris

Every educator is a peace educator could be a true statement if more peace educators took their time to write down the steps that teachers can use to illuminate the rich realms of peace for their students. Peace can be taught in practically every discipline if teachers truly concerned about the fate of this planet and its inhabitants have resources like this book to guide them. Susan Cannon, a middle school teacher in suburban Philadelphia, has in *Think, Care, Act: Teaching for a Peaceful Future* provided concrete ways to teach young teenagers about peace.

The years 11-15 are ideal times to teach young people the benefits of learning how to behave peacefully. Youth that age are eager to learn about the world. Developmentally they are looking outwards at their horizons trying to figure out where they fit in a world that has gone mad with violence. They want to redress the suffering that occurs in their worlds because of cruel aggressive behavior. They are capable of being empathic and responding to the cries of those wounded by violence. They hope to live in a peaceful world so that they can realize their dreams. Their conceptual thinking becomes more complicated as they address issues like human rights, environmental sustainability, and the quest for a just world order. They want to live in a world free from prejudice and the suffering of innocents caused by war. Susan Cannon's pupils, like most children, look forward to building a better future (hence the universal appeal of this book).

Susan Cannon has what she understatedly calls a modest goal, "to change the prevailing belief in the inevitability of war." This goal is a challenging goal. If war was that easy to stop, every teacher would be a peace teacher. The ending of war is a struggle that humans throughout their history have addressed, often through education, teaching skills of nonviolent conflict resolution, arbitration, mediation, and reconciliation. Ms. Cannon teaches these and many more aspects of peacekeeping, peacemaking, and peacebuilding to her students. She also teaches critical thinking skills; works with her students to set ground rules for how they should treat each other throughout the school year; challenges them to articulate their feelings about race; builds a caring classroom that promotes compassionate behavior; encourages them to use respectful speech; urges them to assess their consumption of popular media; involves them in service learning projects where young people learn how to be good citizens on this planet; helps them envision a culture of peace; and prompts them to act upon principles of justice.

This book is divided into three main sections: think, care, and act. Each chapter has a description of interesting lessons and activities for middle-school-aged pupils. In addition Susan Cannon explains how to use resources outside her room like the student council, debate club, and the Model UN to sophisticate students' thinking about the complex challenges of creating a peaceful world. She explains how to engage students in lessons about violence in their lives and how to respond nonviolently to conflicts and problems. She provides at the end of each chapter reflection questions for the reader.

The author of *Think, Care, Act* is well aware that teaching about peace challenges students to think through and replace many violence promoting prowar messages young people receive from the culture. She is concerned that her students can not easily conceive of a culture of peace, although they can readily imagine the culture of war like the one they live in—replete with violent media, news, games, and history lessons that extol the conquest of the "other." Her sophisticated understanding of how to address these complex issues will help other teachers choosing to grapple with these difficult challenges. If more teachers follow the guidelines she provides in this book, every student can learn about peace.

ACKNOWLEDGMENTS AND HEARTFELT THANKS

Over decades of learning and teaching as a student and colleague, I have gained inspiration and knowledge from teachers. I thank all those who have shared knowledge with me over the course of my lifetime—as my teachers and friends. As I further reflect on my approaches to teaching kids to think, care, and act, I have built my philosophy using input from the true experts—the students I have taught. To them I am grateful, every day.

Thanks to the Peace Education Series Editors at Information Age Publishing who saw the potential in this book: Ian Harris, Ed Brantmeier, and Jing Lin. Their wise suggestions have made my voice for peace education stronger and clearer. I especially appreciate Ian Harris's contributions, both as editor and as the scholar on whose work I built my initial peace-education efforts. I am honored by his generous foreword. Thanks to George Johnson, Sarah Williams, and the Information Publishing staff for efficient and flexible help. Thanks to the editors of *Friends Journal* who published portions of the *Introduction* and *Afterword* in the March 2009 issue. Thanks to Tom Lickona, Phil Vincent, Ian Harris, Matt Newcomb, Heather Dupont, Cynthia Stern, Christine Weiss Daugherty and Chuck Daugherty, Anne Morrison Welsh and Bob Welsh, Usha Balamore, Marie Ellen Larcada, and anonymous reviewers who read early drafts. Your insightful suggestions have made the book better. Thanks to Kathy Hirsh-Pasek and Tom Lickona for advice through the process. Indeed, Tom's early enthusiasm helped me begin this project in earnest, and the enthusiasm of my gifted colleagues Matt and Heather kept me going.

At the Episcopal Academy, I am fortunate to have colleagues and friends who make it fun to come to school! Thanks to Linda Lew, Lisa Fox, and Charles Collins for technical help and steadfast support. Charles took delight in helping me edit the photos in this book, seeing the importance of bringing the classroom strategies I described to visual life for readers. Thanks to Mike Letts and the legal and administrative staff at the Episcopal Academy who helped me obtain parental consents and other important information. Thanks to Brian Hecker for website assistance and Cathy Hall and Paul Merchant for computer help. Thanks to the parents of my students who saw promise in this project and supported me with consent forms, notes, and enthusiasm. Food and friendship kept me energized during long days of editing after school, and I thank the gracious and talented cafeteria staff for their friendship and delicious support.

I have had the good fortune to have my teaching enhanced by energetic, knowledgeable, generous, and creative colleagues with whom I have collaborated over many years. They have helped form my talent and outlook as a teacher. Foremost among them are Usha Balamore and Crissy Cáceres, along with Heather Dupont, Melissa Goins, Andy Hess, Charles Hollinger, Roberta Howlin, Naomi Knecht, Susan LaPalombara, Dorie Leahy, Linda Lew, Mark Luff, Fran McLaughlin, Matthew Newcomb, Kim Piersall, Courtney Portlock, Laura Russell, Steve Ramirez, Kris Ryan, Lauren Smith, Linda Smith, John Spofford, Susan Swanson, Angela Womack, Wei Yang, Bert Zug; and other members of the *A-Team*, Lower, Middle, and Upper School faculties and staff among numerous others. Administrators such as Ham Clark, Jay Crawford, Mark Devey, Anna Hadgis, Jackie Hamilton, Mindy Hong, Steve Morris, and Jo Walker supported and encouraged my initiatives, with Steve and Jo going above and beyond in helping me fulfill my vision of education. The Episcopal Academy has afforded me the opportunity to teach eager students and to experiment and extend the boundaries of the classroom to the global community. I am particularly grateful for the opportunity, through my sabbatical award in 2005-2006 (and as a Faculty International Travel and Study Fellow in 2010), to have taught in China, Japan, Canada, Denmark, and the United States. These experiences have enriched my global understanding and stimulated my hope in the strength and potential for peace education.

I would not be the person and teacher I am today without the loving nurture of my friends and family. Sufi sage Bawa Muhaiyadeen embraced the world's "funny family" and modeled how to lovingly and wisely teach a room full of people with different interests, levels of understanding, and needs. Among the people in that room are lifelong friends who are like brothers and sisters to me, asking meaning-of-life questions together. I also thank my own brother, Richard, and sister-in-law, Cheryl, who are lifelong sources of friendship and support. Friends in the Saranac Lake Quaker Meeting have shared encouraging and enthusiastic conversations about peace and global citizenship as well.

Both of my parents provided me with the security of a loving home, a lifelong love of learning, and the love of all kinds of people that fuels my work for peace. My mother, Sylvia, buoys me with unfaltering confidence and pride and shows me the true power of a mother's love, patience, and acceptance. My father, Fred, introduced me to the wide world of people, teaching me how he cheerfully made friends with everyone he met—even as he experienced the inner torment of a veteran. My son, Bajir, has been a steadfast and creative source of support and enthusiasm, reminding me that the travel is hard, but the journey has its reward. I wish him and Maki the best of adventures as they become a global family. My son, Lateef, has been an unwavering and honest critic and advisor, teaching me about what works with kids in the classroom and life. I know he will heal both hearts and bodies as he works to infuse equity and compassion into health care.

From puppeteering to peace activism, my husband, artist J. Kadir Cannon, has literally been by my side for the entire journey. His parents, Phyllis and Vernon, were the first couple to show me how to live an alternative lifestyle as Kadir and I embarked on ours. Kadir painted the beautiful vision of peace that graces the front cover of this book and the anguished antiwar art in the introduction. Kadir's devotion to peace, his humility, his creative vision and talent, his perseverance despite obstacles, his curmudgeonly love of humanity, and his encouragement and love are lifelong treasures that nourish me as we work for the unseen harvest together. Peace.

INTRODUCTION

Teaching Students to Think, Care, and Act for a Peaceful Future

"I had a modest goal when I became a teacher ... I wanted to change the world."

—Howard Zinn (in Ellis & Mueller, 2004:
Howard Zinn—You Can't be Neutral on a Moving Train)

"A culture of peace will be achieved when citizens of the world understand global problems; have the skills to resolve conflict constructively; know and live by international standards of human rights, gender and racial equality; appreciate cultural diversity; and respect the integrity of the Earth. Such learning can not be achieved without intentional, sustained and systematic education for peace."

—Global Campaign for Peace Education, 1999

"War is hell. I don't wish it on my best friends or my worst enemy. May my children, and my grandchildren, and my great-grandchildren be spared from it, forever. Amen."

—Private First Class Fred Gelber
(Personal interview, November 23, 2000)

Figure 1.   Private First Class Fred Gelber, 1945, Italy.

I believe in the culture of peace. I believe in daily peace building on a personal, institutional, national, and international level. I believe in regular, not random, acts of kindness. I believe in the power of teachers and students to be peace builders.

In many ways, my journey to becoming a peace educator started at home with my father, Fred.

LESSONS FROM MY FATHER

From my earliest memories, I can see images of my father in uniform. There were the tiny photographs (fading even in my childhood) that he shot in Italy in World War II. There he was holding up the Leaning Tower of Pisa or posing with a buddy in a foxhole. In my memory, I can hear the stories, often funny, of how he and a buddy jumped waist-deep into a pigpen under orders to take cover, of getting stranded up a telephone pole when he was stringing wire as his jeep buddies sped away under German fire. My father told these stories over and over again, and they always ended with his loud belly laughs, as if he were trying to persuade us that the war had been fun.

But, I also hear the screaming. My father screamed in his sleep often, sometimes nightly, especially after watching a war movie. "Don't let him watch it," my mother would plead. "He'll fight the war all night if he does." But my dad always wanted to watch; it was as if he had to. He paid for each viewing with refreshed images in his nightmares. He would awaken my mom as he kicked and twitched, flailed and yelled, working the covers off his bruised and purple legs, battle-scarred and discolored from freezing in the Italian Alps in the winter of 1944.

My father had written my mother every day during the war, and we have over 1,000 letters he sent her, full of love, loneliness, and longing, but missing any mention of war's horrors. He never talked seriously about the war until he was in his eighties, when my sixth-grade son conducted a video interview for a school project. Again, my dad told the funny stories, but suddenly, after two hours, he got serious, calling for his Army-issue Bible, a battered leather-covered copy that he had kept in his pocket every day of the war. He read the Twenty-Third Psalm aloud. "'The Lord is my Shepherd; I shall not want.' I read that verse every day in battle," my father confided, looking straight at the camera, telling the truth finally, even though he knew we could not fully understand it:

> War is hell. That first battle was my baptism by fire. I was one of the walking wounded.... Those times weren't a vacation and it wasn't a game. There were thousands of dead people lying around—not just one—but thousands.... There were dead soldiers everywhere.... War is hell. I don't wish it on my best friends or my worst enemy. May my children, and my grandchildren, and my great-grandchildren be spared from it, forever. Amen.

"Okay," my father concluded. "Now you can shut off the camera." Unfortunately, we couldn't shut off the war in his mind.

The Secret World of War

The combat veteran lives in a world apart. The civilian coworker, friend, wife, husband, child, parent—knows nothing about this world. Aware of our ignorance, countless poets and writers have tried to translate the soldier's and veteran's inner life to the rest of us. As I went searching for peace builders during my sabbatical year, I encountered two of them early in the process. Former war correspondent Chris Hedges writes compellingly about war's horrors in two books, *War is a Force that Gives us Meaning* (2003a), and *What Every Person Should Know About War* (2003b). His work does much to help ordinary citizens like me understand the realities—not the myth—of war. In a newspaper commentary in 2005, Hedges explains how war "distorts and damages those sent to fight it."

> No one walks away from prolonged exposure to such violence unscathed....
> Our leaders mask the reality of war with abstract words of honor, duty, glory,
> and the ultimate sacrifice. These words, obscene and empty in the midst of
> combat, hide the fact that war is venal, brutal, disgusting.

John Crawford, an Iraq War veteran, was a senior in college when his Army Reserves unit was sent to Iraq. An accidental soldier, he published his war writing in his book *The Last True Story I'll Ever Tell* (2005). Reading it and talking with John, I understood more clearly the transformation from student to soldier he had undergone. "They wanted me to act like a man, but I was feeling like a little boy," he said. "I never wanted to hate anyone; it just sort of happens that way in a war."

After my father's death, I asked my 90-year-old mother, "How did Dad go through all he did and still carry on a normal life?" "He fought the war every night for 60 years," she replied, and turned away. He wasn't alone. Millions of veterans of combat, soldier and civilian alike, are living with the demons of war both in their daily lives and in their nightmares. And every day, in numerous countries around the world, more men, women, and children are becoming living and dead casualties of war, military and civilian alike.

As a daughter, a sister, a wife, a mother, and a teacher, I want to know why we are allowing this as a global society. I have not raised my two sons to kill other mothers' sons. I am not teaching my students so they can kill the students of other teachers. In my classroom, I refuse to support the myth of war anymore. I want to create a culture of peace.

BUILDING A CULTURE OF PEACE

I am a teacher with a modest goal: to change the prevailing belief in the inevitability of war into trust in the path of achieving security, justice, sustainability, and peace through peaceful means. I work to reach this dream by empowering the minds, hearts, and hands of the adolescents I teach—one student at a time. Step into my middle school classroom and you will feel energy, passion, and urgency of mission—along with a healthy dose of humor—in my students and me. I think you'll wish you could have been in my classroom—as a student or fly-on-the-wall observer—as one of the

Figures 2 and 3.   Human costs of war. J. Kadir Cannon's *Anguished Art* series depicts horror of war for soldiers and civilians.

following events occurred. They highlight the way a group of adolescents can learn to think, care, and act.

- In an American history classroom, students have spent two weeks designing ideal communities in the Americas of the 1600s, with the requirement that every rule and decision "will result in the most fair, sustainable, and positive outcomes for all involved," including Native Americans, Europeans, Africans, men and women, children and adults. I've stayed in the background as they've created and debated the goals and rules for their communities. It's been a complex assignment, in which students have analyzed historical facts and aimed to rewrite history. In reflecting on their thinking they say, "We had to use critical thinking. I would think of something and debate it with myself." "You can't go back in time and change stuff, but it did make me think in a new way." "I learned how to make a successful community, which we will have in the future." "I learned that you need to think *beyond*."
- In an English classroom, after weeks of reading, discussing, role playing, and debating the book, *Roll of Thunder, Hear my Cry* (Taylor, 1976) I've asked my students if the racially charged novel should remain in the curriculum. A Black girl who has been active in our class discussions responds, "This was the first time I thought my classmates really understand some of the things I have to go through every day. It made me angry, but after we discussed it, I felt better. I think students should read this book in sixth grade. This is the grade when racial discrimination begins." Meanwhile, a White boy shows new empathy and resolve, stating, "Children can't change the past, but they can surely change the future, and the sorrow and sadness that the kids share will make the children reading the book unite and ban racial cruelty forever. Thank you for having us read it."
- It is near the end of our year in sixth-grade history, and I introduce my students to our final project. On the board for their homework assignment, I simply write, "Change the world! Details coming soon!" Gasps. Puzzled murmurs. Excited chatter. Finally, Kimberley pipes up, "Mrs. Cannon, are we really going to change the world? I always wanted to be one of those people who change the world." Her enthusiastic reaction is a high point of my year, as students begin planning world-changing projects ranging from educating their peers about the Iraq War and the election process, to collecting supplies for inner-city soccer programs and a school in Ghana, to cleaning up a local park and cooking at a women's shelter.

How do we get here year after year? What's the buzz?

Figure 4.   Students analyze William Penn's role in American history.

Think, Care, Act

First, in each class, I provoke my students to think critically. It is good teaching and learning, and they eagerly walk into my classroom expecting nothing less than some kind of challenging surprise. Ian Harris and Mary Lee Morrison (2003) agree that students must learn to create knowledge actively if they are to become peacemakers. This tenet is a foundation of my teaching. To engage students in the process of creating their education, we set ground rules together on the first day of school. I inform them, "I will not tell you *what* to think, but I *am* going to *make* you think." They set goals to become active thinkers: evaluating information and asking questions during the year. As we complete each unit of study, we stop to consider our own thinking and performance—and that of others—critically and respectfully. Students offer me informal "report cards" on my teaching and their learning in writing or conversation. They give their peers positive feedback and constructive criticism—as do I. Students become invested in creating the atmosphere and learning of the classroom.

Second, we build a foundation of compassionate care to support our classroom and personal endeavors. Again, we create this safety net together, as students set goals in September for courtesy, friendship, and respect for each other. I model and express the expectation that our room will be one where it is safe for each person to offer heartfelt reactions or unpopular opinions out loud and on paper without threat of ridicule. If they fall short—using expressions like, "That's retarded (or ghetto, or gay)," I interrupt conversations to guide them to use respectful speech. I teach them to accurately express their opinions without hurting others. Further, I invite them to share aspects of their personal lives, forming a family-like classroom community. With such caring, I agree with Nel Noddings (2005a), who believes that we teach our students to care by becoming members of caring relationships with them.

Third, we embrace the idea that students become empowered by taking action, as does Rahima Wade (2007). Thus, we study the lives and impact of those who have helped change the world, examining their steps in doing so. I plaster my walls with inspirational photographs, posters, and quotations. I frequently refer to Nobel Peace Prize winners such as Wangari Maathai of Kenya. She faced ridicule, jail, and physical attack, but reminds us still that change takes time, struggle, and perseverance. We use her advice in our daily academic, athletic, and social endeavors as well as when we take action to help others—in our classroom and beyond.

Like many dedicated educators, I share Howard Zinn's "modest goal ... to change the world." But I have a very specific change in mind: to empower the youth I teach to ultimately create a peaceful future. Thus, in my zeal to push my students to think critically and ask questions, to care for each other and humanity as a whole, and to act effectively for the good of others, I have a bigger dream. I want to make my students feel capable of using their talents to think, care, and act for economic and human justice, cooperation, sustainability, and peaceable security over the course of their lifetimes. The outcome—over the course of generations, perhaps—is a global culture of peace.

Envisioning a Culture of Peace

What is a culture of peace? Let us remind ourselves what it is not. In the introduction to their 2008 conference, Peace and Justice Studies Association hosts condemned our current global culture of war, warning that numerous institutions—politics, media, economics, the arts, education, and even families—are contributing to the problems of a global war culture in which wars and injustices continue to rage unabated. They further chided the art and creative media communities for glorifying war and failing to promote peace.

In contrast, in a culture of peace, politics and economics would advance and be enriched by cooperative interactions among nations, corporations, and groups. Self-interest would be replaced by mutual interest. In a peace culture, education, family, religion, and the arts would celebrate inter- and multicultural diversity and understanding. Media, rather than depicting and thereby promoting gratuitous violence, would certainly contain content about struggle and conflict, but coverage would enhance understanding of nonviolent solutions to disagreements among people and nations. Conflict would not go away, but our systematic approaches to it would be transformed drastically.

The Global Campaign for Peace Education [GCPE] (1999) provides a working definition of peace culture that I share with my students and colleagues. This conceptual framework expresses the foundation on which this book is organized and envisions the peaceful future to which my teaching aspires:

> A culture of peace will be achieved when citizens of the world understand global problems; have the skills to resolve conflict constructively; know and live by international standards of human rights, gender and racial equality; appreciate cultural diversity; and respect the integrity of the Earth. Such learning can not be achieved without intentional, sustained and systematic education for peace.

Harris and Morrison (2003) further clarify the potential outcomes of such purposeful education: "Education for peace is essentially education for compassion and empathy—for oneself, for others, and for the earth" (p. 32). When I am teaching adolescents to build a peaceful future, these definitions describe how that future looks for me, and for peace educators around the world.

PEACE EDUCATION AS AN UMBRELLA CONCEPT

I call the holistic teaching and learning that promotes such a culture of peace *peace education*, and I envision peace education as an umbrella, encompassing education's best efforts to empower youth to change the world for the better: critical and creative thinking education, civics education, character and moral education, multicultural and antibias education, gender-equity education, conflict resolution and antiviolence education, social justice and global education, service learning, environmental education, and twenty-first century education to name major strands of teaching for the greater good. Betty Reardon, Alicia Cabezudo, (2002) and a group of global educators use the term "comprehensive peace education" (p. 19) to describe the broad outcomes envisioned and multiple strands of education employed in the effort to teach for peace.

Theoretical Underpinnings

Thus, my comprehensive peace-teaching philosophy stands on the shoulders of giants in a variety of fields. To create a democratic classroom atmosphere in which critical and creative thinking and questioning are active components, I look to Paulo Freire, John Dewey, and Maria Montessori who provide models and philosophies of such education. To critically teach history, I rely on the work of Howard Zinn, James Loewen, and Bill Bigelow. In creating caring and inclusive classroom communities I respond to the call of Nel Noddings, Parker Palmer, and Michael Thompson. To understand my roles as a multicultural, antibias, and gender-equity educator, I study Sonia Nieto, Peggy McIntosh, Elise Boulding, and Carol Gilligan. To appreciate the impact of character and moral education, I lean on the work of Thomas Lickona and Matthew Davidson, who promote practices to elicit both excellence and ethics.

In employing social justice, environmental, global, service-learning, and twenty-first century learning frameworks, I am inspired by many Nobel Peace Prize laureates, the United Nations, Rethinking Schools, and organizations developing initiatives in which youth can learn and serve, such as *PeaceJam, Teaching Tolerance,* and Jane Goodall's *Roots & Shoots.* I revere basic tenets of world religions that promote peace, and appreciate the work of healers like Jon Kabat-Zinn and Rachel Naomi Remen, who utilize the mind/body/spirit connection in seeking inner peace, compassion, and health. And of course, to understand the power of nonviolent social change, forgiveness, and reconciliation, I consult the writings of Mohandas Gandhi, Martin Luther King, Jr., Thich Nhat Hanh, and Wangari Maathai, among others.

Bringing these sections of the peace-education umbrella into a whole for me and countless teachers globally are Ian Harris, Betty Reardon, and other peace-education scholar/practitioners, who provide theoretical underpinnings and ground educators in the historical roots of peace education. By documenting research and effective practices in a variety of settings, they encourage us to fly on the wings of possibility toward a peaceful future by teaching for peace.

A Moral Imperative

What is peace education, and how does it differ from plain, old-fashioned good teaching? There are similarities and interconnections with character, multicultural, and social-justice education. Peace education is multidimensional, encompassing a wide variety of curricular content, from subject areas to socialization. Peace education complies with numerous content standards, and is applicable to all ages of students in various

Photo credit: John Spofford

Figure 5.   Students keep peers safe on ropes course.

educational and community settings. So, how does it differ? Teaching for peace requires a leap of imagination.

Peace education aims to change an existing belief system—a culture of acceptance of war as a method of solving international problems—to a new paradigm—one in which human rights, social justice, sustainable development, social action, and creative diplomacy are promoted as effective paths to national and international security. Peace education helps children see themselves as integral parts of one human family and as capable actors for positive social change on a local and global stage. Recognizing that it is a long-term process, I see education for peace as a priority, a passion, and a promise.

Negative and Positive Concepts of Peace

I have good reason. Educational, media, and other institutions are drowning our children in a sea of war culture. Too often, we fail to teach children a positive conception of peace as a natural part of the local and global landscape. On any given day, for example, I can ask my students to draw pictures of war, and they have no problem getting started, quickly filling the page with explosions, blood, and guns. Early in the year, however, when I ask them to draw pictures of peace, they sit at their desks, stare at the page, and ask me what I mean.

Researchers such as Orlando Lourenço (1999) have long studied this phenomenon. They find that our understanding of war and peace is developed during childhood and becomes the enduring basis for our subsequent ideas about interpersonal and international conflict. Lourenço describes studies with 8- to 16-year-olds showing that they understand war long before they comprehend peace. Further, when children finally articulate an understanding of peace, they begin with negative peace (absence of war and violence) rather than positive peace (presence of cooperation and respectful interactions).

Lourenço expresses the moral urgency of actively teaching for peace. Further, he asserts that peace education should be overt and is best when it includes both major components of moral development theory: Lawrence Kohlberg's emphasis on justice and fairness and Carol Gilligan's principles of care and empathy. Such linking helps children see peace as a positive condition that includes constructive interpersonal and international relations, respect and empathy for all, and cooperative conflict resolution for the common good, rather than simply as an absence of conflict or violence.

Teaching Positive Peace

I wrote this book to help teachers in various settings realize we can infuse peace education principles and practices into our existing curricula and school cultures. We can employ multi-faceted and simultaneous components throughout the school year and the school environment. We can conceive of peace as positive, and we must actively help our students make this discovery. We can introduce students to a multilevel description of peace, such as that offered by Harris and Morrison (2003), beginning with the global level:

> Peace implies that governments respect the sovereignty of nations and will use methods other than force to manage conflicts. At the national level peace implies law and order, self-control, a respect for others, and the guarantee of human rights. At the cultural level artists create peaceful images to counteract some of the violent images propagated through the mass media and entertainment industries. At the institutional level administrators use organizational development techniques to resolve conflicts. At the interpersonal level individuals can learn how to arbitrate conflicts and negotiate agreements. At the psychic level peace implies a certain calm and spiritual connectedness to other forms of life. (p. 14)

With such a clear definition in mind, how do we teach for peace?

First, we must help our students to **think** critically—especially in the face of constant media bombardment—to provide them with what scholar Noam Chomsky (1989) calls "intellectual self defense" (p. viii). Numerous studies document the harmful effects of television viewing on children and adults (Vincent, 2006). For example, a vicious cycle ensues in which violent programming desensitizes us to violence and can even stimulate violence in viewers. Disrespectful discourse in sit-coms, dramas, and campaign ads fuels a flurry of thoughtless, negative, and demeaning language in society-at-large. In contrast to these negatives, we can help students recognize positive role models and heroes in the media as well. This exercise can be both encouraging (in that they celebrate positive role models) and frustrating. ("Mrs. Cannon, there are so many more news stories about bad people doing bad things!" a student complains.)

Further, news content, delivered in 30-second sound-bite-style "coverage," hardly begins to educate citizens about issues on which they must make thoughtful decisions. Discussing war reporting, for example, Katherine Covell (1999) decries the video-game-like coverage of the Persian Gulf War, writing, "The implicit message to North American children was that war is a game which the United States wins" (p. 117). It is our job as educators to help students see through the "game" of war and understand its dire consequences. We must also help students assess their media consumption and take control of their media-based learning, by researching from a variety of news and reference sources, for example. Media evaluation should also include online news and entertainment, as well as new media, such as YouTube, blogs, wikis, Tweets, and social networking sites.

Second, we must teach children to **care** about their classmates and to know them on a deep rather than superficial level. By discovering our similarities and celebrating our differences, we turn the classroom into a caring community of learners in which respect, fairness, friendliness, and appreciation are the daily norm. In addition, we should teach students to be citizens of the world, part of the global human family: embracing what Nobel Peace Prize winner Jane Addams called in 1907—lacking a better term—"cosmic patriotism" (2002, p. 40). To do so, we must break barriers of ethnocentrism and nationalism and investigate the common humanity behind the history and news stories of people in other countries, sometimes communicating with them via letter, Internet, or e-mail. On our journey to becoming culturally competent, we can build the study of a vast variety of cultures into our studies of our own country's history, as well.

In our study of care we must also include the recognition that every human being is entitled to such rights as equal access to water, resources, education, and others outlined in *The Universal Declaration of Human Rights* and *The International Convention on the Rights of the Child* (Reardon &

Cabezudo, 2002). We must introduce these documents to our students and actively teach them that peace without social justice is not really peace at all.

Finally, however, it's not enough for our students to think and care, we must also teach them to **act** positively, honorably, and productively to create the change they wish to see in the world—locally and globally. This third of my goals for teaching invites students to feel powerful in the face of daily fears—many of them absorbed from incessantly violent media messages. Writing about social action and media, for example, Bonnie Winfield (1999) states that taking action combats negative media imagery and helps youth develop empathy and efficacy that can lead them to feel hopeful and empowered.

I am not talking about the occasional bake sale. By investigating root causes of social ills and injustices from bullying to poverty and pollution, students can create informed and pragmatic action plans that deeply concern and engage them in service and social action (Berdan, Boulton, Eidman-Aadahl, Fleming, Gardner, Rogers, & Solomon, 2006). Whether they are enacting daily kindnesses like befriending a classmate or educating peers about a global cause, students begin to see themselves as capable, admirable, and secure classroom and global citizens.

Imagining What Might *Be*

Middle school children are the perfect age to embark on this journey to the future, and I share such aspirations with my students from the beginning to the end of the year. Numerous researchers write about adolescents' receptiveness—and need—to engage in such questioning of present and future society. Nancy Carlsson-Paige and Linda Lantieri (2005) observe adolescents can envision the *possible* versus the *status quo*. Tony Wagner (2010) asserts they must do so in order to live in and create the world of the future. Like many middle school teachers, I perceive that my students' sense of moral engagement with the world is developing, and their ability to move from concrete to abstract analysis of problems is enhanced. Their focus—while still *all about me*—is also becoming team-oriented and globally curious. On the first day of school, for example, when I ask students how they want to change the world, the majority want to "end war," "end poverty," or "make peace in the world." They are quickly developing into powerful young individuals who are ready to think, care, and act for a peaceful future.

Thus, while I begin each year by explaining the academic curriculum, I also discuss the need for all of us to become thinking, caring, and acting individuals in general. As we set goals and ground rules together, I make sure students know they can feel safe to disagree with my opinions as long as they formulate theirs thoughtfully. Because I write frequent newsletters home and include their families in classroom and homework explorations, my students and their families know I care about them as individuals and a group, and that I respect their families and traditions. I expect them to show this kind of respect to each other as well. Finally, they soon learn that I believe that aspiring to develop our ability to think and care, while an urgent objective, is not complete without bringing our insight and compassion into active engagement to improve the lives of our classmates, families, school, and world. The classroom walls say it, even when I do not.

The Unseen Harvest

I grew up listening to the nightly screams of my father, a man who had endured and perpetrated the horrors of war as a combat infantry soldier. I am the wife of an artist, whose work has been infiltrated by his reaction to the atrocities of war. I am the mother of two sons of military age, and I cannot imagine these most gentle of young men killing other mothers' children. And I teach eager young adolescents, whom I believe can change the world.

Irwin Abrams was an internationally recognized historian and biographer of Nobel Peace Prize laureates. In his nineties, he continued to write and lecture in the cause of peace, and in the course of my research, I sought his advice. I shared with Irwin my quandary over the urgent goal and slow pace of peace education. It's such a long-term solution to an imminent problem. "What do I answer those who criticize peace education as being too slow to be effective?" I asked. "What do I tell myself?" is what I really wondered.

Without missing a beat, Irwin replied, "We work for the *unseen harvest*. There are consequences" of the work we do.

Critical, pragmatic optimism, based on historical fact in the struggle for human rights, helps me continue the long-term process of teaching for peace. Howard Zinn (2002) also espouses the historian's long view, "To be hopeful in bad times is not just foolishly romantic. It is based on the fact that human history is a history not only of cruelty, but also of compassion, sacrifice, courage, kindness" (p. 208).

Thus, I am inspired in moments of doubt by *A Force More Powerful*—the book (Ackerman & Duvall, 2000) and video (York, 2000). They document numerous nonviolent peace and social change movements. In March 1930, for example, Mohandas Gandhi launched his campaign of civil disobedience against the British with a 240-mile march to make salt from the sea. Seventeen years later, India gained independence from Great Britain. I take heart by remembering that in December 1959, Reverend James Lawson began training young Black college students in methods of nonviolent social action. These courageous students began a campaign of sit-ins at segregated lunch counters in Nashville, Tennessee, in February 1960. Four months later, Nashville lunch counters were desegregated. I am reminded again and again that whether the results come slowly or quickly, those who work for a just cause must not lose hope, must be well organized, and must continue to strive for the harvest of peace, justice, and common good. Gandhi said we must start with the children if we want to achieve real peace. So, how do we begin?

EMPOWERING ADOLESCENTS

Numerous researchers affirm what Harris (1999) asserts, "Youth who are frightened cannot focus on their lessons" (p. 315). Children learn better when teachers use various peace education strategies to tackle the interpersonal, local, and global forms of violence that frighten their students. Teaching for peace can improve the classroom and school climate as well as the local and global culture. It can positively impact students' lives in the present and the future as well. Shouldn't we be teaching for peace every day?

Adolescent Idealism

And shouldn't we be aiming our efforts toward the student most ready to embrace the concepts and goals of peace education—the middle school child? Harris and Morrison (2003) describe young adolescents as ready to learn to think for themselves, think about the future, and consider the wider world. They are entering the "age of idealism, as young people's capacities for abstract thinking increase, an ideal time to discuss international institutions, world order, cultural differences, civil and human rights" (p. 157).

In my own adolescence, I was a school-loving child, comfortable with the good-student role I played in the classroom. Yet, it was not in school that I first felt the power of being a thinking, capable person. I stayed several summers with my grown cousins who attracted a diverse group of conversationalists to weekly dinners at their home in New York. As a teenager, I felt mature just sitting around the table with their guests. However, I soon became aware of their friends' treatment of me as an adult, their openings for me to join the intriguing conversations about politics and

Figure 6.   Students attend international Model UN conference at United Nations.

social-justice issues, and their willingness to consider my ideas as valuable as those of the various professionals gathered around the table.

What does this kind of treatment do for a young person? It made me feel smart—more smart than grades on a report card had. And, it made me feel powerful, that I, too, could change the world for the better.

Hypotheses for Teaching for Peace

As a middle school teacher and a student of moral development, I make the following assumptions in my work to design a multifaceted peace-promoting curriculum for my middle school students. Many of these assumptions can also be made for younger and older students:

1.   Adolescents, while egocentric and self-absorbed, have more anger, fear, and hope about social injustice, global warming, international relations, global security, and issues of war and peace than we think they do, and their fears undermine their academic and social suc-

cess. They need the opportunity to understand their fears, empathize with others, and act upon their hopes in a safe and supportive environment.

2. Media bombardment does not help them evaluate information effectively. They need guidance to become informed and to think critically about historical, current, and future events. They also need assistance recognizing the culture of consumption and dissatisfaction various forms of media may cultivate in them and in society.

3. Teaching adolescents about—and giving them opportunities to become—exemplars of nonviolent, courageous action for peace and justice is a crucial and often overlooked part of their education. Often, this means supplementing textbooks that overemphasize military heroes and military approaches. For example, allowing middle school students to speak the words of Nobel Peace Prize laureates, to discuss and debate nonviolent prevention of deadly conflict, and to develop and implement social action projects on the local and global level will help them envision peaceful solutions to problems, help build cultural competence, and make them feel powerful in the face of ongoing danger in the local and global community.

4. Teaching critical and creative thinking, cultural compassion and competence, and moral action and leadership—teaching children to think, care, and act—at the middle school level is key to the development of future leaders able to achieve "excellence and ethics" and to peacefully and productively serve their fellow citizens.

ORGANIZATION OF THE BOOK

In the following pages, I describe teaching that elicits such feelings of curiosity, compassion, and capability from middle school students. Beginning each chapter by explaining the thinking that directs my teaching, I share brief summaries of research that inspires me in my quest to become a better peace educator. Next I share my introductions to lessons, classroom play-by-play, and student evaluations. I discuss interactions in history and English classes, as well as school-wide activities, such as advisory, Student Council, and elective courses (Debate, Model UN), detailing what happens when we deeply engage students' minds, hearts, and hands. I end each chapter with reflection questions that invite readers to ponder their own philosophies, practices, and possibilities for growth. To protect their privacy, I have changed student names while describing examples spanning a number of years. I have obtained written parental consent to include student writing and photographs.

Thomas Lickona and Matthew Davidson (2005) articulate the interconnected strands of performance character (doing excellent work) and moral character (being an ethical person). For both strands they recognize "three psychological dimensions of character: *cognitive* ('the head'), *emotional* ('the heart'), and *behavioral* ('the hand')," (p. 20). Awareness of these three realms inspires my teaching. Danny Weil (2004) identifies numerous critical thinking and feeling virtues inherent in being responsible citizens in both local and global neighborhoods: curiosity, empathy, integrity, and perseverance, among others. My shorthand for all the components needed for individuals to build peace is that we think, care, and act.

Think, care, and act. The three are intertwined in my teaching so why have I chosen this progression in my teaching philosophy and the organization of sections of this book? Thinking provides the *awakening*, the awareness that something needs investigation, care, and action. Children in middle school—entering the "age of idealism"—are ready to wake up, to dig up the underlying assumptions and inconsistencies in history books, literature, and media, as well as in teacher and parent pronouncements. They begin to care more profoundly about issues after they have identified the issues in the first place. In the end, their thought and engagement can lead to action for the greater good—and ultimately, for a culture of peace.

- The *Think* section begins in Chapter 1, as I detail classroom activities starting with opening-day introductions to critical thinking in history and English classes as well as metacognitive evaluations used through the year. Chapter 2 discusses cooperative projects involving critical media analysis and political debates. Chapter 3 introduces cooperative projects in which students critically imagine ideal histories and futures.

- The *Care* section begins in Chapter 4, where I detail methods for building a caring community in the classroom and throughout the school. Chapter 5 describes the power of reading, discussing, and debating multicultural, historical, and controversial literature to increase understanding and enhance empathy. Chapter 6 demonstrates the power of writing prose and poetry to promote deep connection in classroom and global communities.

- Finally, we get to *Act*! In Chapter 7, I describe the hands-on Citizenship Action Projects my students undertake as their final projects in sixth grade history classes. Chapter 8 discusses thoughtful, well-organized, school-wide activism of the Middle School Student Council. In Chapter 9, I describe the role of electives, particularly

Debate, Model UN and *PeaceJam*, in which students research and enact global conflicts and diplomatic efforts to solve them.

- The Afterword closes the journey with my summary of lessons learned in the classroom and description of lessons learned worldwide during my peace education sabbatical. In the Appendix, my annotated bibliography of over 100 books on such topics as peace education, character education, critical thinking, and multicultural teaching will help readers extend their knowledge. Included are illustrated children's books useful in middle school classrooms. Other resources, such as student handouts and recommended websites for teacher and student action are available on my website, Teach for Peace, www.teachforpeace.org (Cannon, 2006).

How Can We Achieve What We Dare Not Name?

I invite readers to enter anecdotal doorways into the minds and hearts of my students engaged in peace education. Yes, I dare call my objective "peace education" although other labels are generally considered more palatable and "safe." To teach peace is considered an act of surrender by some, betrayal by others. In a time of unquestioning patriotism and nationalism (in the United States and around the world), educating for peace is seen by critics as "unpatriotic," even "dangerous."

In energetic contrast, I believe peace education will ultimately lead to true, long-lasting national and global security based on justice and human rights. Peace education is a moral imperative, and to shrink from it is a failure of imagination and a disservice to our students. In teaching my students to think, care, and act, I am empowering them to build a peaceful future. I believe in the power of teaching for peace on the day-to-day level. I can't help but believe in the unseen harvest to come.

PART I

THINK!

"The Socratic love of wisdom holds … that to be human and a democratic citizen requires that one muster the courage to think critically for oneself."

—Cornel West (*Democracy Matters*, 2004, p. 208)

CHAPTER 1

CRITICAL THINKING FROM SEPTEMBER THROUGH JUNE

"Knowledge emerges only through invention and re-invention, through the restless, impatient, continuing, hopeful inquiry human beings pursue in the world, with the world, and with each other."

—Paulo Freire (*Pedagogy of the Oppressed*, 1970/2000, p. 72)

"To think critically, young people must exist in an environment of curiosity, creativity, compassion, and safety."

—Pat Williams-Boyd
(*Middle Schools: Curiosity and Critical Thinking*, 2004, p. 92)

"I like to go off topic because I have a ton of different questions."

—Sixth grade student

Think, Care, Act: Teaching for a Peaceful Future, pp. 3–20
Copyright © 2011 by Information Age Publishing
All rights of reproduction in any form reserved.

Figure 7.   Small groups prepare position statements for classroom debate.

CRITICAL THINKING: WHAT, WHY, HOW?

Joseph shines as he realizes he is able to take the perspective of a political candidate with whom he disagrees. Sharon brightens as she declares she is a visual learner. Aliyah glows with appreciation as she understands I am sincere in asking for her evaluation of my teaching. And Ava sits up with a jolt as she reads that past United States foreign policies have funded Al Qaeda. Moments of critical thinking are awakenings for my students, and when students grasp a concept, ask an original question, or interrupt group work to share a new idea, I see light bulbs floating over their heads—just like in the comic strips.

But I don't take critical thinking lightly. Cornel West (2004) reminds us that our ability to be good citizens—indeed humans—depends on our ability to courageously think for ourselves. In this *Think* section of the book, I explore what critical thinking looks like in a middle school class- room and share varied ways teachers can enhance students' courage to engage in such thinking throughout the year. But, first, let's unpack the ideas surrounding critical thinking so we can better recognize it and help our students apply it in their classrooms and lives.

Defining Critical Thinking

Transformative researchers and practitioners from all over the globe use conceptions of critical thinking that are—at heart—the same. Further, they see such thinking as a tool to change the world for the better. Brazilian Paulo Freire (1970/2000) sees critical reflection and committed social action in a deeply intertwined cycle arising from questioning and rethinking knowledge. American Nel Noddings's (2007) definition encompasses reasoned analysis of issues, as well as reflection on moral and social beliefs and action. Tanzanian-born Ladislaus Semali (2004) offers perspectives from elders in his native Chaggaland, who describe critical thinking as *imanya* ("to know intellectually and to be morally or spiritually motivated"), and *kusare* ("to consider all the possibilities ... think deeply"). He concludes, "Critical thinking is a lived activity, not an abstract academic pastime" (pp. 170-171).

Joe Kincheloe (2004) adds that critical thinkers recognize that they are part of a social fabric woven by threads of racial, economic, class, gender, religious, and geographical circumstances and awareness, and that they understand that these connections affect the ways they think, learn, and change. Definitions give us a common understanding of the components and possible outcomes of this deep type of thinking. But how do we *do* critical thinking with students?

Doing Critical Thinking

A friend calls me "a coach in a gym class of the mind." He understands that I energize students as thinkers and doers. Like all good coaching, the process of involving kids in morally engaged and complex critical thinking requires research, planning, working out, playing, and flexibility. I design curricula that engage students in issues of intellectual, personal, social, and moral importance. I get students curious and keep them feeling safe to make mistakes. I invite their input and help them exercise their intellectual and imaginative thinking to make their own discoveries.

How do I accommodate for the effects of background, temperament, and gender on class participation? I allow time for students to come to conclusions at different times, and I let them express their understandings in various ways. I often ask students to write their reflections before sharing them in discussion, for example, and I find such thought-gathering deepens students' thinking. I find that using online discussion boards allows some of my students who would not generally join a discussion out loud to join in vigorously on computer. When I silently count several seconds before calling on students, I allow both girls and boys and impulsive and thoughtful students an equal chance to share ideas. When I invite students to simultaneously share their thoughts in pairs and foursomes, allowing the class to become a buzz of conversations, I allow students to literally find their voices. And, when I seek out students between classes to personally assess their comfort and willingness to participate in class, they report that they appreciate having so many choices.

Importantly, I also arrange the desks in a large, open square, allowing all students to see each other. I sit among them and sensitively moderate, questioning stereotypes and misperceptions during honest discussions. I prod and push past limits gently, and I thoughtfully consider students' deeply held beliefs. In preparation, I research background information, collect a variety of viewpoints, and create diverse situations for learning so that I am prepared to insightfully guide my students to insights of their own.

Becoming Scholar Practitioners

By engaging in such pursuits, teachers become what Carol Mullen (2004) calls *scholar practitioners*, teachers who study school-wide and global issues, create curriculum, solve problems, and lead by example, combining theory with practice to stimulate themselves and their students to think and act.

I was once given a backhanded compliment by a psychology professor who attended my presentation at an academic conference. "I'm surprised at how much theory you use in your teaching," he enthused. "Duh," I thought. Readers of this book undoubtedly know that teachers can both think and act in the field of education. And, if teachers can become scholar practitioners, why can't students?

Children's Literacy Initiative cofounder Pat Federman creates stimulating programs in public schools across the United States. She bemoans the fact that teachers she trains are under mandate to "skill, drill, and kill" their students to prepare for standardized testing. "It's one size fits all and it's not authentic teaching or learning," she reports. Freire (1970/2000) denounces such "banking education," in which "the teachers make communiqués and make deposits which the students patiently receive, memorize, and repeat" (p. 72). As students are denied opportunities to develop critical and transforming thinking, they become apathetic and passive.

In contrast, Nancy Kraft (2004) describes educational situations that enhance *student scholar practitioners'* academic and real-world engagement. These include democratic classrooms in which learning is participatory, thematic, multidisciplinary, and connected to the real world. Such settings invite students to question their teachers, textbooks, media, and curricula, and ask "What if?" questions (such as those posed in Chapter 3). Student scholar practitioners in such classrooms have requisite qualities including curiosity, the ability to live with uncertainty, the ability to "think 'outside the box' and challenge their assumptions," and to have a "sense that one has the individual capacity to effect change—to apply knowledge in a practical sense to make a difference in this world" (pp. 359-360).

What About the Curriculum?

Regardless of setting, teachers are expected to teach a curriculum, however strict or loose the requirements. What we do with this "official" or explicit curriculum leaves room for interpretation. Thus, it is always possible to include an implicit curriculum, the tangential, unplanned topics of discussion that arise from teacher and student passions. The null curriculum consists of what is missing—by design or chance. Leila Villaverde (2004) encourages teachers to be proactive regarding these three components and to change their curricula if important content, perspectives, and possibilities for promoting critical thinking—and ultimately social action—are missing.

How does such course-correction look in my curriculum? I introduce peacemakers of the Americas such as Dekanawida, founder of the Iroquois League, and we compare rights of Indian women with those of English women in the American colonies under their respective laws and customs. I ask students to compare Puritans' search for religious freedom for themselves with their intolerance for the beliefs of others, such as dissenters and practitioners of other faiths. We consider implications for today of the multiple examples of tolerance set by Pennsylvania's founder, William Penn. Further, I invite students to connect the past to the present by asking them to scrutinize the growth pangs of our young country and compare them to modern-day intolerant actions of Taliban religious fundamentalists in Afghanistan, for instance. I pose the questions, leaving the possibilities open ended. I ask students to research, compare, and contrast multiple viewpoints on such issues. I ask them to look at media reports with a lens of inquiry. I encourage them to discuss such ideas with their families over dinner. At times, parents express alarm at the connections I invite students to make, and we add these cautions to our discussions. Finally, we consider ways to employ such concepts in our daily actions.

Essential Questions

This type of questioning, possible in any classroom, brings us to the *Understanding by Design* curriculum design model espoused by Grant Wiggins and Jay McTighe (2005). The best thinking and learning occur, they assert, when teachers act as assessors of understanding (rather than activity planners) while keeping big questions about big ideas (essential questions and enduring understandings) in the forefront. Thus, rather than focusing on activities of curricular units (making masks, staging a Colonial Fair), teachers who espouse this planning method focus first on questions that will elicit critical thinking during units of study (How did African, Caribbean, and European cultures mingle in the Americas? How do events in our country's history connect with events in other countries' histories?) These questions help students understand why the classroom content is important in an enduring, essential manner and help them transfer knowledge from one setting to another.

Acknowledging Purpose

A theme arises as we examine critical thinking and education: students and teachers alike can actively question the *present* and positively affect *the future*. Critical thinkers understand that they are social beings and know that their connections and backgrounds affect their perceptions and those of others. They question, interweave, and curiously explore academic and social issues. Finally, they acknowledge that the purpose of thinking is to ultimately act as a moral force in family, community, and society.

In my opening days in the classroom I express such functions of education to my students. However, William Damon (2008) worries that too few teachers actively intrigue students in the long-term purposes for learning. He exhorts us to openly discuss passions that drive our daily work and help students consider what might give them life purpose—in and out of the classroom—as well. I answer Damon's call, in my daily teaching and in the pages of this book. Undertaking an exploration of the "what, why, and how," of teaching and learning gives me a sense of purpose as I begin a year with a new set of students.

OPENING DAYS IN CLASS

On the opening day of my American history class for sixth graders, I begin the questioning we will employ as we pursue a year of critical thinking

Figure 8.   Vote with your feet, even if you stand alone—Faces decisions game.

together. I greet my new students but don't let them sit down. Instead, I ask them to stand in the center of the room and look around. First, I want them to notice their surroundings. I take care to make the room warm, lively, and inviting. Some colleagues chide me for visual clutter, but I want students to find something to think about—even if they "zone out" on a lesson I am teaching. Thus, I create bulletin boards for each unit of study, replete with provocative questions, quotes, photographs, and posters. Most kids love my room—and say so.

I Can Believe Anything My Teachers Tell Me

After several moments, I begin. For this exercise I ask students to find three photos I have posted on different walls of the room. Abridging the National Writing Project's *Four Faces* lesson (Berdan et al, 2006), I've hung one picture of a child with a joyful smile, one with a negative grimace, and the third with a neutral face of a contemplator. I tell students, "We're going to play a game to learn similarities and differences in our thinking on certain topics. You're going to vote with your feet. I won't hold your opinions against you, and you won't hurt my feelings by being honest."

It's hard to know if they'll trust me on the first day of school, but I hope they will. In a history class I invite students to stand near the photo that expresses their opinions as I make a series of statements like these:

1. History is my favorite subject.
2. Anyone can make history.
3. I have a favorite person in history.
4. I can believe anything I read in books.
5. I can believe anything my teachers and parents tell me.

Sometimes I stop to discuss each question. Sometimes we skip along quickly, just to enjoy the fun of moving across the room and noting where people end up. The last two statements, however, always merit comment. The braver students inspire sincerity in others, so when three-fourths of the class choose the negative face of disagreement when I mention trusting books, they are already thinking critically. I question the other, more trusting, fourth of the class.

"Why can you believe anything you read about books?" I ask one of the students next to the happy face. He replies, "I've read a lot of books and most of them are true, except for the science fiction and fantasy. And anyway, they wouldn't be published if they weren't true." "Why don't you believe what you read?" I ask another student, standing by the negative face. "Books can be written by just anybody. You have to check your facts. They mix things up," the skeptic replies. An "undecided" near the contemplative face is convinced by this argument and joins the negatives.

"Why can you believe anything your teachers and parents tell you?" I ask a shy girl, hiding behind another. About a quarter of the class is standing next to the happy face. She begins slowly, "I've been pretty lucky with teachers. I think they try hard not to lie to us. My parents always tell me the truth." Turning to the negative group, I call on a girl who is jumping up and down to share. "Oh, come on," she begins. "No offense to anyone here, but you can't really believe that teachers are always telling you the truth, can you? Maybe they try. But, sometimes they say we don't have time for recess, and we really do. Or you learn something in second grade, and then in fifth grade you learn it didn't happen that way. And what about the Tooth Fairy and when the goldfish dies and your parents tell you it's just 'gone away.' Sometimes it is for my own good, but my parents don't always tell me the truth." They remain in place, absorbing each side's arguments.

I Want My Parents to Find Me a Spouse

In an English class the questions relate particularly to three novels we read in sixth grade. Each novel has a strong protagonist: Jonas in Lois Lowry's *The Giver* (1993), Cassie in Mildred D. Taylor's *Roll of Thunder, Hear my Cry* (1976), and Koly in Gloria Whelan's *Homeless Bird* (2000). In two of the novels, occupations and spouses are selected for the protagonists by others in the community. Knowing this, I build the day-one questions from the innocuous to the provocative:

1. I like to read.
2. I love to write.
3. I know the parts of speech.
4. I think reading a book can make a person change.
5. I want my parents to choose my job for me.
6. I want my parents to find me a spouse.

The children move deliberately as they assess their relationships with books, writing, and grammar, taking a stand adjacent to photos, or between them if they hedge their bets. However, when I pop the last two questions they scramble *en masse* to the negative face. No one wants a parent picking a job for him or her. "I'll know better than my parents what kind of job interests me," one student protests. And nobody wants their parents picking their life partner. Except Eric. After the marriage question, he stands alone by the happy face while his classmates jump and point from the comfort of their group of negatives. First, I calm the naysayers and praise the one brave voter. "You took a real risk, standing for something that no one else supports. That took courage. Why would you like your parents to choose your spouse?"

"I really love my mom, and she loves me," Eric begins. "I think it would be hard for me to pick someone, and I think my mom would be able to find someone good for me." I have to work to keep the class quiet enough to listen to this sensitive reasoning. "Look," I chide the unruly majority, "It's hard to build a good marriage. You might want to consider asking your families for guidance on this!" "Oh, I'll bring someone home to meet them," volunteers one boy. "But pick for me? No way!" Eric stands his ground, and a year of critical thinking begins for all of us.

Revealing the Hidden Agenda

Finally allowing them to sit, I distribute a handout of the course description, and we preview the curriculum for our year together. Reading it with their families will be their homework at night. But before sharing the academic curriculum with them, I offer them, in print and aloud, my "hidden" agenda for the class. I believe my students learn better when they know where I am coming from and where we may be going together—and why. Yes, I use challenging language for sixth graders (and their families), many of whom have never heard these terms before. I explain the phrases as we go along, trying to tie our study of the past with a purpose for the present and future:

> I want to help you **think** critically—especially in the face of constant media bombardment—to provide you with what scholar Noam Chomsky calls "intellectual self defense." I want you to **care** about your classmates, and to know them on a deep rather than superficial level. I also want to encourage you to be caring citizens of the world: embracing what Nobel Peace Prize winner Jane Addams called—in 1907—"cosmic patriotism." But it's not enough to think and care, I will give you opportunities to **act** positively and effectively—locally and globally! We will do all this by becoming a community of learners, studying our country's early history.

I point to the essential questions posted in big letters on the bulletin boards. On the English board, students might consider, "How do writing and reading help you understand yourself and others?" "Can reading a novel make you change?" "What do characters in books do to overcome obstacles?" "What do you do about things that bother you?"

On my history class bulletin board students read a different set of essential questions. While particular units will have others added for consideration, these are a good intellectual place to start as we consider the purpose of studying history. "How do events in America's past connect with events in the world today and tomorrow?" "How can I know what information to believe from books, teachers, Internet, and media?" "How will this knowledge help me succeed in life and make a positive contribution to the world?"

A Multicultural American History

I also hang a colorful DVD on which the title boldly proclaims, *They Lied to You in School* (Fadden, 1995). The accusation never fails to catch someone's eye. The video, of Mohawk elder Ray Fadden, is one I will show during our year together. Fadden's passionate monologue about the contributions of American Indians to world knowledge is right in sync with the eloquent arguments by James Loewen in *Lies My Teacher Told Me* (2007). They urge us to remember that the story of the Americas is a multicultural one, in which American Indian, European, and African civilizations and cultures clashed, intermingled, and created something new. Loewen warns that most history textbooks instead offer a parade of facts with limited perspective.

Happily, my inquisitive team of teachers and I (and a dedicated group of former colleagues) have designed a history curriculum to allow students to construct a complete and multicultural picture without (we hope) facing a string of disconnected "facts," sugar-coated lies, or omissions. Yes, we teach an early American history course ranging from pre-history to 1776. But, how do we teach it? First, with an inclusive and multicultural curriculum. Second, using a wide variety of source material, from rare use of a textbook (to teach reading skills and to critique missing information), to archaeology and history magazines, to websites, first-person documents, videos, interviews, independent research, and field trips. Third, by giving students numerous opportunities to work individually and cooperatively to construct their own understandings. A teacher in a public school setting might face challenges to such supplementation, but it can be done.

My colleagues and I weave global and current connections throughout our year in early American history. Further, in each case in which we study an oppressed or conquered people, we affirm their status as a capable and inventive culture or civilization. Thus, our first studies of the Americas allow students to investigate the stature of civilizations of the Maya, Aztec, and Inca before their conquest and colonization by Europeans. Prior to studying enslavement of Africans, we study African kingdoms of Mali and Songhai, for example. Additionally, aiming to broaden students' awareness of the *Americas* as more than *North* America, our first cooperative research project is one in which small groups research a country in the Americas (South, Central, North, and the Caribbean), investigating its indigenous culture, European and African influences, current political configuration, and current relationship with the United States. In our American history class, students will gain awareness of the global influences in the Americas and the parallels to globalization today. Further, they will know that "Americans" can live almost anywhere in the hemisphere, not just in the United States!

Goals for Teaching and Learning

Respecting the diversity of beliefs and learning styles in my classroom is as important to me as exploring cultural diversity in the subject material. Thus, further in the handout I explain we will discuss multiple perspectives and invite dissenting viewpoints. We'll learn to actively listen to each other. We'll do cooperative projects as well as individual ones. We'll act out role plays of issues and literature. We will engage auditory, visual, and kinesthetic modalities to help all students become equal partners in creating learning in our classroom. For many students, mine is a classroom where students know their strengths will be appreciated and their weaknesses addressed. "I will challenge you," I promise them, "but this is a place in which you can feel safe."

Finally, in the day-one handout, I invite students to set goals for their own learning—and for my teaching. In addition to reading the course description with their families, students complete a chart on which they set goals—for themselves and for me. I use their ideas to better understand their learning styles and to engage them in shaping this class from the beginning.

How do they react? Middle schoolers have lots to tell a teacher who will listen. They write a flurry of requests like "make the class interesting," "explain everything clearly," and "don't give much homework." But some pieces of advice show deeper consideration. Olivia knows herself well as a learner, writing, "I love to imagine things. I like to work by myself on handouts, but on projects I like to partner up." Morgan also refers to her learning strengths, "I am a visual learner so drawing diagrams on the board helps me." John writes, "If I don't understand something the first time, explain it in another way." Natalie requests, "I like to go off topic because I have a ton of different questions."

Meanwhile, Mia understands her emotional needs, writing "I don't like being criticized, especially in public." Alyssa agrees, writing in bold letters, "DON'T YELL PLEASE. The louder you get the more scared we get!" Ella requests, "Share your own experiences of your educational journey with us." Nathan proposes, "Give me a chance as a new student, and I'll give you a chance as a teacher." Finally, Lily's teaching rule for me is "Try your best to be honest with me and my fellow classmates."

For some sixth graders, taking ownership of their learning goes beyond the typical goals of "do the work, pay attention, behave in class." For example, Leah's rule for herself is "If you don't understand something, 1st ask yourself, 2nd check your book, 3rd check with your friend, 4th ask a teacher." Sabeena sets a goal of "Studying. I will use different techniques. And I won't laugh at others' mistakes." Lucas is ready to help the entire class by "acknowledging a classmate if they are speaking to me. Or if a classmate or teacher is speaking to the whole class, I will only focus on the person that is speaking." (He actually succeeded!) Finally, Jerry and Ismail each assert a simple rule for thinking and learning in this class, "Ask more questions!"

How Can I Change the World?

At the close of class I point to Howard Zinn's words hanging above my desk, "I had a modest goal when I became a teacher ... I wanted to change the world" (Ellis & Mueller, 2004). Helping students see that I have purpose for my effort—even though (or because) it is the first day of class—is important and Damon (2008) would agree. I ask students to consider how they will use their knowledge to change the world. This sampling of first-day responses shows a motivated group of kids who are ready to think, care, and act for a peaceful future:

"I want to stop war." "I want world peace." "I want to wipe out cancer." "Stop global warming." "Stop pollution." "I would make Africa a rich continent so that everyone would have medicine and food." "Everyone would be given free medical care." "I would have people with different opinions and backgrounds learn to get along." "I would change the way the economy works." "Find better use for our trash." "Stop illegal poaching of endangered animals." "Stop the racism that still goes on even if it is hidden and not like it used to be." "Peace in the whole world."

We've got a lot of work to do.

STUDENT EVALUATIONS THROUGHOUT THE YEAR

It's a given that teaching kids to think critically requires developing a stimulating and meaningful curriculum. I follow day-one introductions with a year of critical thinking opportunities, designing lessons because research says they will be effective in meeting my goals, or because students have expressed interest in exploring a meaningful tangent, or simply because I think they will be fun to try. I evolve as a teacher by keeping my critical-thinking head in the game. And, my greatest sources of inspiration are the formal and informal evaluations of their learning and my teaching I invite my students to give me.

Metacognitive Postcards

Lickona and Davidson (2005) urge us to be thoughtful about our teaching and to collect student reactions to our practices. Sonia Nieto (2004) also encourages us to ask students for feedback. She discusses research that confirms that middle school students want teachers who expect a lot of them and teach relevant curricula in an effective manner. How teachers teach is important to students!

Figure 9.   Student teaches peers about women's suffrage movement.

Typically, after a unit or project is over, I request that my kids "write me a postcard" on a three-by-five card, answering questions I pose on the board. I ask them how I can better teach the material, I ask them to explain a big idea they will remember, or I ask their opinions on whether we should continue to study the topic at all. For lengthier critiques they express their opinions of specific high-points and low-points on full-pages of feedback, online or on paper. "I give you grades all the time," I explain. "I need to know how effectively you think I am teaching and how well you are learning so I can keep improving as a teacher."

We are all engaging in *metacognition* (another term I teach them on the first day of school)—we're all thinking about our thinking. I believe the evaluation process makes them better students, and I know their evaluations make me a better teacher.

Evaluating Videos

An example from history class illustrates the process. I honestly cannot decide which of two videos will give students essential background on the history and impact of slavery in the United States. The older video, Knowledge Unlimited's (1994) *Pride and Prejudice: A History of Black Culture in America,* ask a unique "What if?" question that European Americans rarely confront: What if the diverse peoples of Europe had been kidnapped from Ireland, Denmark, Poland, Italy, and Germany, and enslaved in a country far away from their homes? The newer video, *Shaping America: The Slave South* (2004), focuses more on factual representation of conditions of enslavement, agriculture and economics in the North and South, and methods of slave resistance. Unable to decide, I show both videos, explaining my problem and asking students to review each of the films for me. Yes, my indecision costs me class time, but helping me make the decision increases students' motivation to view the videos critically.

While most students prefer the newer video, it is apparent from their evaluations that they "get" them both. I am impressed with the detail of Kimberley's review:

> The *Pride and Prejudice* video pushed us and was important to show that people were stripped of their culture, identity, and freedom, and it had a great quote from W.E.B. du Bois. I liked how it flipped slavery onto a European question at the beginning. But *Shaping America* showed us how "spin" was used when they called slavery a "positive good" instead of an "evil bad." It told more stories, showed more statistics, was more interesting, and showed examples of runaways.

I collect their notes, and after we discuss the pros and cons, students suggest a compromise: if I have time to show both, do so. If not, I should show the beginning of *Pride and Prejudice* and all of *The Slave South.*

Evaluating a Multicultural Debate

Tying together our studies of the colonization of the Americas, students prepare a debate to compare how each of the three founding cultures of the Americas: Indian, European, and African has contributed to present-day civilization in the Western Hemisphere. The debate is meant to be provocative, and the students are well-equipped after months of research, projects, and cooperative work to defend each of the cultures as crucial. At the end of the debate, I ask for their feedback. "Did the debate help you or confuse you?" "What would you change about the way I taught this?"

Their replies are affirming. "It wasn't confusing, but it did make me think about the bad and the good." "It helped me understand the complex cultures of America." "It made me think about other peoples' opinions, and it made me wonder what would've happened if something was changed back in history." "It was a fun, open-ended way of learning." "I wouldn't change anything in the way you taught it, but I would change how the Europeans treated the Africans and the Indians."

Evaluating Research Projects

For the entire winter trimester students research a topic of their choosing somehow related to the history of the *Americas*. In this three-part project, students appreciate the opportunity to select and research, write about and make multimedia projects, and finally teach the class about a topic on which they become experts, uncovering topics relatively unknown to American student or their parents. The project is challenging and rewarding, and after almost 12 weeks of work, students are quite ready to tell me what works and what doesn't.

Suggestions for future years' students are fairly uniform, "Pick a topic you enjoy because you're stuck with it for over two months!" Or, "Don't wait till the last minute to do everything." Suggestions for *me* to employ in future years are varied and helpful: "Let us pick topics more recent than up to ten years ago." "Don't make us use the online note-taking system if we prefer note cards." "Give us class periods to work on our media." I incorporate these critiques in my planning by scheduling more note-taking lessons and more in-class work time, for example. Thus, the research process gets better each year.

Aside from questions about nuts and bolts of the project I ask, "What is the one thing you learned about your topic that you think might help you in your own life?" Dorothy Dix's researcher writes that he will remember, "If you think something isn't right, then stand up for it and do something about it!" Clara Barton's biographer has learned, "Even in hard times, one person can make it better." A girl who has researched sharpshooter Annie Oakley reports, "I learned that if you try hard enough you can have a good career, even in something that is gender-dominated." Finally, "Rachel Carson has taught me that if you persevere, you will always accomplish your goals eventually."

Evaluating the School Year

It's June and the kids are ready for summer. However, they are also experts on our curriculum and my teaching—what works, and what doesn't—so I ask them for one last evaluation. Often gratifying but sometimes grueling, their evaluations are my first pieces of summer reading. I use a variety of formats in asking students to evaluate my teaching, including answer-on-a-scale questionnaires, short-answer questionnaires, and long-answer evaluations. I invite students to assess study-skills lessons and homework, books and topics, and me and my teaching.

I start by asking about big ideas, "What is an idea about our course topics that you will remember from this year's class?" One history student writes, "I will remember the BIG IDEA that the Americas were not made by just one group of people. It was many different people including Europeans, Africans, and Native Americans." Another appreciates learning "History is EVERYWHERE!" That history is not inevitable is an important idea another student realizes, "History is unpredictable. People do unexpected things." Learning they can make a difference is of lasting importance to several students. One writes, "I'll remember 'You can make history.' You don't have to be important to do something good. This encouraged me." Another student "will remember that anyone can change the world, and teamwork helps everything."

Several English students appreciate that "Poetry and prose are meant to express yourself in very different ways." Lots of kids recognize "how much reading can help you understand yourself more clearly." Numerous English students remember our discussions of *Roll of Thunder, Hear my Cry*. "It was intense," one writes. "I will always remember racism exists." Another reflects on our discussions of *Homeless Bird* and India, becoming aware "that India is not only poverty." Another reveals that our readings "taught me how important family is."

Kids appreciate some things about my teaching, "She looks at different points of view." "Mrs. Cannon strongly promotes both differences in opinion and full class participation." "I like it how you use every type of learning (seeing, hearing, feeling)." "Does things like throwing us the tennis ball as an example of a direct object." "We understood WHY this was written before we read it. Provides good background info." One student welcomes the opportunity to evaluate a teacher and writes, "Thanks, Mrs. Cannon. This is great! You're the only teacher who has done this."

They criticize as well: "You could have more patience." "I think Mrs. Cannon could answer more questions and more than once, even if it's annoying." "Personally, I think you were a little unfair towards me, and at times were mean."

I save student comments from year to year, sometimes re-reading the positive ones when I'm running out of steam and need a lift. But I also re-read the negative comments to keep my teaching honest and to give me a kick in the pants to improve. Am I so focused on projects and due dates that I forget to give a kid a break who needs one? In my interactions with students, do I show favoritism to some and "meanness" to others? Am I so focused on helping kids learn to think that I forget how they feel? And don't I know that how they feel is going to impact how they learn? I can't please everyone, but it is my job to be the best teacher I can be. In discussing promoting critical thinking among my students, I appreciate the way they promote critical thinking in me.

Questions to Consider:

1. What motivates you to teach? What are your joys and hopes? Can you share these with your students? How?
2. How do you conduct your first day of school? How can you include students in goal-setting for your year together?
3. How do you promote critical thinking in your students?
4. How does your teaching style interact with students' various learning styles? Do you vary your approaches to reach all of your students?
5. When can you invite your students to evaluate you? What do you hope or fear to learn? Are you willing to change in response?

CHAPTER 2

MEDIA LITERACY AND CURRENT EVENTS

Examining 9-11 and Presidential Elections

9-11 MEDIA INVESTIGATIONS

"My personal feeling is that citizens of the democratic societies should undertake a course of intellectual self defense to protect themselves from manipulation and control and to lay the basis for more meaningful democracy."

—Noam Chomsky (*Necessary Illusions*, 1989, p. viii)

"Nothing stimulates thinking like controversy.... Balance and fairness must characterize the school's approach to controversial issues."

Thomas Lickona and Matthew Davidson
(*Smart & Good High Schools*, 2005, p. 92)

*"I wonder when did they stop liking America?
I personally believe they are sending a message to us."*

—Sixth grade girl

Think, Care, Act: Teaching for a Peaceful Future, pp. 21–35
Copyright © 2011 by Information Age Publishing
All rights of reproduction in any form reserved.

21

Figure 10.   Students read "peace news" hallway bulletin board.

The anniversary of the appalling attacks of September 11, 2001 comes quickly during the opening days of school. The tragedy offers a host of important learning opportunities for our students and our country. Yet, this event is too often covered in the mainstream media with a harmful absence of critical thinking and background information. In the May/June 2002 *Columbia Journalism Review,* journalist Russ Baker (2002) chastises fellow members of the press for "wrapping themselves in stars-and-stripes graphics" rather than asking tough-minded questions about the attacks and the American response. He continues with a helpful clarification that it is necessary to "distinguish between patriotism, love of one's country, and nationalism—the exalting of one's nation and its culture and interests above all others. If patriotism is a kind of affection," he writes, "nationalism is its dark side."

Intellectual Self Defense

As complex as it is, September 11 is our first opportunity to put a current event under the critical thinking lens and to analyze concepts like patriotism versus nationalism, objectivity versus sensationalism, resilience versus victimhood. Linguist and social critic Noam Chomsky (1989, 2005) discusses how citizens can learn the intellectual fortitude necessary for such evaluation. He acknowledges that engaging in such critical thinking may be time consuming, but everyone must and can do it, simply by learning to ask important questions and being willing to do the work to get the answers. Chomsky especially considers it the duty of educated and privileged people to go beyond the superficial and research the issues of the day so they will be able to make responsible decisions as powerful people in society.

This type of research must (and can) be done with middle school children who are awakening to their world and will soon be in responsible positions. Yes, it is important to approach the issues in a developmentally appropriate manner. Thus, in contrast to Lower School's No-TV Week in which we engaged students in seeking alternatives to TV-watching, we actually ask middle schoolers to pay attention to the effects of TV and other media—as critical consumers—during the week of September 11.

William Kealy (2004) warns that media literacy is a vital skill for people in a democracy. Further, he writes, it is dangerous for media to be controlled by the few and marketed to the many who passively consume it. But critically thinking about TV and other media is difficult! There are many processes at work as various media suck us in and disarm our critical viewing. To promote media literacy, Lickona and Davidson (2005) cite five useful questions from the Center for Media Literacy to help us analyze media (p. 98):

1. Who created this message and why are they sending it?
2. What techniques are used to attract and hold attention?
3. What lifestyles, values, and points of view are represented in this message?
4. What is omitted from this message? Why do you think it was left out?
5. How might different people interpret this message?

Media and Emotions

My colleagues and I guide our students to employ such questions and evaluate the impact of news coverage during this week of TV viewing. We also use the research of Robin H. Gurwitch (n.d.), modifying ideas from her *Building Strength through Knowledge* lessons for our students. We share her objectives for such an examination, knowing the tragedy shook the sense of security of our country and its people. We express our intention that students will learn to consume and evaluate print, online, TV, and radio media critically. We explain that we are exploring the way media can affect our emotions. We want students to be able to step back emotionally and learn skills to enhance their emotional and intellectual resilience as they encounter media that may disturb, puzzle, or manipulate them.

As we introduce our new students to the assignment, we explore such terms as *patriotism, nationalism, emotions, empathy, empowerment, resiliency, media, opinion, fact, sensationalism, manipulation, terrorism, and isolationism.* We will use these terms as we discuss current events issues and the media throughout the year.

Involving Families

Family participation is key to a meaningful outcome. Indeed, in a letter home to families explaining our rationales, we strongly encourage adults to actively participate in the exercises, to discuss their own understandings and feelings with their children, and to listen to their children's responses. We assure families that we are not asking them to immerse themselves in media coverage of 9-11:

> Rather, we ask that they and their families discuss any media coverage to which they are exposed in terms of radio, TV, print, and Web-based coverage they encounter of the events related to 9-11-01. We ask students to record media coverage nightly on a simple log. Importantly, we ask them to EVALUATE their perceived effects of the particular media on them.

The media log contains several categories. First, we ask students to determine the emotional effects of specific media coverage in a category called "Promotes Healthy Mental Outlook vs. Hindrance to Healing." Some children feel it is emotionally positive to watch a remembrance of the events or coverage of a memorial service. Others find these images have a negative effect on them emotionally. Jerry, for example, favors a *Philadelphia Inquirer* article that "talked about teaching kids about 9-11 the correct way" over an Internet site that "had sad photos." Jesse finds NBC's *Today* show comforting because "the host explained that although 9-11 was a great tragedy, it brought the country together." But Audrey feels that the "*New York Times* website *Ceremony at Ground Zero* article would make people feel worse because relatives and friends are more and more affected by the services."

As they tackle the second category "Informational and Factual vs. Sensationalism," we note that some sixth graders are quite astute at seeing sensationalism for what it is. They appreciate historically comprehensive coverage while chastising channels for repetitive replaying of the burning Twin Towers, manipulation of images, and intrusive interviews. Robert analyzes these differences:

> Informational and factual—This video falls into this section because the video is by someone who saw it happening from their apartment and their natural reaction to what was happening without anything added.

> Sensationalism—This video falls into this category because it tries to create emotions of fear, hate, and sadness by showing the pictures of the people involved, showing multiple scenes of the second plane crashing into the tower, set to emotional music.

In the last category we ask students to determine whether coverage "Promotes Patriotism vs. Nationalism and Isolationism." This is a stretch for some, so we discuss the difference between open-minded love of country versus blind and ethnocentric nationalism. Emily states that "The *Channel 6 News* promotes patriotism because it showed how the presidential candidates put their differences aside and honored our country." Along these lines, Kylie appreciates that "*NPR Radio* just simply reported and did not stress whether one candidate did more than the other, but instead just showed that they cared." However Layla worries that "a candidate used 9-11 images as a label to show what would happen if you didn't vote for him." And Jesse dislikes a "*YouTube* film that encourages revenge over forgiveness."

What is Terrorism?

After we discuss and clarify these thoughtful responses, students end their investigation by writing reflections on what they know, what they have talked about with their families, and what they still wonder. Angelina kicks off the discussion with a recitation of facts but wonders "how much of a deal people would make if it had happened somewhere not well known like Wyoming or any other state" We discuss what would have happened if it had occurred overseas. Would we have cared as much? Where has terrorism happened before in the United States and beyond? We pull down the map. We learn about Oklahoma City. What is terrorism anyway? We look up definitions of terrorism.

Later in the day, with my Model UN class of seventh and eighth graders, I deepen students' thinking about what is an act of terror and who is a terrorist. Students in small groups agree on their own definitions of terrorism. Using questions and scenarios created by Bill Bigelow (2008) we ask if governments or corporations can commit terrorist acts, if terrorism can affect just one person or many, and whether the term applies to destruction of property, for example.

Back in sixth grade, most students label the perpetrators of 9-11 as "terrorists," but some write more specifically of "Middle Eastern extremists," or "the Taliban," or "Al Qaeda." Most students wonder, "Why would anyone do this?" But again, there are some students who deepen our conversation. "I wonder what was going on in the minds of the terrorists, and how could we have reacted differently, and if there is a possibility that it could have been prevented," asks Albert. Valerie writes, "I wonder when did they stop liking America? I personally believe they are sending a message to us."

Having had detailed discussions with his parents, Jesse has an ironic sense of past history, writing, "I wonder why Al Qaeda and Osama bin Laden had to attack us, even though we helped him." Jonas has a more personal connection that he's pursued with his family, too. "About three years after the attack my cousin joined the Marines and was launched to Iraq. I have two questions. Why did we invade Iraq, and how can we get out safely?"

Complexity, Contradictions, and Controversies

Only by asking my students to articulate their understandings and questions am I able to debrief misperceptions. Sensitively, with regard to the variety of opinions and levels of understanding in the room, I complicate their thinking with historical background from balanced reference sources connecting American foreign policy over past decades to possible reasons "why they don't like us." Responding to Jonas's questions I am thus able to detach Iraq from the events of 9-11, inviting students to join him in questioning the root causes of the war in Iraq. Later, in my seventh and eighth grade debate class, I continue this sort of dialogue.

Lickona and Davidson (2005) see controversy as crucial to promoting critical thinking, but emphasize the importance of employing fairness and multiple perspectives in classroom approaches to controversial issues. An article we discuss in my debate class echoes this sentiment. Written for educators, it also stimulates thoughtful discussions with sixth through eighth graders in the first week of school and throughout the year. Pedro Noguera and Robby Cohen (2007) write that educators have a responsibility to discuss such controversial issues as multiple perspectives on the role of United States in world affairs and the contradictions in U.S. policy over time. They note, for example, that few Americans are aware of the support given to Al Qaeda and Osama bin Laden during the 1980s in an attempt by the United States to weaken Soviet control in Afghanistan. Few are aware of the close relationship the United States once had with Saddam Hussein. Most of my students are indeed surprised when they read this information, and a complex discussion ensues. My students appreciate the authors' thesis that teachers should help students understand that such contradictions exist throughout history and should provide materials that convey divergent perspectives on the same event.

If the only knowledge students (and sometimes parents) have comes from superficial news coverage, teachers have to work extremely hard to bring historical perspective, controversies, and multiple sources of information into the classroom. And students appreciate it! Further, if the only emphasis on current events is on negativity and violence, students do not appreciate the tenacity of local and global heroes working nonviolently for justice and peace. Therefore, using websites such as peaceoneday.org (n.d.) we celebrate International Peace Day, September 21, with an analysis of neighborhood and international peace news. From 9-11 to Peace Day, students appreciate the chance to interpret media influence on their lives.

Student Evaluations

As our study of 9-11 ends, I ask my students to write anonymous evaluations of the unit, answering three questions: "What helped you learn about 9-11? What should I change about teaching it? Should I teach it at all?"

Absolutely, they reply. "I really liked the 9-11 discussions and worksheet. It was useful because I always had a lot of questions from 9-11 and talking to my parents really cleared it up," writes one. Doing all of these activities "helped me learn safely," writes another. "It was good to get together as a class and tell where we got the information from." "I don't think you need to change anything because I understood it. We do this not to relive the past, but to make sure we know what actually happened."

We can inoculate students to resist the mind-numbing impact of media in their lives. By giving them tools with which to engage with various media, questions to ask about the origins and purpose, and opportunities to discuss their emotional and critical reactions with parents and teachers, we can introduce a lifelong habit of critical—versus thoughtless—media consumption to our students and families.

PRESIDENTIAL ELECTIONS DEBATES

"If schools are to live up to their role in preparing students to be 'full participants in our society,' they must also teach them how to engage in their communities as active citizens, and they must teach them how to operate in a political democracy."

Figure 11.   Students record election issues survey results.

—William Damon (*The Path to Purpose*, 2008, p. 173)

*"Most teachers believe that politics should be kept out of
the classroom. But it never is."*

—Bob Peterson
(*The Complexities of Encouraging Social Action*, 1994, p. 40)

*"The debates we had in class were really,
really interesting to me, and I mean it."*

—Sixth grade boy

Teacher Bob Peterson articulates a clear set of guidelines for teachers to
use to help students feel safe while confronting controversy (1994). As do
other researchers and practitioners, he first exhorts us to examine multiple points of view. Next, he urges us to share our personal opinions as just
that—personal opinions! Further, we must make sure students are confident that their grades are not affected by differences of opinion with their

teachers. But finally, he warns that a teacher who professes to hold no opinion on issues is not credible to students. Worse, he asserts, an apathetic and unengaged teacher is a poor role model.

Teachers who worry about discussing politics with their students might want to rethink their fear. Researchers like Damon (2008) say we should instead worry about the lack of political engagement among the nation's youth, regardless of the increase in young voters in 2004 and 2008. Students do not know about or engage in daily activities of civic life. While some youth are apathetic, others are hopeless; they don't believe they can get involved and make a difference, even if they knew how. Predictably, Damon chides media as part of the problem, noting that the attention to scandal rather than substance promotes cynicism in young people, rather than civic engagement.

Happily, however, Damon cites research indicating the effectiveness of classes and other activities that teach students how a democracy actually functions. Although the research was conducted at the college level, Damon asserts that the implications are most applicable to secondary school students who are just beginning to explore political knowledge and engagement.

Issues Versus Personalities

Taking this mandate seriously, my sixth-grade history colleagues and I continue our media examination through the year, especially during presidential election campaigns. The introduction to our week-long investigation began this way during the contentious 2004 campaign. We invited students and families to engage in a civil discourse on the issues rather than the media's focus on differences in personalities and attack ads. We expressed our goal to promote critical thinking and political engagement. "In the long term," we wrote, "we hope students will take active interest in becoming informed citizens who vote and participate in their communities."

We introduce and discuss enduring understandings and essential questions:

1. How can citizens become involved in the election process?
2. What are the important issues of the election?
3. What does civil discourse look like and sound like?
4. What news and Internet sources offer balanced versus biased information?

Being able to have "civil discourse" on the issues, however, requires groundwork. In 2004, we start our investigation by asking students to list what they already know about the election process. Making a huge chart on the board, students show they know there are candidates, political parties, voters, campaign ads, and personalities, but they have little concept of the issues that separate the predominant political parties, Democrat and Republican, and candidates, George W. Bush and John Kerry. This gives us a place to begin.

2004: Top Issues for Adults

Our next step involves interviewing adults. Teaching our students the difference between asking someone to *name and summarize multiple sides of an issue* versus asking someone's *opinion,* we assign students to interview three adults. Their question: "Name the top three issues that are important to you in this election." Without putting adults on the spot to reveal candidate preferences, the results will lead us into the rest of our investigation. The interview process seems to get adults invested in researching the issues themselves!

The classes are abuzz. Through superficial exposure to the media, students have intuited the personality issues of this election ("Bush is friendly; Kerry is snobby.") But, they have little grasp of the complexities facing the country. When they return to classes the next day, they are full of explanations of controversies on gay marriage, Supreme Court nominations, the Middle East, and nuclear proliferation. But as each teacher compiles the results of the interviews, three other issues rise to the top. I send an e-mail bulletin to the faculty and family community using my students' data:

> **Election 2004: Top Issues:** Currently, the concerns of approximately 95 adults in our community have been tallied. Please help our students research and understand all sides of the top issues:
>
> **# Mentioning—Top issues:**
> 75 War in Iraq (and concern for troops, draft...)
> 54 Economy (taxes, deficit, jobs...)
> 38 Homeland Security (global terror, Patriot Act, privacy...)
> 21 Healthcare (insurance coverage and premiums, prescription drugs...)
> 10 Environment
> 9 Education

Students take the rest of the class period to select one of the top three issues to research (and ultimately debate), forming small groups.

Researching issues, not candidates, each student outlines various positions on the war in Iraq, the economy, or national security. Working cooperatively, students identify the central issue of their topic ("Was the war in Iraq justified or not?") and form a resolve or thesis to debate ("The war in Iraq was justified by good reasons."). They continue their research for homework.

2008: Economy, Healthcare, War

In 2008, we refine and repeat the process as John McCain and Barack Obama become candidates for the major political parties. When students conduct issues interviews in this election cycle, three concerns again rise to the top: the economy, healthcare reform, and the war in Iraq—complex problems for all citizens and political leaders, let alone 12-year-olds. Here lies the beauty of family involvement: adults at home have taken time to explain their top issues. Thus, students come to school with lists as well as background knowledge. As we clarify the boundaries of discussion for each debate ("We agree we're going to include taxes in economy, right?" "Shall we research Afghanistan as well as Iraq?"), the children form three cooperative groups based on their interest in a topic.

In 2004, we conduct our research without connecting issues to a candidate. However, in 2008, the students and I decide the concerns are so complex it will be easier to investigate the two major party candidates' positions on the issues. Notice that students have formed groups based on topic interest, not party or candidate allegiance. While many of the students indeed have a favored candidate (or their families do), they place their personal viewpoints on hold as we research multiple perspectives to inform our discussion.

Again the class is buzzing. With the help of educational websites, family input, and teacher research of the issues, kids build working understandings of the complexities. Again, I help define terms as students read candidate position summaries from the elections websites at various newspapers and networks, as well as Justice Leaning's (n.d.) www.justice-learning.org , and Gale's (n.d.) *Opposing Viewpoints Resource Center* website (available through our school's reference database). With the help of our librarian and working as a teaching team, we vet media websites and online subscription sites to save search time. To give the kids a chance to compare these supposedly "objective sites" to obviously partisan ones, the students also read each candidate's website.

Kids who "get" the concepts explain them to others. But they invariably get stuck, and I field questions. "Mrs. Cannon, why do they call Democrats liberals and Republicans conservatives?" "How does the stock market work?" "What's the stimulus?" I walk a fine line of balance as I explain issues without injecting my opinion (unless they ask):

> Democrats—and there are probably more liberals in that party—generally believe that it is important for the government to directly help poorer people. They think it is the government's job to make sure everyone has their basic needs met, believing that as people get jobs, they won't be poor anymore, and this will help the economy. So (raising my arms up from my waist) Democrats try to bring people up from the bottom. Republicans—and there are probably more conservatives in that party—usually believe that government should help businesses by not making too many rules on how to run them. They believe that when businesses do better (lowering my arms down to my waist) the money will eventually help the poorer people. They believe the economy will improve this way.

I use a tennis ball to explain the stock market, a mimed kick in the pants to explain the stimulus. I do whatever works to bring these terms to working life for the kids. They continue the research for homework, filling in the pro/con T-charts in their packets.

Figure 12.   Students compare candidates' websites.

Civil Discourse on Civic Issues

When they enter class the next day, students compare their T-charts, adding to their notes by sharing information with group members. The moment of truth arrives when I ask them to divide themselves into two teams within their issue groups. Circulating among the groups, I flip a coin to determine which team will represent which candidate! The coin toss elicits cheers and groans as some kids will represent the candidate they personally like—or don't. I am nonplussed, knowing that they will learn each candidate's position, regardless. Lickona and Davidson (2005) discuss various types of debate format but agree that the objective should be to promote critical thinking and civil conversation. We are walking in the shoes of others, and no matter how those shoes pinch our feet, we will begin to understand and respect others' viewpoints!

Debate days are glorious as students arrive prepared with informative speeches supporting "their" candidate and critiquing the other. They deliver speeches and cross-examine each other as their opponents and members of other groups take notes on each issue. The homework assignment each night is to react to the debate in writing and to share their reactions with adults at home.

Student Evaluations

Here's how Andrea sums up her debate on healthcare:

As I listened to the speeches, I got an idea of how the candidates would deal with this issue. Obama plans to help the people who can't pay for healthcare insurance first, while McCain plans to help the people who already pay for healthcare insurance first

These debates were well fought, and when we finish them, I think I will have more information to remember than there is room in my head. If I were old enough to vote, I would vote for Senator Obama. Even though he is inexperienced, he has great new ideas that I think would work efficiently.

Jerry has made a decision based on the economy debate, writing,

Obama is going to get our economy going by cutting taxes for the lower and middle class.... Another thing was that he was going to invest money in hybrid and fuel efficient cars. This is the major plan that got me to vote for Obama because I am a tree hugger and don't like to depend on foreign oil.

Joseph has been soaking up every word while waiting for his turn to debate the wars. He has also been discussing the candidates at home. He writes:

> The debates we had in class were really, really interesting to me, and I mean it. First, I admit I was really nervous. I don't know how the candidates can speak so calmly. Secondly, it was really interesting to me to listen to each candidate's ideas. I didn't know they had so much in common, but they still have more differences than similarities. And lastly, representing my *un*desired candidate was really interesting to me. It made me think about Senator Obama much more deeply, not shallowly, and I really got to understand his ideas.
>
> However, for my candidate I have chosen Senator McCain. For the war in Iraq and Afghanistan, he wants to send even more troops to these places, says we should help rebuild Iraq's cities which have been destroyed, and wants to pressure Iraq's neighbors. This is a more aggressive plan than Senator Obama's which I think will help us win the war.

Everyone is developing an opinion based on research, but Adrian questions why we have limited our investigation to the two major candidates. He writes that he is curious about third parties' positions on each issue. "You almost never hear about the independent parties in the news, so it might be a good idea to get one person for each issue to represent the independents in the debates." This is an important idea to consider for our next election.

While voting isn't everything in a democracy, thinking is. These students are preparing to think, care, and act on issues rather than personality in local and national elections. Examining media coverage of 9-11 and the elections allows students to think critically about current events. How about inviting them to employ critical imagination about history or the future? Chapter 3 examines asking the powerful question, "What if?"

Questions to Consider:

1. Are you comfortable when your students raise questions about politics, terrorism, race, or other controversial issues? Are you able to discuss controversial ideas with students, friends, and colleagues in civil ways, acknowledging multiple perspectives?

2. How would school families or administration react to discussions of controversial issues in your class? How can you involve them in the process to reduce fear and promote dialogue?

3. Do you regularly take time to critically discuss current events with your students? What format works best in your classroom? What are the obstacles?

4. Within your curriculum or school setting, where are opportunities for analyzing media's various effects? Can you spare 5 minutes? Forty minutes? Several lessons?

5. How can you increase your own media awareness? How critically do you read newspapers, watch TV and movies, and use Internet sources? React to this question: "Do you use media or do media use you?"

CHAPTER 3

USING CRITICAL IMAGINATION

The History *Utopia Project* and *The Giver Utopia Project*

THE HISTORY *UTOPIA PROJECT*

"The world is not always as we might wish. Self-interest, greed, envy, and brute power too often prevail. Although we cannot rewrite the realities, we can imagine different scenarios."

—Joan Goodman and Usha Balamore
(*Teaching Goodness*, 2003, p. 191)

"We understand Columbus and all European explorers and settlers more clearly if we treat 1492 as a meeting of three cultures (Africa was soon involved), rather than discovery by one.... The process of exploration has itself typically been multiracial and multicultural."

—James Loewen
(*Lies My Teacher Told Me*, 2007, p. 65)

"You can't go back in time and change stuff, but it did make me think in a new way."

—Sixth grade boy

Think, Care, Act: Teaching for a Peaceful Future, pp. 37–49
Copyright © 2011 by Information Age Publishing
All rights of reproduction in any form reserved.

Figure 13.   Small, cooperative student groups design utopian communities.

When the 500th anniversary of Columbus's landing in the Americas was to be commemorated, there was a global glut of plans to celebrate this anniversary. There was controversy as well, much raised by Indian groups throughout the Americas who felt this date should be mourned not praised. I was interested in questioning the significance of this anniversary with my students, thinking critically, "What if ... the Spaniards had not come to conquer, but to cooperate?" I was teaching third grade at the time, and the idea of mindlessly celebrating was not palatable.

Rethinking the pageant the school was planning, I collaborated with fellow teachers in Lower School to create an alternative to history: an event in which we helped students understand both the facts and possibilities for a better way. As Joan Goodman and Usha Balamore (2003) explain, teachers and students in each grade of our school committed to studying a piece of the complex puzzle. Pre-K and kindergarten classes studied American Indians, while second and third-graders studied the Spanish and Africans of the 1500s. First graders studied the forces of wind and water that affected Columbus's trip. Weeks later, when third and fourth graders came over the hillside carrying their cardboard ships, they were ready to cooperatively meet the confident younger children and invite them to share stories, music, and cultural perspectives as equals. What a "New World" ours might have been!

Critically Teaching History

When I moved to sixth grade and teaching American history in middle school, I returned to the idea of questioning Columbus's impact. These older students are now ready to connect history of 500 years ago to current trends in international exchange. Further, they are able to consider the impact of ethnocentrism, interpreting the world solely from one's own cultural perspective. I teach them this term on the first day of school, and their homework is to discuss ethnocentrism with their parents that evening. "First, you'll impress your parents with the big word. Second, you will have an interesting discussion about your family's heritage and how your family members rise above an ethnocentric view of the world—or don't!"

Our textbook at the time, like many that sociologist James Loewen (2007) critiques, overemphasized Columbus and European conquerors and downplayed Indian and African contributions. Yet, Loewen does not ask educators to embark on a voyage of Columbus or European bashing, nor does he want students to feel guilty about events in the past. Rather, he asks teachers to assemble primary documents and other resources and take time to allow our students to discover a more complex picture of the Columbian Exchange. This we do as we examine the tenacity and innovation of European explorers such as Columbus. At the same time, we uncover the long-lasting effects of the genocide and system of slavery they perpetuated among conquered peoples.

Columbus Conundrum

What is a teacher to do to promote critical thinking about Columbus and later conquerors? Bill Bigelow (2008) steals a student's purse! When his class complains, he replies, "What if I said I *discovered* this purse, then would it be mine?... Why do we say that Columbus discovered America" (p. 15)?

I start digging for information. I collect complex critical thinking on the subject from such sources as Zinn's *A People's History of the United States* (1980/2005), Jared Diamond's *Guns, Germs, and Steel* (2005), and *Rethinking Columbus* (Bigelow, Miner, & Peterson, 1991). I travel to the Smithsonian Institution in Washington, DC, taking notes on displays. I buy the exhibit-related book *Seeds of Change* (Viola & Margolis, 1991) and pore over what will become a valuable classroom resource. I read multiple sources until I have sufficiently built my multicultural knowledge to be able to teach 1492 as a complex multicultural series of events.

Taking the maxim to heart, I "seek knowledge even unto China." There I learn about China's brilliant navigator Zheng He, who set sail with a fleet of ships over 400-feet-long, journeying from 1405-1433 on seven voyages throughout Asia and Africa (and—some claim—as far as the Americas in

1421). I encountered him when I taught near Nanjing, China, during the 600th anniversary celebrations of his first voyage. Thereafter, my colleagues and I expand the notion of European exploration to include Asian accomplishments as well as Arab and African trade and innovations.

Inspired by a Chestnut Hill Academy teacher workshop on creating curricular word and number puzzles for groups of students to solve, I create the *Columbus Conundrum*, a multistep, multiday problem that has students using the Internet, encyclopedias, and books on the Columbian Exchange to evaluate its impact on native peoples of the Americas as well as Europeans, Africans, and other global cultures. I ask essential questions leading to the big ideas I want the students to discover as they work on this project:

1. What Indian and African civilizations were well established before the arrival of European explorers?
2. What were positive and negative effects of European exploration on the Americas, Europe, and Africa?
3. How did the encounter of 1492 create a true NEW WORLD through cultural clash and exchange?

Eventually, interested in taking the idea of "What if?" further, I ask students to completely reimagine the purposes and results of such voyages. Thus, we embark on a new project of discovery.

Reinventing History

One of the most engaging projects I have devised to help students think critically about American history is *The Utopia Project*, in which small groups of students reimagine early American settlements, designing sustainable and just communities and colonies, and figuratively righting historical wrongs. We take several weeks, using a variety of resources to grasp the historical accounts of diverse American Indian cultures, global exploration, and European colonization. We also study African kingdoms and trade prior to the 1500s. We build a solid knowledge base of "what was."

Now, I ask students to employ critical imagination to gain deeper understanding of "what could have been." Utopia (*n.d.*) is defined as an "ideal and perfect place or state where everyone lives in harmony and everything is for the best." This is what we set out to create—in the past.

Casting them as European trade and settlement organizations, I divide students into small groups with a very different mission from historians' familiar formula for plunder: "God, gold, and glory" or Diamond's (2005) triumphant trio of "guns, germs, and steel."

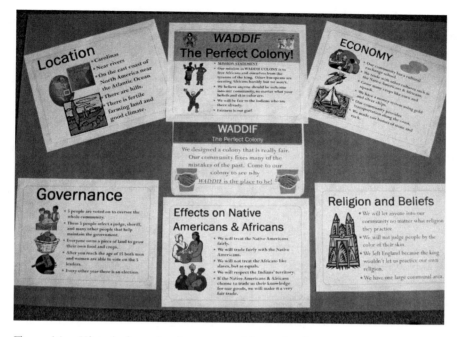

Figure 14. Historical utopia plan prepared for review by peers.

Your mission is to design an ideal community in North America from 1600–1700s. Everything you decide to do must be chosen because you believe it will result in the most fair, sustainable, and positive outcomes for all involved.

Reading Newbery Award winner Lois Lowry's (1993) provocative novel *The Giver* in their English classes, students are already grappling with the idea of utopian communities, as this novel is seemingly set in such a place. Simultaneously, while studying early European colonies in history classes, they have assessed colonists' successes and failures guided by my encouragement to use critical thinking to reevaluate the myths of American history. This project gives cooperative groups of middle school students the chance to reinvent history and imagine an ideal world. Who better to do the job?

A Fair and Equal Utopia

Since the investigation is grounded in events of the past, their multi-part task first involves researching and summarizing the causes and effects involved with actual North American settlements of the Spanish,

French, Dutch, and English in the 1600s-1700s. Ultimately, students use this information in a written introduction to their redesign of history. Second, groups must revise the attitudes and expectations of the European settlers they have researched by writing a culturally inclusive mission statement. Third, they design the specifics—location, economy, governance, religious beliefs, effects on Indians and Africans—their rethought settlements will entail.

The ideas fly. I circulate among the groups, listening and gently coaching. The task captivates the participants, and I am not needed for much besides clarifying requirements. Thus we enter the type of student-driven "Forum Discussion" Heidi Hayes Jacobs (2006) describes. With limited teacher input, such discussion facilitates uninterrupted critical-thinking exchange among students. Their creative thinking improves as well. Po Bronson and Ashley Merryman (2010) report on the creativity boost this type of activity (fact-finding plus divergent and convergent thinking) gives students. By studying and then redesigning the past, they are inventing new ways to build communities as well as new ways of thinking about history.

Devising mission statements leads to disagreement and compromise, but the egalitarian spirit is strong. One group has created a settlement in Georgia with a mission statement promoting equality of race, gender, and religion:

> Our mission is to create equality among our community. No matter if a person is Black, White, or Native American, they would have the right to vote, even if they are a female. The community will vote for a leader for the colony. In our utopia there will be absolutely no slavery. Religion is free and open. Africans and Natives can worship freely without being forced to be Christian or anything else. We are looking to create a fair and equal utopia, staying away from mistakes and errors made in the past.

One group creates "a cultural exchange school." Another forms a government "made of one man and one woman from each religion." A third promises, "Everyone gets supplied with what they need. The old must be highly respected."

The WADDIF colony asserts:

> If the Native Americans choose to trade their knowledge for our goods, we will make it a very fair trade. We will not treat the Africans like slaves, but like equals. We will not judge people by the color of their skin.

The Terranovans will make a new beginning, proclaiming: "We live in peace with the Native Americans and the Africans. There are systems made through the government in which no one will ever be homeless or hungry."

Student Evaluations

Students prepare formal proposals (including maps and housing plans) to present to their classmates, as I empower listeners to be members of a *Committee on Settlement* with the power to choose a proposal to "fund." As groups make presentations, classmates evaluate and rank their proposals, writing at least one positive and one negative appraisal of each.

During the design and critique process it is obvious to me that students find the project invigorating and exciting. Regardless, I formally elicit students' opinions on the value of the *Utopia Project*: "Did it help you think in a new way? Was it a waste of time? Did you learn anything you might find useful later in life? Do you have ideas to improve the project?" This evaluation process provides another opportunity for students to think critically and helps me refine my teaching practices.

Students' comments confirm my observations. "Maybe it did take a long time. But it was a lot of fun to work together to design something people in the past couldn't even do." "We had to use critical thinking. I would think of something and debate it with myself." "You can't go back in time and change stuff, but it did make me think in a new way." "I learned how to make a successful community, which we will have in the future." "I learned that you need to think *beyond*."

I, too, am energized by such projects, and seeing the engagement of the students makes me feel confident of accomplishing the first of my educational imperatives, teaching students to think. But critical imaginings are not relegated to the history classroom. *The Utopia Project* is a hit with my English students as well.

THE GIVER UTOPIA PROJECT

"Peace education, by providing students with a 'futures' orientation, strives to recreate society as it should be. In a violent world, children can often become enmeshed in despair.
Future studies attempts to provide young people with positive images of the future and give them reason to hope."

—Ian Harris and Mary Lee Morrison
(*Peace Education*, 2003, p. 34)

"Helping teens find and develop their voice must begin within the small community of the classroom."

—Thomas Lickona and Matthew Davidson
(*Smart & Good High Schools*, 2005, p. 43)

"The class learns about leadership without being bored and falling asleep."
"This was fun because we get to use our imaginations and argue." "It
involved a lot of reading, talking, sharing ideas but most important of all ...
LISTENING!"

—Sixth grade students

The Utopia Project in history class is partially inspired by English class read-ing of the futuristic novel *The Giver*. I teach English as well as history, and my English class is getting bogged down in confusion about the restrictive rules of the community in which the protagonist lives. "The Elders are in control of everything and things are not working out too well," complains one reader.

"Do you think you can do better?" I challenge. I am eager to get the kids out of the book and actively doing a cooperative small-group role play, so I make them "Elders" themselves.

First, we analyze how Lowry's Committee of Elders handles questions of community security, family structure, food, and technology. Initially, there is much to like in this seemingly utopian community. All members

Figure 15.   Student depicts his group's physical plan for ideal community of the future.

are provided with food, housing, and healthcare. An ethic of cooperation is fostered from the earliest years of children's lives. All adults work at a job for which they are suited. The environment is clean, and people are safe. However, Lowry's Elders achieve these ends with questionable means. They spy on the population electronically, remove choice from most elements of life from schooling to jobs to marriage, and enforce community conformity by "releasing" from the community those who break the rules.

The book provokes critical examination of a society's need for security versus citizens' needs for independence of thought and action. Seizing the opportunity to think complexly about security concerns in the United States and globally since September 11, 2001, we take a detour from reading to connect with current events. "What freedoms will you give up so that the government can keep you safe?" I ask. "Is it okay for the government to listen to your phone calls to your relatives overseas? Do you want a government agency to be able to keep track of websites you visit? Will you willingly take off your shoes and have someone search your back pack before you are allowed to board a bus? Are there places this happens? Are there laws that protect people from being taken away for 'questioning?' Are those laws followed? Are certain groups being targeted for investigation more than others? Is this fair?" Of course the discussion takes the rest of the class. Students continue talking about these issues with their families for homework.

Create a Just, Sustainable Community

The next day, I give students their *Utopia Project* groups, trying hard to match student who have not worked together on other projects. I also partner kids from different backgrounds and those who are detail-oriented to big picture, or concrete to abstract. Finally, I give them their directions and become an active observer:

> You are working as a Committee of Elders to design an ideal community for about 1000 people. You aim to create a community that is safe, fair, sustainable, ecological, healthy, and happy. As you have read, this is difficult to do. To work effectively as a group, each of you needs to speak respectfully and listen deeply to each other. For example, if someone has an idea you dislike, don't ridicule it. Listen and see if there is any good in it. Your job is to think, speak, and listen.

Part of my growth as a teacher is to continually evaluate my students' responses to my teaching. Now, as they design their communities, I take notes on their deliberations. Yes, as do Harris and Morrison (2003), I want young adolescents to envision the ideal future, knowing this process is an important component of peace education. But my other two priorities are that they learn to confidently express their ideas and that they learn to practice deep listening. In these goals I have worthy company, as well. Lickona and Davidson (2005) urge teachers to give their students opportunities to develop voice, even if it means relinquishing control. The classroom is the first place many young people will learn to speak out. While some teachers may be apprehensive about letting students take responsibility for running their own discussions, the benefits outweigh the risks.

Yet, there need to be limits. Thus, I have structured safe conditions via directions that require students to pay attention to each others' thinking: to truly listen to classmates' brainstorms and to deeply consider the reasons group members support proposals or disagree with them. They actually have to write down the reasons with which classmates defend their positions. This is an important step.

I circulate among the groups to listen and watch them work. My class is dispersed, with two groups in the classroom and two more down the hall. Teachers walking by marvel at how engaged students are. One remarks, "They were all working so hard I wondered who was teaching the class!" The students are—that's how high the level of engagement is.

Deep Listening in *Wetopia*

Lucas, Dean, Gianna, and Zaden are animatedly discussing whether guns should be permitted in their community, called *Wetopia* ("because *we* made it together"). Lucas wants to allow guns, and Zaden wants no guns. Gianna wants some people to be authorized to use guns, while Dean promotes nonviolence education. The group goes off on a discussion of why nonviolence education is important to their community. This they can all agree on. Here is an excerpt from Dean's reflective essay:

> One rule in particular we thought was important was "Non-Violence." Lucas said we should have this rule "So people don't harm other people." Zaden agreed, saying, "So people don't die." Gianna took a different approach, with the response, "So people don't have any angry feelings and fight." I believe "non-violent education" is important because kids would grow up to believe in non-violence and would not commit crimes.

Aaron, Raymond, Paige, and Keith have a free-flowing discussion of such issues as freedom, homelessness, weapons, and community service, using a "touch the book" system to decide whose turn it will be to speak. Paige's essay sums up their unanimous views on family structure in their community:

We believe that a family can have as many children as they wish as long as they will be able to support them. With everyone having a good home that would eliminate the amount of poor people. It'd make more loving families if the parents weren't worrying about caring for everyone. It'd give more freedom to the families. I also think it would make for a safer and caring environment.

Their agreement on the structure of the family contrasts with the spirited disagreement among four girls working together. Olivia, Mary, Sabeena, and Lily, not particularly involved with each other as classmates before this project, are enmeshed in the particulars of family planning. Aiming to reduce the divorce rate, Mary suggests arranged marriages, like those of *The Giver*. Finally, they compromise, as Olivia reports:

The rule my group disagreed on the most was a child-birth rule we made up. In this rule the parents were only allowed to give birth to two children and then adopt two children. In the family there would be two girls and two boys. Sabeena disagreed because she thought that more attention would be paid to the biological children. Lily thought that the parents could share experience with their children and adopted ones too. Mary liked that the parents wouldn't have too many children. I just agreed with all of the ideas, because I thought they all made sense.

Money is abolished in one community, affirmed in another. I sit in with both groups, offering critiques of one group's concept of a magical credit card ("People, the money has to come from somewhere!") and giving examples of community ownership. Later, Ashley catches me up, "We're thinking about whether every job should earn the same amount of money or if hard jobs should get more money. Eric interjects, "We should pay a level salary, like $20.00 for two hours of work." Finally, Pauline reports their decision in her essay:

The thing we disagreed upon most was the idea of no money. We didn't know why we should work if we receive no reward, and if someone works harder than another, that they would not get additional rewards. We agreed that there would not be as much stress and hatred, but we still thought it would be better if we would have money.

Student Evaluations

Whole-hearted discussions of bullying, racism, money, property ownership, education, religion, violence prevention, and alcohol and drugs, continue for 3 days—in all groups but one. This group cannot get over recent personal slights, and two of the participants alternate between ignoring each other and making rude comments. I eventually have to park myself in their corner and moderate discussion, affirming each member's good ideas until they make some progress in their planning. They start making real headway as they discuss equality, "All people treated equally means not bullying. Saying racist comments *is* bullying people."

Finally, even for this group, there are positive evaluations of the project as a whole when I pose the questions, "Why do this? Have you learned anything meaningful from this project?"

Aaron replies,

> One is we have to see how hard it is to run a community. We also need to know how to become a leader, because for lots of jobs you need that characteristic. Also, it lets us take a break from what we normally do. It lets us talk and express our feelings.

Cheryl sees immediate benefits:

> I believe the Utopia project helped our class significantly. The project gave us the experience of working with a group. We learned not to argue and to reach out and accept other group members' thoughts even if we did not agree with them. The project helped us learn how to express why an idea is a good or not-so-good one.

Louis values the experience because, "If you work in a group in the future, and if you understand how to make rules, you could make good and fair rules in the future." Pauline also has a future orientation. "L.P.M. would be a big project to develop, requiring a lot of time, but any community with any of these qualities would be worth the effort." Mason agrees,

> We thought it was fun because we enjoyed making a society the way we wanted it by customizing our own rules. We all believed that it was important because it could help us with future problems and cooperation, because we had to work together.

Priya gets the last word:

> It's fun because we get to use our imagination and create something we never would have created unless we became architects.... The thing I was most proud of is that we had a church, synagogue, mosque, and Hindu temple, so all could worship the way they pleased.... We get to learn how important survival and security are, because in real life we have our parents to help us do those things, but when we grow up, we'll have to do them ourselves. That's why we all loved doing this project.

Critical and Creative Thinking

Let us reflect on how critical thinking plays a part in a peace-oriented classroom. Whatever the setting, critical thinking is key to student classroom and civic participation. From day one, we can invite students to think and question history, current events, and school policies. We can provide them with tools, like focus questions, time to collect their thoughts, and civil discussion frameworks. We can model flexible critical thinking for them as we give students opportunities to evaluate our curricula, our teaching, and their learning. Finally, we can give students opportunities to exercise critical imagination—creative thinking—on the past, present, and future. Helping students envision what could be, instead of what was or is, starts them on the path of building the peaceful future.

Using critical imagination on the past and the future, my students are growing increasingly able to use critical thinking in the present. Thinking together in cooperative groups also builds a caring classroom community. In the next section, we examine how students exercise compassionate care for each other and the global community.

Questions to Consider:

1. In your classroom, how willing are you to relinquish control—for 5 minutes, for several days—to allow students to work independently under your guidance? Do you feel that you must have "all the answers" as a teacher, or are you willing to discover and build knowledge alongside your students?

2. What do you do to encourage your students to deeply listen to each other when they share ideas? Do your students see *you* listening to them?

3. How can you tweak your curriculum to include critical and creative explorations of history or literature? Can you start with one topic or unit that lends itself to such investigation? Are there colleagues with whom you can brainstorm ideas intra- or interdepartmentally?

4. Do you encourage your students to ask "What if?" questions about history, literature, and current events? Do you consider alternative viewpoints and help your students see history as a series of choices made by individuals and groups?

5. What do you do to intrigue your students to think about the future and the kind of world in which they want to live? Do *you* think about these things?

PART II

CARE!

CHAPTER 4

CREATING THE *A-TEAM*

Building the School-Wide Safety Net of Care for Students, Teachers, and Families

"Be clear and unapologetic about our goal. The main aim of education should be to produce competent, caring, loving, and lovable people."

—Nel Noddings
(*The Challenge to Care in Schools*, 2005a, p. 174)

"The connections made by good teachers are held not in their methods but in their hearts—meaning heart in its ancient sense, as the place where intellect and emotion and spirit and will converge in the human self."

—Parker Palmer
(*The Courage to Teach*, 2007, p. 11)

"We're your child's advisors. But we like to think that we are your advisors, too."

—Roberta Howlin,
middle school teacher, to sixth-grade parents

Think, Care, Act: Teaching for a Peaceful Future, pp. 53–64
Copyright © 2011 by Information Age Publishing
All rights of reproduction in any form reserved.

Figure 16.   Sixth grade teachers dress as school virtues for Halloween.

While building a caring community is simultaneous and inseparable from developing critical thinking, the following three chapters are distinctive in their description of steps in the affective realm designed to help children feel locally and globally connected, accepted, responsible, and respected—prerequisite feelings for peacemaking and moral life. Character educator Philip Vincent (2004) describes the intertwined intellectual and moral components of education as being equally crucial. Yes, we want smart children who can reason well. Yet, we must also help our children develop into kind and caring people of good character. If we don't, we are not truly educating them—we are *miseducating* them.

There is nothing sentimental or trite about caring, argues Nel Noddings (2005a), urging educators to place care at the heart of our mission. She asks that we teachers see ourselves as parents of a diverse family. She encourages us to embrace this role and to make our first goal "to produce competent, caring, loving, and lovable people" (p. 174). Noddings further clarifies the multiple dimensions of care in her vision of education. We should engage students in learning how to nurture themselves, family members, others in the global community, the environment (including plants and animals), and even material goods and ideas. Indeed, she sees such care as critical for furthering students' intellectual pursuits.

Thus, the second of my three imperatives is teaching students to care. In many ways, they are innately equipped to do this. Scholar Martha Nussbaum (2002) tells us to see ourselves in relationship with others—local and global neighbors—with similar needs and hopes. My aim is to inculcate a caring that begins in our classroom and extends to the global community. As a teacher, however, I realize that I can't teach children to care about classmates or humanity without first demonstrating my own sincere love and respect for them as individuals.

First You Have to Love Them

The book *Living Between the Lines* (Calkins & Harwayne, 1991, p. 11) begins with a conversation between the author Avi and a teacher, " 'Well, first you have to love them,' Avi says. 'If you can convince your children that you love them, then there's nothing you can't teach them.' " Such caring assures students *and* assures me. Parker Palmer (2007) discloses the fears and self-doubt (I call it stage fright) even veteran teachers feel during the first school days of September. What allows teachers to overcome this anxiety? Connecting with kids, heart to heart. Good teachers weave connections with their students, Palmer says, using multiple strands of instruction styles and subject matter, but most importantly, through heartfelt, human ties.

The student evaluations I have collected through the years indicate I am weaving those connection with most of my students in terms of my relationship with them as individuals. But, what about their connections to their other teachers? What about their relationships to each other in the classroom—and out? What about the relationship between the school and their families? Between their teachers and their parents and guardians? Among their teachers? My students are not operating in the vacuum of my classroom. How do we promote a culture of compassion and connection school-wide?

Principles of Good Practice

Fortunately, as in many schools, there are several structures in place in our middle school to enhance connectedness and cooperation among students, teachers, and families. Both our faculty and student handbooks contain "Principles of Good Practice for Middle Schools," espoused by the National Association of Independent Schools [NAIS] (2008), that help shape the school-wide climate. Similar in scope and content to the beliefs expressed by the National Middle School Association [NMSA] (2009), our handbooks affirm that middle schools should support individuals' self-respect and uphold justice and fair play. They should invite families to form home/school partnerships. They should create school atmospheres that enhance understanding and respect for differences. Finally, middle schools should offer students opportunities to participate as active, appreciated, and responsible members of the school, home, and global communities.

Connecting With Families

Among the first of many steps for bringing these principles to life in school is establishing a strong school and family partnership with honest and frequent two-way communication. Families and faculty members alike get this message from our head of Middle School, in letters, in person, and in the handbooks.

Ongoing follow-ups strengthen the home/school partnership. First, three "official" conference days are scheduled during the year (one before classes even begin), allowing for face-to-face meetings between parents/guardians and advisors, who act as intermediaries between the home and school on behalf of the child. Second, in addition to extensively written trimester comments about students' academic progress, faculty members write parents less formal, more frequent progress reports about positive and negative efforts of children in their classes. Third, phone calls and e-mails are other typical means of communication, as are impromptu chats at sports events or in the hallways, or others scheduled as needed. Fourth, several morning and evening family workshops are offered through the school year as well, including anti-drug-and-alcohol workshops, cyber-bullying and technology teach-ins, and a "Can We Talk?" night in which parents and students engage in role plays of typical middle school situations and discuss family and student responses.

Lessons on Living

Further steps help students become part of a connected community. For example, in each year of Middle School, students take an ungraded class designed to give them time to engage in self-discovery and age-appropriate exploration of life issues. In sixth grade it is Resilience Class, replete with discussions, role plays, and cooperative activities concerning managing time, handling successes and failures, and dealing with tensions with family and friends, for example. In seventh grade, the course

self-control
faith
honesty
courtesy
kindness

generosity
gratitude
courage
respect
sportsmanship

Courtesy of The Episcopal Academy.

Figure 17.   Episcopal Academy sweater and school virtues *(Stripes)*.

shifts to Health Class with exploration of the changes students undergo physically and emotionally as they undergo puberty. Finally, in eighth grade, students use Decisions Class to analyze everyday (and potentially life-altering) moral and ethical decisions which they face as adolescents. Each year the students also take Religion Class, culminating in the eighth grade course in which they examine, write about, and share individual life philosophies in "Faith Papers," many of which the authors read to our assembled Middle School. Catholics, Episcopalians, Baptists, Muslims, Jews, Buddhists, Hindus, Atheists, and Agnostics have shared their beliefs with their peers and teachers in this manner.

Underpinning each of these initiatives is our school's active chapel program. Spanning grades pre-kindergarten through 12, chapel celebrates the spiritual aspirations of all members of our school community. While Episcopalian in tradition, chapel services are inviting and egalitarian in nature, and chaplains and student Chapel Councils energize the school population with games, heartfelt sermons, and entertaining role plays. School-wide chapel themes are examined each year throughout the school, with past themes including the school motto: *Esse Quam Videri—to be, not to seem to be*, as well as such virtues as honor, unity, or faith, or explorations of what it means to "do justice, love kindness, walk humbly." In all, the chapel program connects our community as an active assembly program might in another school.

The Lower School chapel program involves the community in active exploration and celebration of the ten school virtues, known as "Episcopal Stripes" because of our 10-stripe sweater design. Self-control, faith, honesty, courtesy, kindness, generosity, gratitude, courage, respect, and sportsmanship are qualities that are given special value and attention throughout our pre-K-12 community. By the time students get to Middle School, they (and their families) are thoroughly familiar with the virtues expected of all in our community. Thus, when we want to lift up our community behavior, teachers, administrators, and students will often exhort each other to "live the Stripes." Indeed, faculty and students alike are encouraged to commend each other by writing short "Stripes Cards" when we catch each other "living the Stripes." It is our long-term hope that our graduates will employ these virtues in their personal and public lives to change the world for the better.

Athletics are part of the lifeblood of our school, as well, and athletic teamwork fosters many warm and lasting relationships among students and between teacher/coaches and players. Our school's ideal for teachers is that of teacher/counselor/coach. Thus, a teacher may teach students English in the morning and teach them to pole vault in the afternoon! Sixth, seventh, and eighth graders have the opportunity to become teammates, playing field hockey, soccer, water polo, football, basketball, lacrosse, and a host of other team offerings, including cross country, dance, and Ultimate Frisbee. Our handbooks describes the goals of the athletic program in Middle School as being developmental in nature, designed to teach skills, sportsmanship, teamwork, active engagement, and graciousness in victory and defeat.

Community connections are woven in other arenas, as well. Theater productions foster a sense of family among more than 75 Middle School actors and technicians who work together for weeks to perform productions of a musical and a drama each year. Often, the rest of the school engages with the productions by discussing socially relevant themes raised in the plays in classes or advisory. Choral and instrumental groups of various sizes encompass students of each Middle School grade. And elective courses and lunch bunches, such as Newspaper, Video Production, Origami, Robotics, Diversity Lunch, Book Club, and my own Debate, Model UN, and *PeaceJam*, offer students self-selected groups with whom they become affiliated in shared areas of interest.

But an even more personal kind of teamwork helps fosters the kind of relationships that help kids feel like part of a sixth-grade family.

We're Always Going to be the A-Team

Founded in 1785 to educate boys, college preparatory Episcopal Academy became co-ed in 1970. Until September 2008, each of the grades throughout the school was named "Form," after the English system. Thus, when I taught third grade, I taught D Form, and when I teach sixth graders, I am teaching A Formers. This background information is by way of explaining our reaction to the news one year that "A Form" would change to "sixth grade." Our team coordinator, Laurie Smith, exclaimed, "I don't care what anyone says…. We're always going to be the A-Team!"

We A-Team teachers are indeed a team. Middle school teachers are a special breed anyway, but, in all humility (actually, we brag about it), we see ourselves as one of the closest and best teams in the school for building an academic and personal safety net for our students and each other. Yes, we meet weekly to discuss students' progress and difficulties in both academic and affective domains. Certainly, we seek each other for impromptu conversations about interactions with specific kids. But we also play nonsensical games with each other, we sign our e-mails with mystifying nicknames, and we create multidisciplinary academic "extravaganzas" together. Further, we support each other when hardships strike, and we cheer each others' personal joys in school and out.

Our themed Halloween costumes are legendary, with group efforts including dressing as Hogwarts teachers, Peanuts characters, and the school virtues—down to the last detail. Our teamwork can also result in hilarious impromptu performances, as during one overnight field trip with the sixth grade, when we sang a rousing barbershop lullaby of "Goodnight, Sweetheart, Goodnight" in front of each motel room door of our students. We sang the song ten times, one for each group of rooms, getting more creative with dance moves and harmonies with each rendition. The girls clapped and giggled; the boys cringed and hid behind the curtains. But overall, the students loved it, because they could see how much we loved being with them and with each other. Thus, we bring to life the vision of caring camaraderie Noddings (2005a) articulates.

We can be serious, too. As the A-Team, we teach at a point of transition in our K-12 school. Our students leave the familiarity and coziness of self-contained classrooms to enter the fast-paced middle-school world in which they move from class to class and must meet numerous teachers' expectations. Keeping track of belongings is a new challenge, as well. Students have lockers and need to transport items from room to room, as opposed to keeping their books in desks and cubbies in a lower school classroom.

Further, being an independent, versus a neighborhood school, we have students who have lengthy bus rides or commutes. Some rise at 5 A.M. for a school day that ends at 4 P.M., followed by another commute that may get them home at 6 P.M. Some have demanding after-school activities, such as athletic, music, religious lessons, or childcare responsibilities. Then there's homework. It's supposed to be limited to 20 minutes per class, but with six classes, or overzealous teachers' assignments, that time may amount to more than two hours. And, of course, in addition to academic concerns, there is the social world of middle school, with its demands for "being cool," having friends, and feeling accepted. Add to this mix the expectation of parents for academic excellence and social success that sometimes presents itself as brow-beating or overprotectiveness. We teachers are not sure, some years, whether the students or parents are more anxious.

Advisory Program

Happily, our year begins with individual meetings with parents and guardians of the children who will be in our advisories for the year. For these eight to ten children, we will be special mentors, helping them with academic, social, and family concerns. We teach each of our advisees in one of our subject-area classes as well. Some of us will coach them on athletic teams. My colleague Bert Howlin explained our role to a group of incoming parents, and I have repeated her explanation in my meetings

Photo credit: John Spofford.

Figure 18.   Community-building advisory games.

with parents since. She assured them, "We are your child's advisors. But, we like to see ourselves as your advisors, too." For some parents, especially those of first-borns who haven't been through middle school before, this welcome assurance helps them see us as allies who will help them guide their children through early adolescence.

Our advisory program has formal and informal components that go far in building a caring community in school and between school and home. We have role-play-based discussions of bullying, peer-assisted locker cleanouts, creative get-to-know-you art projects, and serious group and one-on-one conversations about friends, social demands, parents, sports, and grades. In exploring a variety of activities such as those described by Rachel Poliner and Carol Lieber (2004), we become a school family.

Making it Personal

Before meeting my advisory parents, I do some homework. I write each of my advisees a letter, usually enclosing something fun and intriguing to make them feel special, welcome, and curious. For example, one summer after I taught in China, I enclosed Chinese currency in my letter. I also enclose a letter to families that serves as my introduction and lets my advisees and families know I want them to get to know me as deeply as I will get to know them. I give them my contact information, including my home phone number (families rarely use it, relying instead on e-mail). More often than not, kids and family members are interested in my kayaking, my sons, or some other item from my personal introduction. Or, they will thank me for recommending such minutia as making copies of the class schedule to post on the refrigerator or locker.

Before meeting families I often read reports about my advisees, hoping to follow up on Lower School teachers' insightful comments during my chat with parents. Other years, however, I delay reading these reports, hoping to make my own observations and avoid having other teachers' experiences prejudice my ability to set high expectations for each child. This is a delicate dance: on the one hand, there is valuable information to be gained by reading these files early, and I generally do this. However, some research (Nieto, 2004) warns teachers away from reading others' outlooks on children before getting to know students oneself. Usually time dictates the answer: I read the folders when I can and set my expectations high for each child.

During our meeting as an advisor and parent/guardian team, I aim to foster just that: a team to coach and support each child in my advisory. I have sent in advance the list of questions that I will be asking during our initial parent conference, so that parents can gather their thoughts. One of the most powerful questions was prompted by a visit to our school by psychologist Michael Thompson: "What are your hopes and fears for your child this year?" This question often opens up the discussion in the most fruitful manner of all.

"Last year he didn't have any good friends," a mother confides. "I'm worried that he will be lonely this year." Another worries, "He's really disorganized. Do you have any tips for me to help him get started?" A mother frets, "Over the summer she fought with her best friend, and she's worried about who she will sit with at lunch." A father shares, "Her grandfather is in the hospital. I'm worried that his illness will affect her schoolwork."

These concerns are important for me to know, and I take notes while we talk. I reassure parents that I will support the child and family, and I offer pragmatic suggestions like color-coding folders for each subject, packing lunch to avoid long lines in the cafeteria (and to get a good seat with friends), and role playing phone calls with a shy child to build confidence in making friends. I tell parents I will alert other teachers about a sick relative, so the entire A-Team can help a child cope. Catching them in the hall informally, or sitting in a circle in my room, I will be able to follow up with my advisees individually and in the group yearlong.

The Middle School Journey Begins

When school begins the next day, we teachers meet our new students in homeroom, tour the school, and share details about school practices and student schedules. We play get-to-know-you games, like the *Same Game* I designed to help pairs of kids explore their similarities and differences. But our initial days are not so much spent in the classroom as they are in engaging in adventure team-building activities with the entire sixth grade. Some years we have gone on camping trips; other years we have played cooperative games on campus.

Some of our most effective opening events have been ropes-course "challenge by choice" activities led by adventure-learning instructor Craig Erb and his team. Craig asks us to agree to personal interaction pledges that help us throughout the year. He calls it the "Full Value Contract" and explains it so the kids understand it, "We'll keep each other safe in body and spirit. We'll use put ups, not put-downs. We'll listen if someone else is talking. We'll let go of emotional garbage." Every person of the 100-member A-Team—teachers and kids—must agree before we can even touch a rope or wire.

Teachers throw tennis balls around a circle with our advisees as we all struggle to learn names, we and our students cross pretend shark-infested waters using teamwork and strategy, we act as spotters for students balancing on wires, and we are lifted (literally) over walls or in flying slings by the students we will teach the next day in classes. In this way we embody core teaching truisms Michael Thompson has come to value: the best teachers love the age group they teach and let their students know it, they know they will motivate their students most effectively by creating a caring community, they believe there are many ways to learn outside of school, and they appreciate that they and their students are taking personal risks by revealing themselves and trusting each other every day (Thompson & Barker, 2004).

Student Evaluations

Students see the value of these team-building efforts. Payton writes, "I have learned more about trust and that you have to listen to others' words. I feel like I accepted many ideas that were great and used them. I relied on my teammates to help me and I felt like they were there." Johanna agrees, "All the activities really helped us learn to trust each other."

Some years, after discussing the opening activities in advisory, I incorporate students' comments into an informal newsletter to families:

> We talked about the ropes course, and everyone agreed "it is worth it." "It helped us learn to work together." We learned much from our challenges, such as: "Esse Quam Videri … perseverance … trusting … listening … being supportive … being there…." We learned on the ropes course to promote "physical and emotional safety" for ourselves and our classmates. I was especially impressed at the friendliness and cooperative nature of this particular group of advisees. They persevered without fighting, listened to each others' ideas, and had good-natured attitudes that made the day fun for me, too.

Kids appreciate having an advisor as well. Shares one advisee at year's end, "From the beginning to the end of the year, you were ready to help me if I needed it." Another, new to the school, writes, "Every time I was feeling down, you always had something encouraging to say to lift up my spirits. I knew that every day you were around I would have someone to talk to." Larry Dieringer (2004) writes that students will succeed in school when they feel physically and psychologically safe, feel like they are respected members of a group, and feel like someone cares about them. Advisory, the A-Team, and school-wide community-building efforts make that care happen.

Some years, we follow the group activities of the ropes course with a paired challenge of canoe tripping down a local river. Partnered as girls and boys, new students with old, they bump, bash, scream, argue, laugh, and float down the river, while we teachers referee and rescue. Some canoes make bee-lines, some play bumper cars "gently down the stream" as the rapid life of a school year is fast approaching. But we watch the barriers break as the A-Team begins to form. The middle-school journey begins.

Questions to Consider:

1. How does your school promote a spirit of community and acceptance? What opportunities and obstacles exist within your school to improve the sense of community?

2. What interactions with your colleagues best support you as a teacher? What interactions detract from feelings of camaraderie? What can you do to enhance your teaching team?

3. How do you communicate with families to build a home-school partnership of care? What obstacles exist? What new methods might you try?

4. What obstacles make it hard for you to communicate with students in your class? How do you overcome these barriers to build a classroom community of care and trust?

5. Do you find ways to learn about your students' lives and interests out of school? Do you help them see you as a person with a life and interests out of school?

CHAPTER 5

READING MULTICULTURAL, HISTORICAL, AND CONTROVERSIAL LITERATURE TO ENHANCE EMPATHY

"In spite of teachers' reluctance to broach issues such as racism, slavery, inequality, genocide, and so on, a number of studies suggest that discussing them can be tremendously beneficial to students if they are approached with sensitivity and care."

—Sonia Nieto (*Affirming Diversity,* 2004, p. 104)

"My assumption is that the novel is both a literary work of art and a representation of human experience, including specific experiences of gender, race, ethnicity, and class."

—Michelle Loris
(*Using the Novel to Teach Multiculturalism,* 2007, p. 62)

"They've got to learn this stuff."

—Sixth grade girl

Think, Care, Act: Teaching for a Peaceful Future, pp. 65–81
Copyright © 2011 by Information Age Publishing
All rights of reproduction in any form reserved.

Figure 19.   Students disagree on literary character's options.

Literature is a powerful tool for enhancing students' empathy—for class-mates, people in the past, and people halfway around the world. Michelle Loris (2007) sees novels as artistic vehicles that transport readers into diverse forms of the human experience. She is gratified, for example, that her college students unanimously report that they are challenged to think about life in new ways by the novels they read in her course on multicul-tural novels. They further realize they share similarities and differences with diverse members of the human race and, even more importantly, they appreciate these connections.

As this chapter reveals, novels allow middle school students to attain such understandings as well. Our reading of each novel starts with two essential questions: "How can reading literature help you understand yourself and others?" "Can a novel make you change?" Additional ques-tions allow students to consider emotional components specific to each novel we read.

HOMELESS BIRD

For example, while reading the novel *Homeless Bird*, by Gloria Whelan (2000), we wonder:

1. What do characters in the book do change their situations?
2. What do you do about things that bother you?
3. How can teachers and students challenge stereotypes when studying cultures different from their own?

Challenging Stereotypes

Set in contemporary northern India in a rural village and the pilgrimage city of Vrindavan, reading *Homeless Bird* allows us to explore issues of Indian culture and history, to view commonalities and conflicts in attitudes among rural, urban, traditional, and modern Indians, and to explore a variety of beliefs about marriage and gender roles. However, without a teacher's thorough introduction to modern Indian culture in all its diversity, this book could mistakenly convince students that all Indian girls are forced into arranged marriages at age 13—as is the protagonist. To avoid this error, we investigate gender bias in education and birth rates, but we also view videos about Indian economic advancement and the growing middle class. We peruse *India Today* magazines seeking female athletic champions, Bollywood stars, and Parliament members, noting that female representation India's Parliament is among the highest in world governments. We interview our own families about marriage customs as well. We conduct days of investigation before we even begin the novel.

Student Evaluations

Many students consider *Homeless Bird* their favorite novel we read together. Both boys and girls appreciate the perseverance of the protagonist, Koly, and the kindness of Raji, the boy she befriends. We discuss Koly's ability to thrive in spite of traditional gender role-limitations that initially hinder her progress. Using the book as a jumping off point, I invite students to consider such personal issues as the qualities they will look for in a mate, real-life reflection Noddings (2005a) worries is far too infrequent in schools. My students, male and female, seize the opportunity.
Writes one sixth grader:

> I am looking for someone caring and kind. Someone smart and dedicated. I would enjoy spending my life with someone talented, passionate, and thoughtful. Perhaps someone is out there for me, like for Koly and Raji, but I don't intend to marry for a long time.

They also value the knowledge they gain about a culture new to many of them:

> The 6th grade was introduced to Indian and Hindu life—something we hadn't learned about before in our other classes. This connected with some topics we learned about this year such as religious freedom. This added to our understanding of world-wide religions. Learning about Hinduism was important because it's unlike other religions we have studied, especially my own.

For my students and for me, the book's benefits outweigh the dangers of stereotyping. Readers meet a wide world unfamiliar to many of them, with characters their age who overcome adversity. They have a new corner of the world about which to care and new role models who inspire them to persevere.

MY BROTHER SAM IS DEAD

We can use literature to promote compassion in history class as well. Poet W. D. Ehrhart teaches English and history at The Haverford School. A former Marine and Vietnam veteran, he offered a workshop on his techniques for using poetry to unlock multiple perspectives on historical issues. The medium of poetry, Ehrhart posits, makes issues in history—especially war and peace—come alive. Many scholars (Loris, 2007) agree that novels serve this function also.

Thus, at the end of our year studying the history of the Americas, we read the 1974 historical fiction book, *My Brother Sam is Dead*, by James and Christopher Collier. The novel depicts the Meeker family's anguish as the elder son, Sam, joins the Revolutionary Army to confront the British. Writing from the perspective of the confused younger brother, the authors cleverly convey the depth of debate about the war in 1776. The Colliers force readers to confront their own ambivalence toward war, as well, and to evaluate their beliefs about the United States Revolution.

Questioning War Through Historical Fiction

I value the book because it does not pull punches. With youthful swagger, character Sam argues, "I am an American, and I am going to fight to keep my country free." His father, a veteran of the French and Indian War, gloomily rebuts his arguments with graphic warnings of war's human costs, "You may know principle, Sam, but I know war" (Collier & Collier, p. 21). He proceeds to tell Sam of the horrors he has seen on the battle-

Figure 20.   Students discuss justifications for the Revolutionary War.

field: friends and enemies maimed and killed, personal injuries, psychological wounds, and the cries of families who have lost loved ones.

Teaching in a time in which the United States is involved in wars in Afghanistan and Iraq, I want students to question the morality and human costs of present-day war as well. Indeed, Noddings (2007) urges us to place such study in the core of the curriculum. Thus, I drop in and out of the novel to ask provocative questions tying past to present: "Terrorists attacked us, so we must attack them. Do you agree?" "Civilians will be killed by bombs we drop on 'bad guys.' Is that acceptable?" "Saddam Hussein is a brutal dictator, so we should invade Iraq. Does this follow?" I push them further: "Some colonial Americans did not want British soldiers in their country then, and some Iraqis and Afghanistanis don't want Americans occupying their country now. Can you see a parallel?" "Some British called Minutemen 'terrorists.' What do you think?"

I want young citizens to question the founding myths of the United States and feel compassion for those left out. "Was this a war of independence for American Indians? For Africans?" I teach them about numerous, successful, nonviolent economic initiatives the colonists used to gain independence from British taxation—using Gene Sharp's *Disregarded History* (1976/2010), for example—because I want them to feel the responsibility of choosing war: "Is it true that the only way to independence and freedom was to fight a war with the British?"

I take time to strengthen the trust required for such controversial questioning in time of war. I invite them to discuss these questions with their families, and we bring opinions from home into our discussions as well. This connection to the home is important, because children understand that I value the family culture upon which they base their opinions.

Even students who have been otherwise unresponsive in class participate energetically because their hearts and minds are engaged in these issues. One argues, "Sam is fighting for freedom, and I would do the exact same if I didn't have freedom. Mr. Meeker is saying, 'You can't get rid of injustices by fighting,' but you actually can." Another counters, "I agree with Mr. Meeker, because so many people die from war and the problem usually never gets solved." A third adds, "Fighting only continues the cycle of violence and solving the problem for <u>one</u> group. A fourth supports him: "I agree with Mr. Meeker because it takes a more subtle approach and people can protest rather than fight. They can fight but not physically. War never solves anything. It only causes death."

I use discussion, magazines, maps, and videos to supplement the Collier brothers' excellent research. I know I've complicated kids' thinking about the Revolution and war in general, but I also want to help them find empathy for the soldiers and civilians caught in war's web. Thus, for example, in addition to historical videos about the Revolution, I show my classes the video interview in which my father, a World War II combat veteran, talks to his grandson about his personal experience of the nightmare of war. I show a segment of *You Can't Be Neutral on a Moving Train* (Ellis & Mueller, 2004), a documentary about the life and work of Howard Zinn. Also a veteran, Zinn debunks the idea that humans are inherently violent and that young men are eager to go out and kill each other.

Student Evaluations

As we finish the book, I ask students and families to read an article by Anthony Swofford, Gulf War veteran and author. His 2004 commentary—*The Homecoming, and Then the Hard Part*—expresses in modern terms some of the horrors of war—horrors civilians cannot comprehend even when they "support" the troops and the cause. He describes the emotional tedium, suffering, loneliness, and disorientation soldiers experience while home on leave among civilians:

Ribbons, flags and parades help convince families and the citizenry that our cause is just and that the price paid by the few—death, heinous injury, a long-term psychological disorder—is worth the gain for us all.... Those who greet him at his homecoming party will have no idea what he has endured.... It's likely the soldier will return from leave early.... He'll be living among the soldiers he served with.... He'll be safe.

Talking about the novel, article, and videos elicits new understandings from students. "I never thought about the mental aspect of a soldier. It must be very hard to witness these things," offers Jamie. Layla replies, "Even though we can watch videos and hear stories about war, we will never really know how it feels to be in a war." Nancy tells the class that she's already learned a lot because her cousin is in the army, but, she says, "I also realized war is much worse than people think. Half of the stuff isn't on TV."

They begin to consider the long-term effects of war. Monica decides, "War is like a scar on a soldier's heart. You can't forget and you can't really move on." Adrian agrees, "It really must be terrible to have scenes of carnage replaying in your head, while no one understands." Pat sums it up for all of us: "Even though we act like we know what war is, we will never know." I hope she is right.

Should we read such a heavy book? Yes. Elisa writes, "All sixth graders should read it. It will change everything you think about war and the risks you had to take. Once you are caught up in a war, you can't get out." Jonas agrees, "It has an exciting plot in the sense that you don't know what is going to happen next. It also illustrates the fact that it is very hard on a family when a member is a soldier at war. I would recommend this book especially for the sixth grade, because in sixth grade you need to learn about war to educate yourself." *My Brother Sam is Dead* plays a strong role in provoking questioning and enhancing empathy in the sixth grade history curriculum.

ROLL OF THUNDER, HEAR MY CRY

In hundreds of sixth grade English classrooms in the United States, students read Mildred D. Taylor's (1976) Newbery Award winning novel, *Roll of Thunder, Hear my Cry*. But, should they? Students are emotionally moved when confronting the horrors of slavery's Middle Passage in my American history classes. More subtle, however, is some students' seeming apathy about racial prejudice underlying reality today. Can a novel move student apathy to empathy? Can adolescents connect wondering how racial issues affect people in a story to how racial issues affect their lives?

Figure 21. Students debate merits of reading *Roll of Thunder, Hear my Cry.*

Race Matters

After spending weeks reading the novel, we ask such questions in a formal debate in our English classroom. One aspect of my lesson planning is to give these young students the historical context needed to understand the book. This I must do with sensitivity, as the novel, set in Mississippi in the 1930s, is unflinching in its treatment of racism and institutionalized injustice. Author Taylor succeeds in bringing to life a loving and determined Black family in the protagonists, the Logans. Unfortunately, they and the Black sharecropper families around them are surrounded by White racist antagonists (individuals and a system) who make life (and reading) unbearable. These are tricky waters into which some teachers are afraid to wade.

However, we must. Including "the respectful mind" as one of his *Five Minds for the Future* (2006), psychologist Howard Gardner urges teachers to help students directly face such conflicts among diverse groups of people, with the explicit goal of promoting positive connections in the future. Sonia Nieto (2004) also encourages teachers to break the cycle of injustice and racism, and she cites numerous studies that describe the benefits of teaching about these issues in a courageous and sensitive manner. Thus, wholeheartedly and with care, I begin to introduce my students to the world of the Logans, the Jim Crow South, and the personal background that makes me know this book is important.

My students of all backgrounds are savvy enough to realize that even in an era in which the voters of the United States have elected an African American president, we have yet to achieve a society that has overcome racial inequality and prejudice. Further, while scientists recognize that "race" is not biologically relevant, race exists as a societal construct (Nieto, 2004). Thus, as I do in the beginning of the year in class introductions, I uncover the "hidden curriculum" for my students as I introduce them to the novel. And, I explain why I—a White woman—care about teaching it. In doing so, I aim to help all students—White students and students of color—understand why the issues raised by the book are important to all people, regardless of ethnicity.

"My parents wanted me to go to an all-White, girls' high school," I begin, "but I insisted on attending a co-ed high school where I was one of what seemed to be about 200 White kids in a school of almost 5,000 Black kids. My high school is famous because some big stars went there. But for me, it was huge, it was harsh, and I felt alien. It was the hardest experience I ever had, but it was the best decision I ever made. Why? I was in the minority, and I learned how it feels to be looked at because I was different, an outsider. I learned about Black culture and how my White culture was different and similar. I learned to interact positively with people who were different from me. And these lessons have helped me throughout my life."

I explain that these were times of Civil Rights progress and awful assassinations, when John F. Kennedy, Malcolm X, and Dr. Martin Luther King, Jr., were killed. I tell them I grew up in turbulent, explosive, and hopeful times, and race issues are important to me. "This book is important because it helps us understand how racism and violence work—among people and institutions—and how people like us can work to overcome them," I continue. "We'll be handling some painful information together, but it's important to me as a White person to learn about it, and it's important to me as a White teacher to help you learn about it. Race issues are everybody's issues; they don't just apply to people of color."

The *N Word*

Agreeing with antibias/multicultural educators Louise Derman-Sparks and Patricia Ramsey (2006), my English teaching colleague Matt Newcomb and I know that such work must include families, administration, and colleagues to avoid misunderstandings and confrontation. Together, and with our school diversity coordinator and other colleagues, we discuss current thinking on reading literature with racial slurs, for example. A helpful book is Jabari Asim's (2007), scholarly history, *The N Word*, which tracks debates over such literature. We proceed thoughtfully.

In a letter to families prior to beginning the book, we describe our commitment to read the book sensitively, and we invite adults at home to engage in discussing issues of racial equality and social justice along with us. We welcome their input as we all work to make our classrooms and our world places in which people of all backgrounds can feel safe, respected, and appreciated. Finally, we alert families that language will be an issue in the book and that we will discuss the history and impact of racial slurs with the students to help them understand their power to hurt, within the context of the novel and in the real world.

To students we convey our policy on the author's use of language, cautioning, "We will be reading a racial slur used by characters in the book. However, you are not to use the word in our school, anywhere. When we are reading, we will leave a silence and go on." Discomfort ripples through the classroom when the word is encountered. This is good. We should feel uncomfortable when racial epithets are used as weapons or in jest.

Students read about Civil Rights history and Jim Crow laws, role play scenes, study maps, conduct family interviews, connect current events, write mock letters-to-the-editor, and watch videos. I select carefully from online and video resources, selecting examples of institutionalized racism via discriminatory signs and unequal conditions in segregated schools. I do not show scenes of lynchings, however, although we read about and discuss these. I pause videos frequently, pointing at images of faces, signs, or conditions of school facilities, for example. We take emotional breaks during this weeks-long process—taking time to write kind notes to each other and to explore the similarities and differences of our family heritages, for example. But more or less, we become immersed in the 1930s, in the hot, dusty, racially explosive Mississippi of the novel.

Debating the Book

The novel is compelling in its own right, and the Newbery is well deserved. However, use of the book is not without controversy, and I end our weeks of study by having students debate its inclusion in our curriculum. Using their own reactions to the book, interviews with parents, teachers, librarians, and fellow students, as well as articles summarizing school board debates in Seminole County, Florida, and elsewhere in the United States, my students conduct a formal debate on the merits of reading this novel for sixth graders. I make the debate quasi-role play in nature, in that I invite members of the faculty and our head of Middle School and tell the students that they will be helping the school make a decision on whether to keep the book in the curriculum. Their job is to find convincing arguments for each side of the debate, although they will only present one side. They may not get to present the side they really believe in, but like good debaters, they will work hard to convince our head of school and the "book committee" of the point of view of their teams.

To begin the process, students identify major areas of contention, writing issues on the board, such as language, psychological effects, behavior of characters, history and perspective, realism and violence, maturity level of reader, and literary merit. To structure the debate, they agree that each team should present an introduction and conclusion, and that one member of the team should prepare a short speech about each issue raised. We agree that everyone will also prepare cross-examining questions on each issue. In a small class everyone takes a part; in a larger class, some kids double up on issues or speeches. Thus, everyone has something to do.

Thoughtfully dividing the class into groups is important so each team can benefit from a variety of perspectives, thinkers, writers, speakers, listeners, and organizers. Initially I assign the groups, but not the side of the debate, pro or con. Thus, all students research both sides of the issue for which their team decides they are responsible. At the end of the first day of class discussion and investigation, I flip a coin to determine the sides. For homework that night, students craft their speeches and questions supporting either the affirmative or negative.

The next day, they meet in groups to share their work. They evaluate each others' arguments, making sure critical strands haven't been omitted (and chiding those who haven't done the work). I budget for two class periods of debate and invite our guests to either or both. The fact that our head of Middle School, director of diversity, Upper School debate coach, and other teachers and administrators routinely show up to watch the debates sends a powerful message to my students: "These issues are important."

The teams sit on opposing sides of our "open box" desk arrangement, and our debate begins. Aaron and Janie, a White boy and a Black girl, oppose Olivia and Judith, a Black girl and White girl, on the first issue of language:

Aaron and Janie (Affirmative): "Not all language in the book is bad. This book has vivid descriptions and uses similes effectively. For example, the author compares the Black family to a fig tree, small but strong, with deep roots. The vivid language helps us to picture the sad, red place these events are occurring. Yes, there are strong words used in the book, but that teaches us how Blacks were treated in 1934. It's better for us to read it than to hear it and not know the history. This language is used in the book to teach us about race history and to help us change things."

Olivia and Judith (Negative): "This is not a history class, it's an English class. This harsh language is inappropriate for sixth graders. Racial slurs make Whites look bad and make Blacks embarrassed. We don't want to hear this language in the hall, so why would we want to hear it in the classroom? Why should we have to read the N-word? The author should change that."

Another strong exchange describes the novel's psychological effects on sixth graders. This time, Dean and Teddy, an Asian boy and a White boy, debate Mia and Pauline, two White girls:

Dean and Teddy (Affirmative): "Overall, this book has a positive psychological effect. The author shows a troubled past, and people sticking together through hard times. Through misery, the Logan family fights back. English teachers say the book is good, but we also interviewed other students who say the book has more of a positive effect on them than a negative one."

Mia and Pauline (Negative): "There were only two good Whites. The rest of the Whites were stereotyped. It made White kids feel bad, and some felt angry. It made African American kids feel bad, and it made everyone feel depressed. How can bad stuff not have a bad effect on us psychologically?"

The debate progresses with energized students speaking, listening, and civilly questioning each other (as I remind them to do!). On debate days, kids come to class early and don't want to leave at the end of class. But, finally, the closing arguments are delivered by Paige and Keith, two White students, and Zaden and Lily, an Asian boy and White girl. Interestingly, Paige is a White student who has been angered by the depictions of Whites in the book. "I have family in the South," she complained one day. "I don't like the way this book puts down White Southerners." However, midway through the book, as two important White characters made positive appearances, her attitude changed. Now, although she is defending the book because of a coin-toss, her remarks are heartfelt.

Paige and Keith (Affirmative): "This book is used across the nation. It's won the Newbery Award given for the best literature written for kids. We've seen violence before. We've seen violent movies. We know about Iraq. The slurs and violence are well done, they portray the past, and it's true that some Whites were really racist. This book helps us learn, and teaching kids about the past helps us improve the future. We should definitely keep this book in the curriculum."

Zaden and Lily (Negative): "The novel is full of racial slurs and bad influences. Whipping, beatings, shootings, lying, cheating, stealing, drinking. Parents don't want kids to read about this stuff in school. Some kids don't think before acting, and they might imitate this stuff. There are alternatives to this book that can teach the same issues without such harsh detail. Books like *Sounder*, or *Bud, not Buddy* could be used. Maybe this book is okay for eighth grade, not for sixth. And, some schools don't have teachers who can teach this book appropriately.

Becoming a Multicultural Person

And this is an important point: teachers have to be willing—and able—to get their hands dirty while teaching a book with such emotionally charged racial content. Each year in discussing our approach to the book, my teaching colleague and I affirm our need to take time for careful instruction and lengthy discussion. We must use supplements and sensitivity to make every child feel safe. Yes, we have other material to "cover," we agree. But this novel has both literary merit and the potential to affect readers' lives lifelong. "Let's take time to do this right," we promise each other.

But that's not all that is needed. I draw on my personal experience living in cultures different from my own as well as my long commitment to learning about race history and multicultural instruction. I know Matt, a White male, shares this dedication. Nieto (2004) delineates the steps that are crucial in becoming a teacher committed to teaching such content. We must become multicultural people ourselves to be able to teach multicultural issues with meaning and deep impact for our students:

> First, we simply need to learn more…. Second, we need to confront our own racism and biases…. Third, becoming a multicultural person means learning to see reality from a variety of perspectives. (pp. 383-384)

They've Got to Learn About This Stuff

One class discussion is a particularly good example of how my willingness to notice unequal treatment and to talk about race—especially as a White teacher—opens the discussion to more participation, thinking, and *feeling* from all the students in class.

We are discussing whether such racial humiliation as we see in the novel ever appears in our own lives or school neighborhood. Our school's population groups— a predominantly White student population as well as African American and other students of color—are drawn from the city of Philadelphia and the affluent suburbs. Students in all groups represent a range of economic backgrounds. Out of a class of 16 students, one year, there are 12 White students and 4 Black students. We arrive at the point in the novel when the Black children shopping in a grocery store are rudely ignored, while the White owner courteously serves the White customers. I ask if any of the students have seen such biased behavior in real life. No takers. I intuit that several of the kids of color certainly have. I wonder if some of the White kids may not be willing to admit they have. And, perhaps others haven't been willing to notice.

Determined to push them to more deeply evaluate their personal experiences, I give an example from my neighborhood in which my son's Black friend is followed around our local variety store by one of the White clerks while both boys are looking at toys. I go on to describe two of my neighbors who are routinely stopped by the suburban police for "driving while Black." The White kids look at me without a clue. The Black kids, however, nod in sympathetic understanding—except for Vanessa.

She just puts her head on her desk and murmurs, "I can't believe she just said that." And then the Black kids and I have to explain to the White kids what the phrase means. Local news coverage confirms that neighborhood police and state troopers routinely pull over cars simply because drivers are Black or Brown. This information astonishes most of the White students, and they listen with a mix of disbelief and concern.

My examples finally open the flood gates, and one by one the Black students describe examples of prejudicial behavior directed at them. "When my friends and I went to the mall last weekend," Aliyah explains, "the security guard followed us everywhere we went. Finally, I went and got my mom to tell the guard to leave us alone. They do it all the time to all the Black kids." That such humiliating treatment routinely happens to their own classmates of color is a revelation to many of the White students in the class.

I am sure I am stretching my White students' thinking. Peggy McIntosh (1988/2006, p. 83) writes about her own discovery of "White privilege" as a White woman. "I began to count the ways in which I enjoy unearned skin privilege and have been conditioned into oblivion about its existence," she writes as she lists daily activities such as shopping without being followed by store guards or feeling sure that if a policeman pulls her car over it's not because of her race.

Before this class my White students are comfortably unaware of their White privileges. Now, they are gaining critical life awareness. But does their growing knowledge come at the expense of my Black students' comfort? After class, I speak privately with Aliyah and express my worry. "Is this type of discussion too much for you personally? Are you okay with us talking about race like this?"

"Mrs. Cannon," she declares emphatically, "they've got to learn about this stuff."

Student Evaluations

At the close of the debate, students summarize the arguments and, as a culminating activity, they finally articulate their honest opinions of whether we should read the novel in sixth grade. Year after year, two-thirds of the students, White and Black, express that the book has had an important and positive impact on them overall. One or two kids offer alternative selections or agree we should read it only "if we have lots of discussions." Anonymously, I share aloud the opinions of members of the class, offering excerpts of support, distress, or suggestions for compromises. For many White students, reading the book "was the first opportunity I had to really understand what racism was, then and now, in a way that was not 'watered down.' It was harsh, but good." For several Black students, reading the book with their White classmates provides a breakthrough. Aliyah's comment is representative:

> This was the first time I thought my classmates really understand some of the things I have to go through every day. It made me angry, but after we discussed it, I felt better. I think students should read this book in sixth grade. This is the grade when racial discrimination begins.

Meanwhile, Owen, a White boy, shows new resolve:

> Children can't change the past, but they can surely change the future, and the sorrow and sadness that the kids share will make the children reading the book unite and ban racial cruelty forever. Thank you for having us read it.

But Does it Make a Difference?

To provide a transition from the past in the book to the present in the real world, I show *The Legacy of Slavery* (2005), journalist Linda Ellerbee's frank *Nick News* video, in which she and scholar Cornel West interview a diverse group of adolescents about race issues, past and present. By this point we have read, discussed, affirmed each other, conducted family heritage interviews, and taken the book from a fictional account of a time far away to the heart of our lives at home and in school and community with a diverse group of people. At one point, two students in Ellerbee's video assert what character Papa Logan states in the novel: When kids get to be around 12 years old, Blacks and Whites can no longer be friends.

On an anonymous questionnaire, my students evaluate our reading of the novel, and I ask them if they agree with Papa's (and the video's) assertion. Indeed, many students experience that it is hard to make friendships across race lines. But most have hope, and they appreciate what they have learned from reading the book.

> I did not like to find out that White people did that then. I did not like to find out that my ancestors did this. I am more sensitive toward people that

are offended by racial comments. I would not like for someone to have a stereotype about me, so why should I stereotype other people?

I learned more about my race and what happened back then. I think I learned to appreciate my life, because I have a lot more than people back then. But, I do agree with Papa and the video because last year I was hanging out with everyone, but this year I'm starting to hang out with Blacks. I still hang out with Whites, just not as much.

I don't agree, because I think we're mature enough to know better.

I agree, because—it sounds horrible to say—but I feel a little more comfortable with friends in my race.

I think that people of different races can be friends once they hit middle school, if you really are true friends. I agree that when you are younger, color does not really make a difference because you do not really see a difference. But when you age you do. People of different races can be friends if they don't fall into pressure and think they are better than someone of a different race.

It might be hard to stay friends, and if it doesn't work, at least you tried. But if it does work, you could change everything.

Caring about stereotyping, racism, and institutional injustice; evaluating inter-racial friendships; hoping to "change everything." These are reasons enough for me to keep reading the novel *Roll of Thunder, Hear my Cry*, and other provocative novels like it. Literature can help us understand ourselves and each other, and for the teacher willing to create a safe space in which students and teachers alike can make life-changing discoveries—positive and negative—such novels are an indispensable tool in promoting empathy in the character, antibias, multicultural, social justice, and peace education processes.

Questions to Consider:

1. How multiculturally knowledgeable and comfortable are you? How can you learn more? Are there colleagues and organizations to help you enhance your own multicultural competence? Will your school support this endeavor?

2. What opportunities exist in your school or area for your students to learn about different cultures and ethnicities? Are students of different backgrounds able to become friends? Will families be supportive? How might such interactions occur?

3. Is there a book or story in your curriculum that you worry promotes stereotypes? How do you assess the risks and benefits of reading such a book with your students? What can you do to deepen student understanding? Is there an alternative book to use?

4. Is it appropriate to read about such painful topics as war and discrimination with students? What about language? How do you determine if a book will be "too much" for your students? If a book has difficult material, have you invited families to become involved in discussing the book with their children? What resulted?

5. Have you seen your students gain new understandings while reading or discussing a book? Has this ever happened to you? What happened to facilitate such change?

CHAPTER 6

CREATING A CARING CLASSROOM AND GLOBAL COMMUNITY WITH POETRY AND PROSE

CREATING THE CARING CLASSROOM

"For adolescents these are among the most pressing questions: Who am I? What kind of person will I be? Who will love me? How do others see me? Yet schools spend more time on the quadratic formula than on any of these existential questions."

—Nel Noddings
(*The Challenge to Care in Schools*, 2005a, p. 20)

"What is it about our schools that takes the poetry out of our children?"

—Luis Rodriguez
(Multicultural Resource Center Conference, April 1994)

*"If you were to look at me you would see a kid who is tall....
But if you were to get to know me, you would see ... a kid that is a good friend. A kid you'd want to get to know."*

—Sixth-grade boy

Think, Care, Act: Teaching for a Peaceful Future, pp. 83–103
Copyright © 2011 by Information Age Publishing

Figure 22.   Students edit writing in pairs.

"The essential human act at the heart of writing is the act of giving," writes Peter Elbow (1981, p. 20). Sharing prose and poetry allows students to give each other gifts of themselves in small pieces over time. Certainly teaching content is important. It's what I have been hired to do. However, I can better teach, and my students can better learn, when we create a warm, collegial, even loving classroom community together. John Medina (2008) cites brain research documenting the positive impact of such warm educational environments and relationships on learning. I further believe that experiencing a peaceful classroom community helps students understand that loving, caring communities can be created outside of the family. They also experience the steps such community building requires. Thus, classroom writing and sharing are tools in peacebuilding in our classroom.

Frustrated that schools pay more attention to content rather than care, however, former math teacher Noddings (2005a) argues that schools don't pay enough attention to the questions most on their adolescent students' minds. She urges teachers to take time—in every subject discipline—to explore them. Lucy Calkins (1986) states that adolescents need to write about topics that are personally meaningful and important, as well. My students echo these researchers' findings, writing, "I wish we could write about more things like favorite old friends and talk about our personality." "I'd love to write about the main purpose about one thing: life."

The History Class Writing Community

Such sharing and caring happens in history or debate class as we reflect on current events or share our opinions on political candidates and historical issues. By promoting civil dialogue, I ask my students to respect and care about the person with whom they exchange ideas. (See Chapters 2 and 8 for more on civil debate.) Although history class writing is usually content centered, my students write personally when reflecting on the significance of the memento they bring to school as we create a class archeological "museum," for example. Tying the study of archeology to personal memoir, students write descriptions to help classmates appreciate the personal significance of a baseball, shawl, photograph, or other family treasure.

In critiquing research writing, one of my goals is to create a collegial environment. To benefit all writers in class, I often share student writing aloud to be critiqued by peers, without individual students feeling singled out for ridicule. When I make the classroom safe for mistake making—by stating specific appreciation for what each writer does well, by modeling constructive suggestions versus personal attack, by thanking student writers for allowing us to learn from their mistakes—our research writing improves drastically. Further, our history classroom moves from being solely a place of research and debate to one that includes mutual appreciation, collaboration, and trust.

The English Class Writing Community

However, in an English classroom, writing more typically describes personal memories and emotions, and sharing this kind of writing allows us to get to know each other faster and deeper than in other subjects I teach. Prose and poetry allow us to investigate life questions in response to literature we read as well as experiences that arise in our school and lives. The affective domain—showing my students I care about their deepest questions and asking them to care about each other—is the foundation for much of the writing we do together. Students grow in skill as writers, as we simultaneously build a caring community.

It is important to create this community early in the year. By doing so, I communicate my concern and interest in my students—not only as students, but as people. Starting in September, I want to get to know them, and I want them to know their classmates and me, on a deep, rather than superficial level.

The Treasure in the Mirror

Laying groundwork with a few "get-to-know-you" exercises as I do in all my classes, I launch the first English-class writing assignment with an activity inspired by Mildred Serra and the Borinquen Writing Project (2006). Each child takes turns joining me in the hall where I hold a basket mysteriously covered with a blue cloth. "It's a treasure," I tease, "and you are going to write about it." I ask each child to pull back the cloth and look closely inside. As children gaze into the mirror I've hidden, they smile, look away, straighten their hair, or laugh. They get it. "Shhh. Write about the treasure you saw in the basket. Don't talk to anyone, just write."

With sly glances around the room, they settle in to write about themselves for the first time in a new grade. They finish their paragraphs for homework, and I ask them to share their writing the next day in class. I wonder if anyone will volunteer. I needn't worry. Beatrice starts: "I had seen it many times before. However, I had never really thought of it as a treasure. Now I realize what a mistake it was to think of it as unimportant." Maya adds: "I never thought that what stared back at me could ever be a treasure to anyone or even to me. In the basket I saw my bright, young face. It looked humble and proud at the same time." Emboldened, Julian expresses his worries and hopes:

> When I saw myself, I wondered if I had been true to that person in the mirror. I found many rights and many wrongs. I decided that I was going to make that boy a better person. When I accomplish that, everyone will look at me and think, *great person.*

Angela widens the mirror to include others:

> When I imagine my reflection I don't just see myself. I see many people behind me, helping me, teaching me. All those people—my teachers, my friends and my family—are my spotters in life. They help me be the person I see in the mirror today, the grand and admirable treasure.

We play with their prose writing, taking essential words and turning their treasure prose into poetry. They start feeling comfortable playing with words and writing about themselves. And, when they next walk into the classroom, they look at each other differently, seeming to see each other—and me—for the first time.

One Moment in Time

They will learn more about themselves and forge closer bonds with classmates if they dig deeper into their personal trove of experience and emotion. Thus, I ask students to gather their thoughts, pictures, and mementos for a memory writing assignment. They grin at the possibilities as I do the math:

> Pick one moment from the millions of moments you've lived: 1440 per day, 525,600 per year, 6,307,200 in twelve years! What makes one moment stand out? What one incident do you remember clearly and vividly, for either positive or negative reasons? What are the feelings or emotions associated with this moment that only you can describe?

To prepare for writing, I first ask students to decorate their journal covers: to draw pictures, attach photographs and important objects, or select magazine pictures that represent people, places, or things that are important to them. At least one item must relate to the emotions of the moment they will write about. We spend a class period sharing and explaining the pictures and objects they choose. This is not time wasted! I have found that talking and listening leads to better writing, and talking about pictures allows students to get to know their peers as they collect words and sentences for their compositions.

To encourage them, and to be a contributing partner in the writing community, it is important for me to share as well. So, I model my request, describing my journal pictures of family, travels, favorite vegetarian foods, and kayaks. Finally, I hold high the foot-long, gray feather I am sure is from the great blue heron I encountered day after day while kayaking a lonely lagoon in Ontario one summer. "One evening," I tell my students, "I decided to take a short kayak trip at sunset. I took the long way around a bay I knew well—in daytime." I continue:

> However, as dusk fell, I realized I could no longer see the tiny inlet that would lead me home. I panicked as it grew dark. I had no flashlight, and no one in the family knew where I was. Suddenly, the great blue heron flew over—like some great pterodactyl in the dark—leading my following eye to the inlet I was searching for. The next day I found this feather. It reminds me of how scared I was. And how grateful.

The kids don't know me well yet. But in that 2-minute sharing, they know I will make this a safe place for their personal writing. I can see it in the way they lean forward to share my fear and the way they want to touch the feather when I finish speaking. I partner boys and girls, or old and new students, inviting them to forge new connections by talking with their classmates about their own photographs and pictures.

They write first drafts and edit their essays in pairs and small groups during this writing process and others. I prompt them to give each other constructive feedback: "Can you write what you did when that happened?" "This part confuses me." During peer editing, I confer with students personally, asking about their pictures, paragraphs, and lives. Finally, reading their final drafts aloud from the "author's chair," students feel increasingly at ease about sharing their writing with others.

Again we play with poetry and prose, mimicking Ben Franklin's method of improving his writing by transforming written pieces from prose to poetry and back. We extract essential words from the memory narratives and write poetry to share in class and to publish in our first magazine of class writing. During this process we learn how Jenny feels to be the oldest of four children as she describes her aunt's wedding: "At the reception/Shirley Temples/Only about four years old/No siblings/Peaceful/ Bliss." We grieve with Maya over the death of a schoolmate: "Death seized me, crept over me,/Lives in me, waiting to come out." And we triumph with Rose at her gymnastics tournament: "I flipped like a copper penny/I turned as if I were a spinning top/ I stuck the landing."

Calkins (1986) writes of the transforming effects of such personal, multidraft writing, noting how the community elicits better writing, while better writing creates the community. I believe in the benefits, but this process is something I have had to push myself to take time for. In spite of having to accommodate curriculum and schedule demands—as do most teachers in public and independent settings—I continue to adjust my writing schedule to include personal poetry and prose, such as the treasure writing, throughout the year. The benefits far outweigh the costs.

The Gift of Poetry

Prior to my first year teaching middle school English, my instinct said to begin the year with reading and writing poetry. Poetry had unlocked writing for me as a middle school student, and I knew it would create opportunities for breakthroughs in writing and self-knowledge for my students as well. Thus, I had spent the summer assembling a thirty-page, multicultural, multi-era collection of poetry, ranging from that of Yang Wan Li, a Chinese poet from the 1100s; to Jalal Din Rumi, a Persian poet of the 1400s; to American Emily Dickinson's work of the 1800s; to that of Palestinian-American poet Naomi Shihab-Nye, and former gang member Luis Rodriguez, a Latino poet and educator.

I had heard Rodriquez read his powerful poems at a teacher conference on multicultural education several years earlier. He had spoken to teachers after his reading, and his stinging critique of the education system in our country still rang in my heart. "What is it about our schools that takes the poetry out of our children?" he chided.

I resolved that I would be a teacher who put the poetry back.

Power of the Spoken Word

First, I use the spoken as well as the written word. There is emotional power when I read poems aloud to my students (or when we read them together chorally). The spoken word brings us together in a way that reading the poems silently does not. I warn students not to be concerned if they are bewildered by the imagery of the poems. I assure them with numerous quotes from poets about the affective power of poetry, even if we don't think we understand it. A student ultimately explains it best, "Poetry is a use of words that twist all up in your mind but still make sense."

I begin with an excerpt from Walt Whitman's *Song of Myself* (1867). As he exhorts the reader to spend time with him to "possess the origin of all poems," I define a few words: specter, filter, third hand—and read it again. "It's like he's telling us to think for ourselves," volunteers a student—and we're off. I follow Whitman's plea with a similar one from Eve Merriam's metaphorical but somehow more accessible *How to Eat a Poem* (1986), in which she likens a poem to a juicy fruit awaiting a first, energetic bite. Wanting to keep letting the words of poets wash over them, I practically bombard them with spoken words.

I next share excerpts from Luis Rodriguez's 1995 poem *Don't Read that Poem!* in which he explores the power of poetry to stir the emotions. The first time I recite it, one of my chattiest boys stops talking and almost falls off his chair. He explodes, "That's a poem? That's incredible!" I read it with force, walking around the room, trying to convey the passion with which Rodriguez felt it, wrote it, and reads it himself. Describing a brutally honest poet at an open mic session, Rodriguez writes that he is so overcome with the power of her poetry that his head feels like it will explode. He wants to stand up and scream for her to stop reading.

I ask my students to discern what Rodriguez's words have in common with the remarks by Dickinson, who wrote over one hundred years before him in a letter to a friend, "If I feel physically as if the top of my head were taken off, I know that is poetry" (Ryan, 2006). And how do these writers' thoughts and words connect with those of Yang Wan-Li's words from over 800 years ago? Finally, I ask, "How do these words connect to you?"

Selecting from a poetry anthology, I share one last passage, in prose, in which Cynthia Rylant (1990) describes a boy she calls a poet simply because of the way he notices things nobody else does. She expresses the way he always feels lonely, even though others consider him popular. He simply doesn't feel normal.

Several kids look stunned—as if Rylant has just pried the lids off their hearts and peered in. "Whew," sighs one. "I think I'm a poet." They're hooked.

Who is a Poet?

Because I make myself vulnerable by reading meaningful poems with heart (and including my own writing), my students are willing to see our classroom in a new light: as a place where hearts can safely be shared. I ask them, "If you could talk to a poet we've read, who would it be, and what would you ask about their words?" As homework, they turn their thoughts into a letter to a poet, a definition of poetry, or another personal reaction to the poetry.

A quiet student, who has seemed only half-hearted in her class participation prior to these poetry lessons, finds her voice. With confidence she reads her poem to us. Her classmates sense her transformation as she challenges them to throw out the dictionary definition and use hers instead:

Poet (artist)
A person with a mind as massive as the galaxy itself
Or maybe
A person who desires to show their feelings to the world
It could even be
A person with extraordinary powers…
I hope we're on the same page.

Who am I?

Thus, when I introduce the poems that will elicit kids' writing about who *they* are, we are ready to compassionately receive the classmates who will reveal themselves. My directions are based on my reading aloud poems that are self put-ups or self put-downs. It refreshes young writers to know that poets can brag like Walt Whitman, N. Scott Momaday, and Eloise Greenfield, or self-deprecate like Emily Dickinson, Ronald Wallace, and Sandra Cisneros. In their self-portrait poems I invite students to "brag, question, complain, and soar away from the ordinary."

For young adolescents such sharing requires a leap of faith. When they read, their hands shake. Sometimes we can barely hear them—when a moment before I had to tell them to "keep it down." What do listeners do with these "gifts?" They smile self-consciously. They applaud spontaneously. They look at the readers—seeing them as people with feelings, gifts, and longings the listeners share.

A boy, new to the school one year, reads,

> If you were to look at me you would see
> A kid who is tall....
> But if you were to get to know me
> You would see...
> A kid that is fun
> A kid that is a good friend
> A kid you'd want to get to know

A girl's classmates learn how deeply she is thinking about her identity. Might her words express their longing for self-knowledge, too?

> I am the feather that soars up high
> Up through the clouds, alone
> Trying to find myself as I wave goodbye
> Hoping to know who I am...

And suddenly the pieces of another student's complex personality fall into place as she reveals,

I am.....Beautiful
From as far as the eyes can see
And as well as I know me.

I am not............Hateful
Despite my bad attitude
The negative vibe I give off to some people who give one to me.

Steps in Creating the Safe Space

Students dare to do such deep sharing because I introduce them to poets from diverse backgrounds whom I select because they unveil our common humanity—and I like them myself. For teachers who do not have the time, confidence, or inclination to create their own poetry anthologies, collections like those edited by Paul Janeczko (1990) and Liz Rosenberg (1999) are particularly helpful in letting poets speak directly to diverse groups of children—both through their poems and their commentaries.

While we are becoming a poetry-writing community, I invite all children to share their work every day in class. Some days we share in pairs, so children will gain the confidence to read for the whole group. We applaud for each poet, every day. Everyone feels listened to, heard, and appreciated. We ask questions about meaning and phrasing, valuing the details of writing and the nuances of personality. We publish our work for others to share, on bulletin boards, in a personal portfolio I put on public display, and in a class magazine for which poets choose the poem they deem their best.

Finally, we cap off the unit with a dynamic and rowdy Poetry Slam, adapted for middle school to resemble those held nationally. I invite several teachers and students to do instantaneous "Olympic-style" judging (of content and delivery on a 10-point scale). Kids sign up to perform their poems on a voluntary basis, and we invite an audience whom I whip into a frenzy of warmth and merriment. The readers read, the audience cheers, the judges score, and we have a winner and runners-up. It's all in good fun, and we bring our celebration of poetry to a happy close—for now.

Student Evaluations

Does poetry resonate with the inner lives of children? Does it allow them to give of themselves to others? Does it build a caring classroom? "YES! I LOVED IT!" writes one student. "We could have done more." "I felt like I had more freedom writing poetry." "It's a "fun way to express your mind." It's "a way to get your feelings out."

Others observe increased safety and connection, writing:

Letting other people see your work helps you gain confidence. You can feel like you can show people your writing without being embarrassed.

I didn't know some of my classmates. I thought they were kind of odd and didn't think much of them. But now I think we may have more in common than I thought.

We can put the poetry back in school. In doing so, we create a timeless space for these too-often-harried students to slow down and get to know themselves and each other. We build a community of care.

FAMILY HERITAGE PROJECT

*When students learn to respect and befriend classmates from
different backgrounds and cultures, they are learning an attitude
significant for global citizenship."*

—Nel Noddings
(*Educating Citizens for Global Awareness*, 2005b, p. 122)

*"Everybody born on this earth is something,
and nobody, no matter what color, is better than anybody else…"*

—Mama to Cassie
(in *Roll of Thunder, Hear my Cry*,
by Mildred D. Taylor, 1976, p. 127)

*"My heritage is important to me because in some unseen way, it supports me.
Whatever nationality I am, I will know that my family loves me, and I
should love everyone back."*

—Sixth grade girl

Figure 23.   Students share heritage letters in small groups.

Taking time to "share the love" in our classroom has the payoff of increasing students' fondness for each other and connection with the material to be learned. Riffing on the idea of passing notes in school, I'll occasionally ask students to pass kind-word notes to each other (I read them first!), pushing them to appreciate their peers' unique qualities. Imagine students' delight in reading little slips of paper with such confidence-building compliments as these: "You don't get angry no matter how frustrating things are." "You're a great hockey player." "You write the most exciting stories." "You have a great sense of humor."

Inviting students to express gratitude to our cafeteria staff, teachers, coaches, or family members via formally written thank-you notes gives me the opportunity to teach the lost art of letter writing. Much more importantly, however, the kind-words process helps students feel and express the gratitude they have for those who do so much for them. Psychologist Martin Seligman (2002) and Buddhist Thich Nhat Hanh (2003) agree that counting our blessings—by thanking those responsible for them—increases our joy in being cared for and being caring.

I have written in Chapter 5 about the power of reading *Roll of Thunder, Hear my Cry* to promote awareness and discussion of race issues. Such a book allows us to build caring community through writing as well. In her introduction, Mildred D. Taylor (1976) explains that she wrote the book to introduce her readers to strong, loving Black families.

But, Black, White, Red, Yellow, or Green, isn't it also important to deepen each student's love and gratitude to his or her own family and heritage?

Researching Family Heritage

My aim in this project is to help students understand the philosophy advocated by numerous educators: by exploring similarities and differences of our family heritages, we can better understand ourselves, each other, and families throughout the world (Gardner, 2006; Lin, 2008; Noddings, 2005b). Thus, I ask students to conduct a formal interview of an adult family member, asking specific questions about their heritage:

1. What heritage(s) do I have? (national, ethnic, racial, religious, other)
2. Is it important for me to know my heritage? Explain.
3. What is something you hope I will never forget about my heritage or my family?

4. Is there anyone in our family or from our heritage whom you would like me to emulate?

5. What are your hopes for me? What advice do you have to help me achieve those hopes?

6. Is there a family story you think I should know? (Funny, serious, happy, sad...)

7. Is there anything else you would like to tell me?

In an individual class of students raised in the United States, the cultural roots span the globe: Italian, Hungarian, English, Irish, German, Jamaican, Russian, Lithuanian, Ukrainian, Polish, Cherokee, Vietnamese, Chinese, Chilean, Pakistani, Syrian, Caribbean, Ghanaian, Scottish, Norwegian, Korean, Protestant, Catholic, Baptist, Methodist, Lutheran, Jewish, Muslim, Hindu!

Some years, students take their raw interview data and turn it into a script or story. Usually, however, I use a letter-writing format in which they transform their information into a letter. They choose to write *as* the interviewee, or they write a thank-you letter expressing gratitude *to* the family member for conveying the information. Either way, we actually mail these letters to the parents or grandparents they interview.

For most students, the project is an opportunity to renew family bonds and learn their families' values. One boy is particularly touched by his interview. While he sees his grandfather often, this is the first time his grandfather has shared with him the five "ations." Writing as his grandfather, he explains them and other values his grandfather holds dear:

> Success in life is based on the five "ations:" Education, Motivation, Concentration, Determination, and Dedication. If you follow these "ations" anything can be possible.... Respecting all people of different races, backgrounds, and religions is necessary. We are all equal.

Student Evaluations

Student reflections upon the interview process are overwhelmingly affirming. They appreciate that I conduct the interview unit sensitively, making all students feel comfortable and able to participate with dignity. Adopted children decide with their families whether to interview their birth families or their adoptive families, for example. Many African Americans cannot trace specific national origins of ancestors. We speak openly about the slave trade and how it disrupted family histories.

In some cases, students learn negative things about family members, but turn their ancestors' negative actions into inspiration to do good. For example, one boy's family has engaged him in sophisticated and sensitive discussions of social-justice issues from a young age. Therefore, it is not surprising that he is able to write wisely about his complex family heritage. After detailing many positive and negative accomplishments of his ancestors, he writes, "I will not forget about my more oppressive ancestors so that I never become like them. This was quite a fun learning experience."

An important question for me is whether we should do this heritage project at all in sixth grade. After all, as a third grade teacher in our Lower School, I developed a semester-long family heritage project, in which each student researches the life and values of a particularly inspiring ancestor. Children write reports on a country of ancestry and the life of their "amazing ancestor." They even create a life-sized puppet of this inspiring figure. We invite parents and other family members to our annual International Festival, and our third graders enact a Parade of Ancestors in which each puppet ancestor "speaks" timeless advice.

My goal then, as now, is twofold: to promote respect and empathy in our classroom, and to help students raised in the United States see their tangible connection to people throughout the global community. Except for newcomers to the school, each of my sixth graders has participated in such family research in third grade. Yet, in spite of this prior research, students are positive. One sixth grader's reaction is typical of his classmates' evaluations:

> Learning about my heritage now has meant so much to me. In third grade, we hardly understood the information about our ancestors. Now as 6th graders, we are figuring out our identity. We understand what heritage means. We are able to picture ourselves in our ancestor's shoes. This is why I have found this project utterly fascinating.

A student writes, "It is important for me to know I am from many backgrounds. This gives me more choices and makes me less prejudiced." Another girl learns a similar lesson: "My grandmom told me, 'It is important for you and everyone else in the world to love their heritage because loving your heritage and yourself makes it easier for you to love and respect others and their heritages.'" The student continues, "My heritage is important to me because in some unseen way, it supports me. Whatever nationality I am, I will know that my family loves me, and I should love everyone back."

We will pursue this idea of global interconnectedness in the next section, as my students share their dreams with their counterparts worldwide.

CONNECTING WITH THE WIDER WORLD THROUGH PROSE AND POETRY

"Cyberspace has the potential for bringing together people who hitherto have not been given the opportunity to engage with the 'other.' "

—M. Ayaz Naseem
(*Peace-Education Value of the World Wide Web*, 2008, p. 198)

"We should urge our students to see through many differences amongst nations and cultures and look at the aspirations and wisdom common to all of us as human beings."

—Jing Lin
(*Constructing a Global Ethic of Universal Love, Forgiveness, and Reconciliation*, 2008, p. 313)

"This is a letter to you—you on the other side of the world."

—Sixth grade poet

Figure 24.   Students in Yangzhou (China) respond to dream poems of American students.

Stress and mindfulness researcher Jon Kabat-Zinn (1990) bemoans the fact that children (and adults) are bathed in a steady media diet of negative news and violent imagery. Among the effects of this imagery, he says, is that we create enemies of strangers by promoting *us* and *them* thinking. Instead, he says, we must teach children to start thinking in terms of *we*. Nancy Carlsson-Paige and Linda Lantieri (2005) also urge educators to help students appreciate that the world's future depends on their becoming cooperative, engaged global citizens. To do so, Lin (2008) reminds us to help our students understand our common hopes and dreams.

Internet Postcards for Peace

International writing exchanges are significant, and I often bring postcards written by my students as I travel for educational conferences and teaching overseas. I ask students I meet in host countries to respond to my students, keeping topics uniform so kids will give and get information on a wide variety of high-interest topics. I also post the contents of the cards electronically, so that teachers who are not able to travel abroad may still enable their students to compare and contrast the worlds and lives of students from different places. Internet postings promote global understanding, as M. Ayaz Naseem (2008) recognizes. He has researched online interactions of citizens of Pakistan and India, to conclude that the Internet is a powerful tool for breaking barriers and forging human connections—even among seemingly intransigent foes.

I give intriguing instructions to visitors to the *China Today* portion of my website, www.teachforpeace.org (Cannon, 2006). I have similar instructions, but with American slang terms and topics, on the *Life in the USA* pages:

> Some ideas are very familiar. But do you know what an erhu is, what Children's Day is, who Yao Ming is, why it's good to get red packets…? Do these postcards give you a feeling for life in China for a teenager? What is the same and what is different from your own life?

Compare these "postcards," the first from a Chinese middle school student, the second from a student from the United States, shared online:

Dear Friend,

> I am 14 years old. My favorite holiday is Winter Holiday because I can have a rest. Chinese New Year is in winter, too. I can get some red packets. My favorite place is the biggest beach, because on the beach I can get lots of shells. I eat lots of noodles and dumplings on my birthday.

Dear Friend,

I am 12 years old. My favorite holidays are Christmas and summer vacation, because on Christmas I get presents and on summer vacation there is no school! My favorite place is the beach because it is warm and relaxing. On my birthday, I eat cake.

Children and adults treasure these cards, decorated with colorful, hand-drawn pictures in real life, electronically posted in plain type on the website. Postcards are good for conveying the practical aspects of life in a given country, but sharing dreams forges deeper emotional ties.

The Dream Flag Project

Jeff Harlan and Sandy Crow (n.d.) teach English at the Agnes Irwin School. Their website (www.dreamflags.org) invites teachers to share the poetry of Langston Hughes and the tradition of Buddhist prayer flags with students as a catalyst to get students to write about their own dreams. During a glorious public program at a concert hall in Philadelphia each spring, thousands of students gather to join their dreams and recite poems of peace, hope, and connectedness. The Dream Flag Project has gone national and global, with participants sharing dreams from schools across the United States, and schools in China, Japan, South Africa, and even from Rwandan refugee camps.

"If you could communicate with kids from other countries," I ask my students, "what would you say?" I invite them to write poetry that expresses their hopes for their own lives and for human relationships around the world. We transfer the poems from paper to cloth, eventually creating the clothesline of dreams that connects students' individual hopes to their classmates' and eventually to thousands of students' dreams in our region.

The project is especially gratifying as I prepare to travel internationally, as my prompting question is not theoretical. My students know I will actually hand deliver their messages. Dream flags are cloth poems, light and easy to pack, so I have taken student poems to faraway places to share with students and teachers in Japan, China, Denmark, and Canada.

When I taught in China in 2005 and 2006, for example, there was no more tangible way to convey the care and friendship of American students than to invite my Chinese colleagues and students to read the dreams of my American kids. But everyone wanted to touch the cloth—to hold the dreams—pointing to the words as they read the poems silently, sharing puzzling or poignant lines with friends. Soon, as part of my English instruction, my Chinese students were writing about their hopes and dreams as well. There was palpable energy in the room—because, as one student exclaimed happily, they knew "American students will read and touch my dreams!"

Common Dreams

So, what are the dreams of middle schoolers in the United States? Some are so profound that a Japanese audience with whom I shared them was incredulous. "Middle school kids wrote these?" Yes, they write their dreams joyfully, knowing they will be shared locally and globally. Responding to this opportunity to broaden his horizons, an American boy sends this heart-felt plea to a stranger:

> This is a letter to you
> You on the other side of the world.
> Don't judge a book by its cover
> We are all like you from hat to shoe.

A comic artist in real life, one student wishes the world would be a comic book so he could fix all the problems:

> I would take out my eraser
> And wipe it all away
> No more war
> No more deaths
> The world would be free
> All because of me

Another details her vision of a peaceful world:

> The earth is clean,
> No one is hungry,
> Everyone is happy,
> And healthy,
> And learned.
> There are no poor,
> There is no war....

It is easier for the Chinese students in my middle school English classes in Yangzhou, China to read these poems than to write about abstract dreams themselves. Their English is still somewhat limited. Therefore, two girls collaborate on their wish:

> We hope for no war in the world.
> The people are friendly and helpful.

The birds are flying free in the sky.
Everybody has a forgiving heart.

However, teachers taking my summer workshop in teaching English at Rugao Normal College are quite adept at responding to the dreams of American children with dreams of their own, as in this poem:

My dream is one day
the American students can sit together with
the Chinese students to have a
lesson in my class.
I'll let them communicate with each other
learn from each other
and hand in hand, they'll build a friendship between the countries.

And while many Chinese teachers' dreams include a wish for China "to become a powerful nation," a Chinese teacher/poet recognizes the nightmarish cost of some of the hopes. Her poem helps students discuss the environmental issues that besiege China, the United States, and all developed and developing nations:

I like the blue sky.
I like green trees, grasses and crops surrounded by clean rivers.
I dislike air pollution, water pollution, and noise pollution.
I dislike overuse of natural resources.
I dislike gasses and harmful chemicals from factories and cars.

And who can fail to share the love and hope of this Chinese poet, who teaches fifth and sixth-grade students in a rural school in Jiangsu Province? She could be any teacher, any mother, anywhere. And her baby—couldn't he be any of our children?

How small you are!
How weak you are!
Stay in the cradle smiling.
Everyone loves you.
Mommy will hold you tightly.
You're our treasure.
You're my hope of my life!

Student Evaluations

John Dewey's writings urge teachers to promote international understanding (Howlett, 2008), and Maria Montessori's philosophy of education is designed to encourage global citizenship, as well (Duckworth,

2008). Teachers must engage in the multiple challenges of teaching children to love and be good citizens of our own classrooms, communities, and countries as well as to love and participate in the global family (Noddings, 2005b). Recognizing our common humanity and universal human dreams in our classroom and throughout the world is a powerful step in seeking such local and international engagement. With this recognition our students gain a sense of Jane Addams's "cosmic patriotism," a care without boundaries. And our students "cultivate their humanity" to become the global citizens of Nussbaum's vision: "human beings bound to all other human beings by ties of recognition and concern."

My students in the United States passionately appreciate the invitation to share their dreams internationally. They write, "We made friends without even knowing the people." They understand that by reading others' poems, "You can get many different perspectives." "Everyone's dreams are important, even if you don't know them." "We can help each other achieve our dreams and theirs." "We get to state what we think can be fixed in the world." "When can we do this again?"

We have discussed ways to invite students to care: in the classroom, school, home, and world. Using school values and protocols, classroom reading and writing, and global outreach, we can help students experience being cared for and caring. We can encourage them to share dreams with youth near and far.

Now, students like this writer are ready to act to remedy injustice and create an equitable world:

Dreams are pleasant, but
The action
The movement
That is what affects history....

In the next chapters I describe ways to empower students to act on their dreams.

Questions to Consider:

1. Would you consider inviting students to suggest and pursue writing topics of personal importance? Can you also use subject-related writing to help students explore and share personal insights?
2. How can you make your classroom safe for mistake making? How can you communicate this intention to students and enlist their help?

3. Are you willing to make time for students to share writing aloud, in pairs or groups, to encourage students to connect with each other—and you—in the classroom? Can you think of ways to allow them to connect with peers around the world using electronic and other kinds of exchanges? What are the obstacles? How can you overcome these barriers?

4. Seminal peace educators and educational theorists ask that we help our students become global citizens who care for all of humanity. How do you do this? Do your school and family communities support this endeavor? Do you consider yourself a global citizen? What does the term mean to you?

5. Do you take time to count your blessings, appreciate your family, express your gratitude, and honor your inner poet? How do you feel when you do? How can you teach your students to do these things?

PART III

ACT!

*"We overwhelm children with all the suffering
and evil in the world,
but do we enable them to act?"*

—Sister Joan Magnetti
(in Thomas Lickona's *Educating for Character,* 1992, p. 303)

CHAPTER 7

CITIZENSHIP ACTION PROJECTS IN HISTORY CLASS

*"Peace education does not just mean a peaceful classroom.
It suggests a learning environment in which students are acting to resolve
problems, working with others, and taking on challenging tasks."*
—Ian Harris (*Types of Peace Education*, 1999, p. 311)

*"Taking action allows students to move from a position of
powerlessness to one of possibility."*
—Rahima Wade
(*Social Studies for Social Justice*, 2007, p. 14)

"I learned that you can change the world in small doses, one at a time."
—Sixth grade girl

Think, Care, Act: Teaching for a Peaceful Future, pp. 107–120
Copyright © 2011 by Information Age Publishing

Figure 25.   Cooperative group shows location of action project.

As they learn to question the world around them and feel concern about the problems in it, students who can *think* and *care* need opportunities to *act*. Taking action—big or small—helps them feel powerful in the face of the fears that haunt thinking and caring individuals of any age. Educator Sister Joan Magnetti asks a crucial question (Lickona, 1992, p. 303), "We overwhelm children with all the suffering and evil in the world, but do we enable them to act?" I answer with my end-of-year history assignment: *Citizenship Action Project* or *CAP.*

As spring approaches, I invite my history students to take action to change the world. Here we return to Kimberley and one of the stories with which I began this book:

> It is near the end of our year in sixth-grade history, and I introduce my students to our final project. On the board for their homework assignment, I simply write, "Change the world! Details coming soon!" Gasps. Puzzled murmurs. Excited chatter. Finally, Kimberley pipes up, "Mrs. Cannon, are we really going to change the world? I always wanted to be one of those people who change the world."

Prior to our spring vacation we have just completed our huge Multimedia Research Projects: weeks of study of topics chosen by individual researchers. As our final long-term class project, I ask my students to consider a real-world problem about which they care and act to change it for the better. A perplexed student asks, "But what does *CAP* have to do with history?" "Great question," I answer. "I want you to make history by taking action to improve the lives of the people, plants, and animals around you. Be a thinking, caring, and active citizen, and you'll make history of your own." He nods—this makes sense—and he's on board.

Taking on Challenging Tasks

Awareness of social-justice issues is just dawning on these sincere and energetic middle schoolers, and this project makes them feel empowered to act and be successful at social change. Harris (1999) acknowledges that having a loving, peaceful classroom is not where peace education ends. He urges us to enable students to confront difficult problems and work cooperatively to solve them. Our school's seventh-grade science curriculum includes participation in the Earth Force Project (www.earthforce.org) focusing on environmental activism, and this well-designed curriculum has led to many successful projects.

But I want to get my sixth grade history students active now, in an arena about which they care deeply. I want them to see that taking action is part of their lives every day—every year. Additionally, I want to introduce the history of nonviolent social action movements. So, I give my students a loose timeline and numerous examples of actions they might take regarding problems in the home, school, community, country, and world. Then, with my guidance and the involvement of their families, students work alone or in small groups to devise a project of their choosing.

Teachers all over the world do social action projects with their students, and very clear thinking on organizing for social change can be found in such books as *Writing for a Change* (Berdan et al., 2006). This National Writing Project book details the methodology developed by The Center for Social Action. Influenced by Paulo Freire's educational philosophy, the Social Action Process can be summed up in five stages, inviting participants to ask: "*What* issues and problems concern them, analyze *why* they exist, consider *how* they can take action to change them, take these *actions*, and then *reflect* on what they have done and what has changed" (p. 9).

Timeline for Social Action

My process, honed with my students' input over a number of years, is similar. I keep the initial directions simple, putting them on one sheet of paper and encouraging students to discuss possibilities for projects with their families over the spring vacation. "*CAP* off our year studying American history by making some history yourself! Why? To see the positive effects of active citizen's individual and group efforts to change the world."

1. Identify a problem in your home, school, community, country, or the world.
2. Examine root causes and a way you can work actively to improve the situation.
3. Make a plan and carry it out alone or with others, for a long or short time.
4. Report on your project to the class and community.
5. Evaluate the effectiveness of your actions.

When we return from spring break, students write me informal "postcards" with three or four ideas they've discussed with their families and friends. We start looking for resources to support a variety of projects. At that time, I give them a four-page packet, with inspiring quotations, directions, sample project ideas, and a two-month timeline for the project.

Inspiration From Global Activists and Nobel Peace Prize Winners

More importantly, I give my students an in-depth introduction to the thinking that experienced social activists use as they approach problems step by step. Replete with colorful images of children of all ages, the Roots & Shoots website (www.rootsandshoots.org) depicts groups working on projects worldwide. The Jane Goodall Institute's (n.d.) Roots & Shoots organizes its initiatives into three categories: those that benefit humans, animals, and the environment. These delineations make social action understandable to my students. We also browse books about social change, like Barbara Lewis's (2008) *The Teen Guide to Global Action*, with practical advice and multiple examples of projects initiated by youth the world over.

I bring students digitally to Oslo, Norway, and the Nobel Prize (n.d.) website (nobelprize.org). Showing them pictures, video interviews, and biographies of Nobel Peace laureates, I introduce the ideas of individuals and small groups who see something wrong in the world and work to make it better. Spending time with Peace Prize laureates allows students to meet leaders who use critical and compassionate thinking about root causes of local and global problems in active service to the global community. I further invite each student to consider how the problem they will work on fits into the global picture. Thus, when I introduce them to Wangari Maathai and the Green Belt Movement of Kenya, and they hear why she started this movement that has planted over 45 million trees, two boys look at each other and decide, "We're going to plant trees! It's good for the environment, and that's good for peace!"

Global Security Institute president Jonathan Granoff works tirelessly to promote international cooperation and nuclear disarmament and has represented the International Peace Bureau at the Nobel Peace Laureate Summits in Rome yearly since 2002. And what do these Peace laureates ask us to do? Speaking at our school in 2008, Granoff told us that the laureates urge citizens—especially youth—to demand answers to humanity's three most pressing questions: how to address poverty, protect the environment, and eliminate nuclear weapons.

Big ideas and big issues, yes, but I have found that the encouragement of such exemplars as the Dalai Lama, Jody Williams, and Muhammad Yunus is invigorating to my students. They want to rise to great challenges, even if they do so by taking small steps. Further help from the Nobel Peace laureates comes via the *PeaceJam Foundation* (n.d.) website (www.peacejam.org). In 2006, 10 Nobel Peace Prize winners issued *The Global Call to Action* to youth of the world. Their statement reads like a personal invitation, and I include a copy of it with my directions for the *CAP* project. They ask youth to work alongside them to tackle essential global issues including access to natural resources, disease prevention, eradication of racism, enhancement of human rights, environmental protection, disarmament, and eliminating militarism.

Pick a Project You Love

My young activists have been talking with their families, teachers, and friends to gather project ideas. Choosing a project they care deeply about will make the work much more satisfying. Referring to Goodall's three areas of engagement, I hammer home the point of caring about the project. "Kids have organized their family bathroom schedules to stop fights among their siblings. Kids have decorated nursing homes and worked to stop gun violence. Those are human problems. Kids have educated others about endangered animals or helped train our school guide dog. These are problems involving animals. Kids have taught composting or promoted recycling in their communities. They were dealing with environ-

Figure 26.   Students describe their visits to hospital patients.

mental problems." Or, I will come at the issues using language from the Nobel Peace Prize winners, tying into the Global Call to Action or the three questions of protecting the global commons, addressing poverty, or disarming nations. "Kids have done global projects, like educating others about water pollution, disease in developing nations, and the effects of nuclear weapons and war," I explain. "You have a choice to think small or big, close or far! Pick a project you love!"

I introduce the various ways to do social action: as advocate/educator, as an indirect helper, or hands-on. "Look," I tell them, "I believe in the power of education. Sometimes the first step in problem solving is educating people about the problem." Some kids take the bait and become advocates. Often, students only think of indirect fundraising as an option, so I present alternatives like letter writing, collecting supplies, and direct action. Others plan to get their hands dirty, literally or figuratively. They plan clean-ups of parks, gardening projects, or cooking for the homeless. I want them to choose.

Various times during the project, I lead discussion of the students' *CAP* ideas and elaborate on their thinking, asking them why the issues they have chosen are important to them. We connect their individual issues to the larger ideas of the laureates, trying to learn steps others have taken to solve problems like theirs. In this part of the process, students with similar interests join together. At this point, I also help students understand why their proposals may or may not work.

"Normal" studies resume during the time students are working on *CAP*. We are reading about Colonial history, doing role plays to better understand the ground-breaking actions of such peacemaking Indian leaders as Dekanawidah or socially progressive European colonists such as William Penn, for example. In preparing for a field trip to Colonial Williamsburg, we're trying to understand the cruel impact of the institution of slavery on those who were enslaved, on those who were slaveholders, and on those who benefited from afar. We discuss the irony of our country's founders' principles of liberty and justice, while trade in slaves, guns, and rum was the economic underpinning of the colonies. We talk about those people, slave and free, who resisted slavery, through personal action, boycotts, and legislation. We are talking all the time—in every class—about people's personal choices in history.

But slowly, my students are also formulating their plans and choices as they make history themselves.

Doing Social Action

They often seek me out after class, during lunch, or recess, telling me about a problem they've encountered or a website they've created. "I can't do a bake sale to raise money for the inner-city sports foundation because the school says we're having too many bake sales," grumbles one student. So, we work creatively with our athletic director and get permission for the student to do a lemonade sale at a few lacrosse games instead. "Mrs. Cannon, check out my website about childhood cancer!" And in so doing, I find the student has posted all of her personal contact information, including pictures and phone numbers. "Honey, there are better ways for you to convey the information about the issue without inviting people to invade your privacy. It's not safe. Do your parents know you have this stuff on there? How soon can you get it off?"

About one month after our initial introductions and discussions, I collect paragraphs from each student, in which they outline their proposals. Their plans are varied, ranging from concerns close to home to those far away. One child plans to collect items to send to soldiers in Iraq and Afghanistan, another works to end the wars by educating people, and a third makes brochures about Combat Stress Injury and how to help veterans. They decide to work together. Projects range from money-raisers to educational brochures, personal visits, and petition drives. Some children

Figure 27.   School seeing-eye dog helps students teach about animal rights.

are happy to work alone, while others involve classmates and even family businesses.

Many children are motivated by a personal connection, as is Tanya.

> If two people you loved were diagnosed with breast cancer (as were both of my grandmothers) wouldn't you want to try and help the rest of the people who have this horrible disease? This is why I am making one-of-a-kind pink-beaded bracelets and selling them to raise money for the fight against breast cancer.

Tanya goes on to outline an educational component of her plan, and the recipient of the money, a local hospital's breast cancer center. She is able to donate $400.00 by the end of her project.

Franny's plan is prompted by a family member's illness as well. She has noticed that the rooms of her grandmother's nursing home are "dull and needed some color."

For my *CAP* project I had the idea of buying flower pots and flowers and giving them to people there. To earn the money, I will work at my parents' office for one week after school is finished for the year. Then I will buy the pots and plant the flowers in them. To make the gifts look more cheery, I will paint the pots.

Some students opt to help strangers. Two boys will work together to help homeless children in Philadelphia. In so doing, they'll also have a good time with their talent at drawing comics. One explains,

I think that it is great to turn something I love to do into a commitment for society. I would normally think a project like this was boring, and I did, until we thought of making comics. I think it's helpful for both us and the children.

Mariah has an idea to provide books to hospital patients (and ultimately collects and donates 1,000 books):

So far I have given out the flyers and I have also collected some book donations from a few people. I feel that my donations will help the hospital patients get through their stay at the hospital a little bit better and also help the hospital. This is a great opportunity to meet your community.

Three girls will work together to raise money to send a disadvantaged child to a private school in Colombia. One member of the group has relatives in Colombia who tell her the public schools are inadequate. "So, my aunt decided to start a private school that doesn't cost as much as a regular private school. Also, this project will educate people about developing countries like Colombia."

Many students are passionate animal lovers. One group researches dwindling environments for endangered species. Several students work together to raise funds for a local animal shelter. They build advocacy into their project by making brochures detailing steps for animal adoption and the dangers of puppy mills. Others want to be more hands-on and volunteer at a shelter to socialize animals. When the age barrier for volunteers forces them to regroup, Valerie finds a global project:

First, my mom helped me find an organization working for the cause of animals throughout the world. We are not just talking dogs and cats here. They help animals from chimpanzees to burros to elephants to tigers. They bring veterinary services to poor communities around the globe. I ordered silicone bracelets from www.reminderband.com. So far, I have made almost $100 selling my bracelets.

Colton, also an animal lover, plans an educational project:

> A problem I am trying to solve is the endangerment of raptors, or birds of prey. This is a national problem because most raptors are endangered. My plan is to educate people about raptors, specifically a snowy owl I gave money to rehabilitate. I feel that my actions will only interest some bird-lovers, but not that many people.

Colton's project does interest his classmates, much to his surprise and delight. He continued to work at a raptor center in Vermont subsequent summers.

Students are also motivated to work on environmental projects, local and global. Some plan poster campaigns to promote recycling in school, while others promote recycling at home and in their neighborhoods. One student plans on petitioning a local shopping mall to place recycling containers around the mall. Here is a teachable moment as I ask him, "Have you spoken to the managers? In speaking with them first, you might get the results you want without having to do a petition." He disagrees with my approach, insisting he wants to bring a signed petition with him when he speaks to the mall managers. This is a good opportunity to discuss various ways to approach social action.

One student wants to restore "the nature and life found" on her street. She writes, "Thus far, I have explored adopting my road through the Department of Transportation. I have recruited my family to help me. I have also obtained the supplies I will need, such as garbage bags and gloves. I'm especially proud because I'm doing it anonymously."

Instead of acting locally, two boys want to tackle the whole idea of global warming, so they plan an educational project. They watch the film, *An Inconvenient Truth* (Guggenheim, 2006) and visit the Alliance for Climate Protection website (www.climateprotect.org). Next, they go to Bill McKibben's www.350.org (n.d.) to further research the causes and effects of climate change. Finally, they sum up what they've learned, "Basically, global warming makes the earth warmer and melts the ice on the earth's poles. This will eventually flood the world and make some of the Eastern cities in the U.S. under water." In response, these students make a website to educate fellow students about clean energy, climate legislation, hybrid cars, and electricity consumption.

Student Evaluations

As they complete their projects toward the final weeks of school, students present their project results and posters to the class. They answer questions from classmates and provide handouts of background information. We discuss obstacles they've overcome and plans they have to pro-

Figure 28.   Students teach peers why and how to compost.

ceed. These presentations are gratifying. However, the real excitement comes when these young activists educate the wider school community. To that end, we organize an annual *CAP FAIR* and invite fourth-through-eighth-grade students, faculty, administrators, and families. I create a hallway bulletin board of all the students' posters. Many students display photographs and other props to heighten interest. The hallway buzzes with conversations as students vie for the attention of the guests. Presenters demonstrate exercises to combat obesity, draw comics, explain endangered species, sell snacks and bracelets, demonstrate websites, and answer questions about root causes of problems. They feel pumped, proud, and powerful.

After the *CAP Fair*, I ask students to evaluate the project in writing and group discussion. When I ask if the Citizenship Action Project should stay in the curriculum, Dominic is emphatic:

> I say that this *CAP* project is a great idea because throughout history class, throughout the year, we've just been learning about other people and events. But I've really enjoyed this project, because we've actually done

something to change the world and help our school. Finally, we got to make some history ourselves.

His partner jumps in, "And it's a really good way because it makes you feel good inside when you do something good for other people." Other students agree:

> There are children in the Philadelphia area who have difficult family situations. These children need activities to help them laugh and not dwell on problems that are outside of their control. We made comics designed to help the kids use their imaginations. The stories centered on heroes who are able to overcome challenges and obstacles. We delivered the comics to the shelter. While we were there, a little boy and his mom picked up a comic and started to laugh. We were glad to see our comics were providing relief.

> It was fun working with my friends for a good cause. We could have been sitting at home watching television that Saturday, but instead we were out in the cold having a lot of fun. Picking up trash was disgusting, but we helped the environment around us. We're immensely proud of our hard work and teamwork.

> A big problem in America today is obesity. About 67% of all Americans are overweight.... I'm not trying to be mean, but I care so much about it that I am going to take charge and try my best to see that people in my family, school, and community lose some weight. I personally feel great about what I am doing, teaching people about obesity.

> First is that we saw we have much more than many people, and I have learned to appreciate what I have even more. Second is that I saw that by just doing something little and fun you can make a big difference. When I think about the fact that I sent a child to school, I feel amazed. I gave a child an education. I gave that child a part of their future. Who knows, they can be the future leaders of the world. One thing I'd like to change is for more people to have life, liberty, and the pursuit of happiness.

Changing the World in Small Doses

So, what of Kimberley, so keen at the beginning of the project to be a world changer? Her project—like her reaction—is unique. Partnering with two good friends, her project evolves into a family and global effort. One child's family has connections to the chocolate business. With the help of the World Cocoa Foundation, her family is able to connect the girls with the ECHOES Alliance (Empowering Cocoa Households with Opportunities and Education Solutions, n.d.). Their mission states a commitment to enhancing education and life-skills training for children and families in cocoa cultivating communities in West Africa. The combination of friendship, family support, entrepreneurship, and corporate humanitarianism is impressive and effective.

Group member Natalie explains:

> Through many e-mails, ECHOES found a school in Ghana that was in need of a safe and healthy environment for their students. We began to brainstorm ways that we could raise money. I designed a chocolate bar wrapper and Kimberley designed a necklace. Judith let us sell our products at her dad's café. We also talked to many companies, and they are backing us up, donating a thousand dollars. One is matching the money that we make. Raising money was an important part of our project, but I thought that it wasn't enough. We decided to send photos and letters to the children in Ghana about our everyday lives. We hope we get letters back. This project was fun and inspirational and it helped me make a little impact on the world.

And what do these three world-changers say when asked if *CAP* should stay in the curriculum? Judith, the third member of the group, can hardly contain her smile. "I think it should stay in the curriculum because students always want to change the world, and now, this is our chance to do it. It was a lot of fun, too." Natalie concurs, trying to sum up her enthusiasm in one word, "This is a project that you can do, and it makes you think that you have a *voice*."

Turning to Kimberley, I ask, "When I announced the project, you said, 'Oh, great. I always wanted to be one of those people who change the world.' Did you learn anything about how to do that?" She is beaming. "Yes, I did. I learned that even if it's just by helping a small school in Africa, you're changing their lives and you're helping a lot. And I learned that you can change the world in small doses, one at a time."

Questions to Consider:

1. Are there opportunities in your curriculum for students to study the lives of humanitarians, social activists, innovators, and Nobel laureates through literature, history, math, science, arts, language, or athletics?

2. What opportunities and challenges exist in your school and neighborhood for student activism and service learning? Do students have time for such activism? Do you?

3. Are you willing to let students' social action projects spill over into cross-curricular course work like science teacher Doug Ross of Friends Central School? Scientific stream studies and environmen-

tal projects evolve into writing, math, and social studies collaborations with colleagues. Do you facilitate multidisciplinary student-driven projects alone or with colleagues?

4. Character educator Usha Balamore extends thematic character initiatives into action opportunities. For one project, she transformed an elementary-school-wide *study* of heroes in literature and history into heroic *action* in the home and community. How can student opportunity for action arise from your school's antibullying, school climate, and other character initiatives?

5. Can you involve families and intertwine home, community, and school projects? Will your school support the effort? Are families able to become involved?

CHAPTER 8

STUDENT COUNCIL INITIATIVES IN MIDDLE SCHOOL

"Strive to insure that we are providing a safe and welcoming environment for all members of the community. Inspire service projects to learn about and benefit the wider world."

—Episcopal Academy Middle School
Student Council Mission

"The adults are ultimately in charge, but within that framework, children are given real responsibility for making decisions about certain school matters and for experiencing the growth in character that such decision-making can produce."

—Thomas Lickona
(*Educating for Character,* 1992, p. 341)

Some kids just go with the flow. We control the flow."

—Seventh-grade member of Student Council

Think, Care, Act: Teaching for a Peaceful Future, pp. 121–137
Copyright © 2011 by Information Age Publishing
All rights of reproduction in any form reserved.

Figure 29.   Student Council raises $1,700 to build schools in Pakistan and Afghanistan.

As one of two faculty advisors to Middle School Student Council, I guide young leaders to design school-wide social-action projects to make our school a safe, welcoming, and equitable one. It is gratifying to mentor adolescents as they gain leadership skills and develop community-building, antibullying, antiracism, and charitable social-action projects. But, I took on the challenge of being a Student Council advisor with trepidation.

Heretofore, Student Council's efforts had focused mainly on the social scene, planning Friday night dances. Our Middle School head was eager to find other ways for students to provide leadership, hoping they could be challenged to stimulate different kinds of action for the common good. I was curious what my role might be in advising students to take their leadership in a new direction as well. Engaging in teamwork with colleague Heather Dupont and a group of 15 devoted middle school students, we embarked in a new direction.

It's not that previous advisors hadn't assisted students in planning social action projects like fundraising for schools in post-Katrina New Orleans and *Mix It Up Day*. Indeed, one previous advisor had gotten materials from The Southern Poverty Law Center, whose *Teaching Toler-*

ance magazines and resources are valuable multicultural teaching tools. Using information from the *Teaching Tolerance* (n.d.) website, she and her Student Council members had planned a Middle School version of the nationwide *Mix It Up At Lunch Day*, seating students from different social groups at lunch together.

Mix It Up Day sounded great to us, and Heather and I pitched this idea to our new Student Council members. We were not prepared for the barrage of complaints from the seventh and eighth graders. "No! Everybody hated it." "Kids cried at the lunch tables." "It was so disorganized." "People do not want to try this again," they insisted. So, Heather and I dropped the idea. Essentially, we were asking these kids to lead in a direction with which they were not comfortable.

For our parts, we were trying to balance our roles as advisors with our hopes to get Student Council to add more social action to the agenda. While we are still experimenting with our roles, we have learned some important things about student leadership and faculty mentoring.

A YEAR OF ACTION

Student Council representatives are elected to 3-year terms. Our first few meetings in September allow us to connect with the returning seventh and eighth grade representatives. When they make several encouraging announcements inviting our newest middle schoolers to run for Student Council, we are swamped with 15 qualified sixth-grade candidates for three spots. Happily, after listening to all 15 speeches, sixth graders follow the prompts on their secret ballots: "Think about the candidates carefully. Who will represent your grade effectively? Who will be responsible about attending meetings, making plans, and carrying them out?" After elections, we feel fortunate that we have a diverse group of energized kids.

The Mentor's Role

Heather and I meet together in advance of our first meeting with all of the representatives. We decide we will function as leader/facilitators, inviting all group members to step into leadership roles for various projects. Yes, we take a more directive role than pure facilitators might. But, we think this model is promising with middle school students just learning how to take on school-wide leadership and organize projects from start to finish. We hope that our mentoring will give them the boost they need to experience success. Further, we predict that our eighth graders will step into leadership roles as the year goes on. This is indeed the case. Thus, Heather and I recognize Wade's (2007) view of the adult mentor's dance:

we guide students, support their ideas, and channel their enthusiasm into action plans that will actually work!

Specifically we utilize many facilitation techniques such as these recommended in the *PeaceJam Leaders* curriculum (PeaceJam Foundation, 2007). We set expectations together. We ask questions to promote critical thinking. We listen to students and help them listen to each other. We support them as they explore a multitude of options. We invite them to compromise and be flexible. Without solving their problems, we help Council members determine the steps they can take to do so.

To clarify Student Council's role, we agree on our Mission Statement, which Heather and I refine using school goals and input from student leaders. This mission allows us to be active in a variety of arenas, in and out of school:

> Strive to insure that we are providing a safe and welcoming environment for all members of the community. Inspire service projects to learn about and benefit the wider world.

Meetings and Agendas

Meeting at lunch once in each 6-day rotation provides challenges to reaching such lofty goals, however, and eating while meeting is always hectic. Therefore, we provide an agenda either on the board or on paper, giving kids time to absorb issues we've all agreed to discuss and asking for "new business" to take up. During discussions, Heather and I do what good facilitators do to keep a meeting moving while getting each participant's input. We set times for discussion of each topic, asking kids to be timekeepers. We allow discussions to continue if issues are crucial to resolve, asking kids if we can table other issues until future meetings. We seek input from each member of the group, asking a quiet member, "What do you think? You haven't spoken yet." We help kids stay focused on the ongoing discussion, inviting those involved in side conversations to listen to others and share their ideas with the entire group. We sum up the sense of the meeting before dismissing, using our last few minutes for kids to set priorities and responsibilities for action during the week. It's not ideal to meet for so brief a time, but it is real-world organizational experience the kids—and we—are getting.

Let's see what a year of action looks like for student leaders.

Halloween Fundraiser

We start planning early in the year for one of two middle school dances run as fundraisers by our parent association with music in one part of the gym, basketball and snacks in another. Attendance has been low, but when parent volunteers meet with Student Council to get suggestions for increasing attendance, our kids make proposals with terrific results. They propose a Halloween dance, with a lower admission for those who come in costume. They ask that some funds earned be donated to a low-cost homebuilding charity with which one of our Council members is active. Kids make announcements and signs to post all around school. When there's a good turnout and they raise $239.00 for the charity, they are psyched. This is their first experience seeing the power of their creative and thoughtful ideas in action.

Pep Rally

In October, the planning for a huge all-school pep rally begins. Our school has a century-long rivalry with another local school and the atmosphere is charged during "Spirit Week" in November. The culminating activities are the pep rallies held at week's end. Unfortunately, pep rallies fall into that dangerous category for me as a peace educator. They are occasions in which attitude, language, and actions can easily cross the line from supportive to destructive.

When I taught in Lower School, I was among a group of teachers who worked with our athletic department, upper school team captains, and administrators to change the direction of the pep rally from one of tearing down the competition to one of appreciating athleticism and fair play. From a day I dreaded, the day of the Lower School pep rally became one of child-centered, sportsmanlike fun. Tiny kids entered the gym under a tunnel of hands of the gigantic high school team captains. Kids interviewed team leaders who told us about their sports, their teammates, and their friendships with their competitors. And team captains led us in cheers as we screamed our heads off for them and our school. Kids came away ready to cheer their teams and show good sportsmanship and hospitality to our guests.

Student Council members remember the new-style pep rallies of Lower School fondly and want to recreate such a feeling for Middle School kids. Unfortunately, they meet obstacles (team captains are unavailable, for example) and have to redesign the event entirely. Brainstorming furiously during two lunch meeting sessions, we plan activities for a pep rally extraordinaire.

I take notes and write up the schedule as they design it. Various Council members take responsibility for each part of the program. They ask a teacher to show his photo slide show of athletic teams as the kids enter the theater. They invite Video Class members to create a movie about the upcoming competitions. With thunderous music and hilarious interviews, the video energetically jump starts the program. Student Council members design a trivia game, make announcements, and hang posters informing the student body about bits of school sports trivia in the weeks prior to the rally. Now, they take turns asking questions about the competitions. "How many players are on a water polo team?" "How many years have we had the football competition?" "Who is the captain of our soccer team?" "How long is the cross-country course?" And my favorite questions, "What is sportsmanship?" "What are three ways to show it?"

The athletic department gives us t-shirts for prizes, Heather gets more spirit items from the school store, and the Council kids run the prizes up and down the aisles. Finally, they invite the Middle School Dance Club to perform. Brilliant! The dancers give a dynamic performance to the enthusiastic cheers of students and faculty alike. Our athletic director and head of Middle School take turns leading cheers and setting the tone, expressing their expectations for sportsmanlike and courteous behavior at games. And finally, the entire Student Council runs up the aisle and out the door, crashing through a big paper banner they painted for their dramatic exit.

The event is organized and chaotic by turns, but the kids run it, the audience loves it, and it helps set a positive tone among Middle School spectators. At our next meeting, kids bask in the glow of complements from faculty members and administrators. They reflect on what went well, what didn't, and why. Then, they settle down to write thank-you notes to each of the participants.

Pennies for Peace

There's a lull around the winter holidays, but we come back from winter break invigorated and ready to undertake a new project. Heather has a terrific idea for a fundraising drive: the "Penny War." I don't like the combative language, but the premise is compelling—albeit confusing. Heather explains, "Each grade has a big bottle and people can contribute pennies, silver coins, or paper money. But, all silver coins and paper money count as negative points. Only pennies count for positive points. So, if someone wants to sabotage another grade, they put quarters or dollars in the other grade's bottle. The grade with the fewest points wins the Penny War, and the grade with the most money loses. But it all works out, because the money goes for a good cause." Now the biggest question is what to do with the proceeds. This is where the eighth grade curriculum is helpful.

Eighth graders study developing nations in history class all year. In the winter, they do an interdisciplinary project in which students choose books to read for their English classes set in one of the developing nations they are studying in history. Knowing this, I suggest we give the proceeds

Figure 30.   Student Council runs *Pennies for Peace* contest.

to *Pennies for Peace*, the fundraising organization associated with Greg Mortenson's efforts to build schools for girls in Afghanistan and Pakistan. Student Council kids know of his bestselling book, *Three Cups of Tea* (2007), and several kids in their classes are reading it. We get information and download photos from the Pennies for Peace (2009) website and the kids make posters to hang all around the school. That's how we raise $1,700.00 to help build schools halfway around the world.

Every day, on their way into school, sixth graders gather around the four jars (sixth, seventh, eighth, and faculty), dumping bags of pennies in their jar. Meanwhile, seventh graders are dumping quarters and dollar bills in the jars of the other grades. There is so much noisy enthusiasm for the Penny War that the school secretaries ask us to monitor the racket around the bottles outside their office. Why so much energy? Honestly, I wish the excitement was all about building schools.

In a school in which everyday dress is a school uniform, earning a "dress-down day" is the coveted prize Student Council has announced to the student body. Now that we have their attention, we adapt information from www.penniesforpeace.org to explain Mortenson's courageous philosophy of using education to promote peace world-wide. A mountain climber, Mortenson had been rescued and nursed to health by Pakistani villagers. With gratitude, he promised to help villagers build a school. Years of fundraising later, he founded the Central Asia Institute. Its mission? To improve literacy for boys and girls, thereby improving health outlooks for families of the region. Ultimately, Mortenson asserts, providing education to children—especially girls—leads to stability and peace in regions threatened by extremists.

Pennies for Peace is a win-win contest—except for the sixth and seventh graders. Slyly, donors are slipping twenty dollar bills in their jars. The kids have forgotten about the teachers, and in the end, the faculty "wins" (with the lowest number of points), followed closely by the eighth graders. Student Council awards the dress-down prize to both groups, who happily wear jeans and t-shirts to school after the winners are announced. But *Pennies for Peace*—and the girls of Afghanistan and Pakistan—win as well.

A high-point for Heather and me is when we present the check to Greg Mortenson in person, representing our kids as we greet the bear-hugging, warm-hearted humanitarian. The kids are thrilled at our effort to meet him at an area fundraiser, and they feel pride in leadership that benefits their school and the world at large.

Antibullying

When we enter the busy spring months, faculty and kids notice an uptick of bullying, so Heather and I suggest doing some anti-bullying activities school-wide. Oddly, when we bring these up, the kids are hesitant. We mention our stalemate to our supportive athletic director who offers to make a personal plea at our next meeting. Kim Piersall tells the kids she really needs them to run such a campaign. Well, that's a different story! We're needed. Let's do it! Personal dynamics and worry over seeming *uncool* drop, and the kids plan activities they are comfortable leading: to promote kind words and courteous interactions in our school.

One of our faculty members speaks to the assembled Middle School about being bullied in adolescence, having racial epithets hurled at her in the hallways and classrooms of her middle school. She ends with a plea that our students never treat each other as she was treated. This speech galvanizes our Student Council kids, who propose running an antibullying slogan contest in April.

Each advisory will first address bullying through role plays, personal stories, and moderated discussion. I provide a packet of discussion questions for advisors, selecting issues recommended by Council members: "Why do people bully?" "Where does bullying take place?" "If it happens online, is it still bullying?" "What can bystanders do?" "When do you need

Figure 31.   Student Council evaluates anti-bullying contest posters.

adult help?" Advisories will each invent a slogan to promote kind behavior and curb bullying. There are prizes, Council members promise, as they make frequent announcements requesting participation—not only in the contest—but in behaving in a friendly manner to promote a safe and inclusive environment in our school.

During a subsequent chapel gathering, advisories share their slogans and colorful posters. Before hanging them in the cafeteria for all members of our school community to see until the end of the year, we vote for the winning slogans by secret ballot in our next meeting. We invite administrators to join in the voting. There is much anticipation as Student Council representatives announce the winners. They make the moment a teachable one, reminding their peers that the purpose of advisory discussions and slogan writing is "to help our community become one in which everyone can feel safe, happy, and connected." They finally announce the winning slogans:

In third place: "The Act that Smiles Back—KINDNESS"
In second place: "A bully is one, we are many. If we work together, we won't have any."
And in first place: "TO BULLY OR NOT TO BULLY?—THERE IS NO QUESTION!"

Dance for Malaria Nets

By now, mid-May, Student Council members worry there won't be enough time to plan the spring dance, so they initiate meeting one more day each rotation, at lunch, on their own, without teachers. They return to our regular meetings and report their ideas for an overhaul of the typical dance format. "Great ideas, kids," Heather and I respond. "Write up your proposal so the parent organizers know what you're thinking. Also, you need to get the dress code and location changes approved by the front office."

For a few weeks little follow-through occurs. Heather and I are encouraging, but we won't do these tasks for them. Finally, the kids come through. "We wrote it all up! We met with Mr. Morris! He approved everything!" they report. Next, meeting with the parent association, the kids negotiate having a favorite eighth grade band alternate with the DJ.

Further, our chaplain's friend, a pastor of a community in Tanzania, visits from Africa. After meeting with him personally, Council decides this dance will raise money for mosquito netting and food for his impoverished village. Finally, they announce their idea for boosting attendance: the grade with most representation will win a dress-down day. They explain the charitable purpose to the school and distribute information about malaria and poverty, festooning the halls with posters encouraging all to attend.

Their weeks of meeting on their own pay off, and dance attendance is the highest ever. The band enthralls the crowd with an energetic (and deafening) set of original music. Everyone is happy with the DJ's music, because all kids have helped choose songs. The eighth graders win the dress-down day, buoyed by supporters of the band. And the Student Council earns $550.00 to support the Tanzanian community.

Student Evaluations

The end of the year fast approaching, we wind down with a few bake sales and meetings. Heather and I want to get an "exit evaluation," especially from our eighth graders moving to high school. The kids complete a questionnaire before we talk, munching pizza to celebrate our accomplishments. As we share our impressions of defeats and triumphs, the kids are clearly proud. Snack sales? "I think we need a new system." "Yeah, and more people selling." Halloween Dance? "This dance did not make that much money. We should have pre-planned it better. I liked the theme though." Pep Rally? "It was fun and everyone really got pumped." "This was impressive and we should do it again!"

Pennies for Peace? "Awesome! Both the students and people in Afghanistan and Pakistan gained." "People are still talking about it. Dress down was a great motivator." "Amazing! We raised so much money. We should do this again."

Reactions to the antibullying poster project are mixed. Half the group is for the project. "We should definitely do this again." "I liked the posters a lot. I think it got more people involved and excited about what we were doing." But, the other half deride it, "There was no enthusiasm from the students, and they didn't take it seriously." "This is not an effective campaign." We'll revisit the project next year.

They have no such ambivalence about the final dance, however. The kids are especially proud as this is "their baby." One eighth grader says, "The things we did to make it different (i.e., the band, location, dress code, fundraiser) helped motivate people to come." And how about the way Student Council worked together, meeting at lunch on their own? Kids report, "We were very efficient." "Yeah," quips one, "Some kids just go with the flow. We control the flow." High-fives and applause follow this observation, as Student Council members returning next year vow to make this their motto.

MIX IT UP DAY REVISITED

As Heather and I learn more about helping kids become effective social activists, Student Council projects become more thoughtful, organized, and productive. Examples from a subsequent year detail our growth. Students want to hold a fundraiser for a facial reconstruction clinic in which a representative's father is active. However, the school has a new policy, limiting fundraisers to those established by the school's service learning program. The kids are angry and ready to give up. "Let's meet with Mrs. Swanson from service learning," we suggest. "If you organize your ideas and make a clear proposal—persistently but politely—you may get this project approved."

They divide the tasks. Some research genetic and traumatic facial disfigurement. Some find advisory discussion material to help adolescents talk about how appearance affects security and identity. Some write follow-up questions: "Have you ever felt like an outcast?" "What would you do if you saw someone with any deformity being mistreated?" Others arrange for the father, a doctor, to talk to the school about his work on the issue and the importance of acceptance. They present their step-by-step plan—eventually earning permission to conduct these activities in advance of the fundraiser (which ultimately nets $543.00).

Now, they're ready to tackle something even bigger.

Figure 32.   Student Council paints t-shirts for *Mix It Up Day*.

This year, the kids are receptive to *Mix It Up Day*. They think they can make an impact on school culture, even if it means sacrificing other projects. They're interested in exploring Teaching Tolerance's purpose for the event: to break down barriers of race, class, gender, and other delineations to promote a welcoming, safe school community.

Gathering Faculty Support

Knowing the prior effort had glitches, I consult with an Upper School faculty member who has planned *Mix It Up Day* activities. "Get the faculty on board early," she advises. So, we plan a series of meetings in which the kids will present their ideas and gather input from several key faculty members. We consult Courtney Portlock, our encouraging director of diversity, who hopes we will "educate the community about *existing* prejudices of *many kinds* and highlight the resources of our diversity that make us a rich community." Our athletic director loves the fact that we're doing a "social experiment, trying to make this a normal day with abnormal conditions." We next invite members of Faculty Diversity Council to react to our plans. From each of them we get encouragement: "Sound's great. We're on board. How can we help?"

Taking Time to Organize

As designed by *Teaching Tolerance, Mix It Up* events typically occur during lunch-time, but our kids want to design an entire day of diversity learning. We help the kids divide the tasks, teaching them various community organizing skills along the way. Some adapt a pre-event survey from the *Teaching Tolerance* (n.d.) website as well as discussion prompts and a questionnaire for advisory following *Mix It Up Day*. Others design skits with which to announce the day in chapel. One suggests a game with good ice-breaker questions to leave on the lunch tables. "And how about all different colors of candy?" another suggests.

Our diversity director and head of Middle School help us pay for t-shirts with the message, "I am the face of diversity." With art teacher Naomi Knecht's assistance, we all stay after school to paint 350 t-shirts seven different colors with fabric paint, thus designating randomly assigned social groups with different privileges and restrictions for students and teachers alike. Kids design rules for the day, such as: "Reds may use the downstairs water fountains. Greens must go upstairs. Blues may not use any toys at recess. Yellows can always use their lockers before others." For our *Mix It Up Day* Chapel, Naomi offers to speak about her mother's experience as a Holocaust survivor, and I volunteer to connect our activities to celebrating diversity in school and globally. We meet, plan, and work from November through February.

Two weeks before *Mix It Up Day* Student Council meets with the entire Middle School faculty to summarize our ideas and demonstrate our enthusiasm. Heather and I have kept the faculty in touch, offering statistics and materials from www.tolerance.org on the effectiveness of such activities to promote greater appreciation for differences, and the need for respect, tolerance, and fairness in our community. Most teachers are open and intrigued, but some are skeptical, and many don't want to lose teaching time. The kids ask them to participate as much as they are comfortable, allowing teachers the option of teaching in a "normal" manner or entering the role play in the full spirit of the day. "You can treat kids in your color group as favorites, giving them candy and special seats. Or, you can make your room a safe haven where you treat everyone equally," our spokespeople suggest. The teachers agree to give no tests. The day will be intense enough.

Engaging Families

Head of Middle School Steve Morris energetically shows his support by keeping the families informed via his weekly e-newsletter. He details *Teaching Tolerance's* mission, our t-shirts and privileges, planned Chapel talks, lunch arrangements, and the goals he shares with Student Council. He explains that we have set high expectations for behavior, and that the faculty will watch for negative behaviors that might detract from the purposes for the day. Finally, he invites families to talk with their children before and after the day, to learn what their children are doing to make our school inclusive and friendly for all.

Student Evaluations

Advisory discussions after *Mix It Up Day* yield meaningful feedback from students and teachers. All participants complete a questionnaire in which Student Council asks four questions:

What Did You Like Most About This Day?

"Getting the cool shirts!" "Teachers who actually role played." "I liked that I got to open up and meet new people." "Some teachers gave special things to my color." "I liked the way we learned about racism and how it hurts." "We experienced segregation."

What Did You Like Least?

"That teachers didn't participate as much as they could have." "The fact that my color had no privileges." "Having limits." "Inconvenience." "All teachers hated my color." "We had to stand up in class." "I was unfairly treated."

Did You Meet Any New People?

"I am in 8th grade and I sat with some 6th graders. We did the question game and I learned some fun facts about them." "I didn't realize how many people I didn't know!" "I learned people are cooler than you think." "People bonded over their color."

Would you like to do this again? Why/why not? While 37% of students voted "No," a solid 63% voted "Yes. It was a great lesson in discrimination." Several respondents actually asked "for a longer time period so the feeling could actually sink in." Even in a day, however, many realize the negative impact discriminatory treatment has on learning:

"If school was like this always, we couldn't learn. If you were favored you felt less stress, but if you were oppressed, you tried to be perfect." "I would not like to do this again because discrimination is really awful to feel or watch, even though it teaches you about it. I think we learned enough yesterday to last us awhile."

In my classes, I ask students to write extensive journals which I also share with Student Council. These two students make planners feel their efforts have been worthwhile:

On *Mix It Up Day* I learned how hurtful discrimination is even if you're not the one being discriminated against. I also learned that being favored in a class isn't always the best because then the teacher expects much more from you. Being ignored in class doesn't feel good either. When the teacher treats you as if you're stupid and worthless, you probably won't learn much because you will start to believe it and think that you'll never amount to anything.

When I think of my feelings, the lesson I get out of it is this: stand up for yourself and never, ever judge a book by its cover (or in this case, the color of our shirts). Although I had my own ups and downs, I am glad we have this annual day to teach us more about race, religion, ability, ethnicity, gender, age, etc., and I am looking forward to next year!

Student Council Evaluations

We spend a meeting reading the questionnaires, and initially Student Council kids take every critical comment personally. One is heartbroken that "Some people didn't participate." But as we continue reading and discussing feedback, the kids' spirits lift. We ask, "What are you most proud of?" They're pleased that "teamwork, organization, and hard work" helped them host "such a huge event." "I am most proud of teaching a lot of kids how it feels to be different because I think that now people will discriminate less." "I am most proud of the fact that everyone had an opinion on the day, whether it was good or bad. This means they cared."

We are eager to know, "What is a specific lesson you learned about leadership or organizing?"

Kids understand "the importance of details," "that organization is extremely important," "that if people work together, they can accomplish many things," and "that leadership doesn't always mean being loud and obnoxious." One writes, "I learned that even if we plan a good day, there will be some people who are not willing to cooperate. I learned that I had to look at the positive side of an event and not all the negatives." Our diversity director concurs, "The lesson I continue to learn is to never underestimate the power of collective voices and positive energy."

Our end-of-year exit interview offers one last opportunity for the reflection that is crucial to social action. We ask, "How are you a different person because of your service on Student Council?" Several responses are typical: "It felt good being a leader, and I thought I really helped the school/community." "I see some of the problems throughout the world." "I am more aware, more confident, and have a voice."

Emboldened by their success, the subsequent year's Student Council takes *Mix It Up Day* to new levels of organization and learning. They write specific suggestions for behavior for faculty and send two representatives to a faculty meeting to solicit faculty participation in conveying the lessons of the day. They enlist the aid of Upper School student diversity leaders who have learned training techniques at NAIS's national Student Diversity Leadership Conference. Thus, midmorning on *Mix It Up Day*, Upper School students lead Middle School students in evaluating the diversity climate of the school, stereotypes, and students' personal comfort in our community. Student Council leaders redesign the questionnaires and t-shirts. They take ownership of their roles in planning this day of learning as a yearly event.

Benefits of Activism

With every initiative, we observe in our student leaders the benefits of activism Wade (2007) recognizes. Student Council members use critical thinking and compassion to solve problems in real life. They feel powerful working together to tackle big issues in our school and world.

Can we improve the way we listen to each other? Can students take more initiative? Can we seek and implement more suggestions from the student body, as one outgoing eighth grader suggests? Absolutely, yes. But for now, these Student Council representatives are learning to *think* about what matters in the life of a school, determine what they *care* enough about to work on, and *act* cooperatively to lead their fellow students in making our school—and our world—more welcoming and safe places to live together.

Questions to Consider:

1. What role do Student Council and other student leadership organizations play in engaging your school community in peace and justice issues?

2. Can you think of existing events (dances, athletic contests, assemblies) into which student activism could be incorporated?

3. How does your school address such issues as bullying and discrimination? How are various heritages in your school community recognized and respected? Do frictions exist? What obstacles and opportunities exist for student leadership in these areas?

4. What are the best examples of student leadership and/or faculty mentoring you have seen or experienced? Why did they work? What is the best balance you have found when mentoring young leaders?

5. How do you combat disappointment, fatigue, and stress when working on projects with young people? What do you do if students "drop the ball" while working on projects? How can you facilitate without taking over or burning out?

CHAPTER 9

EMPOWERING ELECTIVE CLASSES

Debate, Model UN, *PeaceJam*

"Through our scientific genius we have made of the world a neighborhood; now through our moral and spiritual genius we must make of it a brotherhood."

—Dr. Martin Luther King, Jr.
(*Facing the Challenge of a New Age*, 1957/2004, p. 181)

"Tell them anyone can be a Nobel Peace Prize winner. They are just ordinary people, educated and uneducated, doctors, lawyers, housewives, volunteers. The thing is: they have done something for the cause of peace."

—Anne Kjelling,
Norwegian Nobel Institute Chief Librarian,
Oslo, Norway, August 2006

"Peace takes more work than I thought it would."

—Eighth grade girl

Think, Care, Act: Teaching for a Peaceful Future, pp. 139–161

Figure 33. Debate class students research gay marriage issue.

Speaking on the 50th anniversary of Gandhi's death, 1977 Nobel Peace Prize winner Mairead Corrigan Maguire (2004) described as insanity the fact that humans continue to produce weapons with the potential to destroy countless people—perhaps the entire planet. Instead, she urged humanity "to take an imaginative leap forward" to "create a new culture of nonviolence" (p. 160).

Maguire (2004) outlines five steps to do so. First, we must teach nonviolence to our children. Second, we must promote nonviolent social change and remove our support from systems of violence and militarism. Third, we must change the emphasis of the media from highlighting violence to covering the countless peaceful initiatives occurring locally and globally each day. Fourth, we can take up the peaceful ethics called for by each of the world's religions. Fifth, we must engage governments of the world in creating and financing nonviolent conflict resolution programs instead of their reliance on violent ones. Maguire's plan seems promisingly rational.

Historian and World War II bombardier Howard Zinn (1995) spent a career studying war and sees it as insane, as well. Because of its mass destruction of humanity, he concludes that war cannot be justified. As does Maguire, he queries, "Is human ingenuity so defunct, is our intelligence so lacking that we cannot devise ways of dealing with tyranny and injustice without killing huge numbers of people" (p. 502)?

Teaching Nonviolence History and Methods

Perhaps humans cannot imagine peaceful solutions because they have not studied successful uses of nonviolence throughout history. Nonviolence educator Richard Deats (2004) praises numerous individuals and groups for their ingenious and courageous efforts to solve conflicts nonviolently, promote justice, and protect the environment. Unfortunately, he notes, nonviolence success stories—from Latin America, Philippines, South Africa, Asia, Europe, and the United States—are rarely taught in schools.

Yet, in 1994, the National Council for the Social Studies [NCSS] supported K-12 programs that promote students' ability to constructively engage in local civic undertakings as well as to help them enhance their ability to see things from a global perspective. They further urged students to learn how to promote peaceful and just solutions to local and global problems. According to the Joint Committee on National Health Education Standards, students must learn nonviolent strategies for managing conflict (2007). The United Nations and other international agencies have devised peace education curricula and standards as well. See United Nations Cyber Schoolbus (n.d., cyberschoolbus.un.org) and Hague Appeal for Peace (2003-2005, www.haguepeace.org) for example.

Along with my daily teaching within my curriculum, I develop and teach elective courses, taking action to fill crucial gaps in our curriculum. Choosing these courses allows students to actively construct their peace education. They grow as peacemakers as they engage in controversy and conflict resolution and delve into the history and effectiveness of nonviolent action, taking on roles of negotiators, diplomats, administrators, or community organizers.

DEBATE, COMPROMISE, AND CHANGE

Researchers Patricia Avery, David Johnson, Roger Johnson, and James Mitchell (1999) indicate that children must experience both cooperation and controversy in the curriculum to be able to understand peace and war. Thus, they urge teachers to incorporate cooperative learning experiences daily alongside discord and controversy to help students learn to resolve conflicts in increasingly sophisticated, nonviolent, and compassionate ways.

The engagement of critical thinking about controversies, the power of role play, and the opportunity to cooperatively act on issues about which students care are elements of my *Debate, Compromise, and Change* elective class, in which we explore the following essential questions:

1. What school-wide, local, national, or global issues do I want to learn about, discuss, and change?
2. Why do I need to listen when others talk? Why do I need to understand others' points of view—even if I disagree?
3. How is a formal debate different from a conversation or discussion?
4. How can thorough research, civil speech, and empathetic listening lead to creative compromises and positive changes in my school, community, and world?

Cats Versus Dogs

In debate class, students learn and practice fundamentals of effective public speaking—and listening. We start by discussing a seemingly innocuous topic: "Cats versus dogs," a topic on which they can speak passionately and factually. Collecting students' ideas on the board, my team-teaching colleague and I list the pros and cons of each pet for city dwellers. "Cats can use a litter box so they don't need to be walked, don't bark, are smaller, and are not dangerous to neighbors," volunteer the cat lovers. "Dogs are playful, can provide protection, can be trained, and can give their owners' exercise during walking," counter the dog lovers.

Inviting four guinea-pig volunteers, we create a resolve: "Cats are better than dogs as pets for city dwellers" and conduct our first mini-debate. We guide participants to use effective techniques, such as employing a logical succession of arguments, offering fact-based examples, and saving personal stories only to expand arguments. Further, we invite students not actively debating to coach both teams during strategic breaks. Some students are naturals, picking up skills of civil discourse quickly, while others need reminders to avoid personal attacks. After all, it's fun to rant, rage, and bluff. So many such behaviors appear in the media daily, many students believe debating means yelling.

Debate and Compromise Versus Structured Controversies

As students end the demonstration debate with closing arguments, we immediately transform participants from opponents and coaches to colleagues: casting them as committee members of an imaginary animal rights organization. We ask "the committee" to recommend a pet policy for city dwellers of our township, challenging them to use perspectives learned from both sides of the debate. In short order, our "pet commission" recommends dogs for house dwellers with yards and cats for apartment dwellers. We now have the opportunity to take action.

In conducting debates in this manner—inviting all members of the class to offer tactical advice during debate, ending in all-class discussions in which students synthesize arguments and propose compromises after debate, and following with action for change—my design differs from the role reversal encouraged by David and Roger Johnson, whose work on structured controversies I admire (Lickona & Davidson, 2005). While they also place students in cooperative groups debating opposing sides of controversial issues, they structure the activity so that students switch positions, re-arguing the issue, but from the opposite perspective.

I don't ask students to re-argue the debate. Instead, I stop the speakers at critical points—after the preliminary speech but before their first cross-examination of the opposition, for example—and allow their observing classmates to coach each team in possible questions to ask and new arguments to introduce. In this way, "audience members" become active in helping to unlock the complexity of controversial issues. They take multiple perspectives and deepen their levels of critical thinking also. Student debaters experience an expectation to perform as well as an atmosphere of cooperation and support. In addition, however, all participants sum up the debate by engaging in a cooperative discussion of compromise. Thus, we build a real-world component of compromising into our debate format. Students employ the arguments they've used and heard to craft workable and equitable solutions to problems.

Choosing Topics

For our next series of preliminary debates, students read simple news articles we have selected for the purpose and choose among issues such as curfews for teenagers in shopping malls, allowing cameras in jury rooms, and whether rap musicians should tame their lyrics. After learning the ropes on these one-class debates, students brainstorm, select topics, and begin research for lengthier ones. Their suggested topics include the rights of able-bodied versus disabled athletes to compete in the Olympics, stem-cell research, the Iraq War, the military draft, use of torture on enemy combatants, the death penalty, gay marriage, the drinking age, homework, school uniforms, the trial of the Jena Six, TV and video-game violence, and social networking behavior. Once the self-selected debate groups have formed, students conduct research during several class sessions, and we invite families to discuss debate issues at home.

While researching background information for school-related debates, students in pairs seek interviews with the school nurse (raising or lowering the drinking age), assistant principal (school uniforms and discipline policy), athletic director (team sports practice schedule), fellow students (homework load), or computer teacher (access to social networking websites in school). They show us their list of research-based questions, and they're off. To further engage the wider community, I maintain a class bulletin board on which I post articles on the issues under debate. We invite students from outside the class to observe and participate in some of our debates as well.

Action for Change

The action for change component comes when we devise our compromise and decide what to do with it. In the case of the debate on school uniforms, for example, students write up their recommendations and give them to the head of Middle School. They provide statistics that acknowledge that three-fourths of students surveyed agree that uniforms help them focus and save time. However, they also observe that the Upper School dress code allows for more flexibility and regular dress-down days than does the code for Middle School. So, they offer three recommendations:

Unrestricted dress-down days more frequently, e.g. once per month
Consider allowing pants with pockets/rivets for girls
Consider allowing sweaters (vs. blazers) for boys

While no immediate uniform change results, the students get to see the process of debate, compromise, and change in its entirety. Happily, the following year, the school adopts the sweater recommendation.

Outside Guests

Occasionally, we invite outside guests. During one class, student debaters cross examine an assistant district attorney. The visit, sponsored by a local bar association allows our guest to interest debaters in participating in Mock Trial in high school as well as in serving as jurors as adults. He explains the justice system and then takes questions on one of our recent classroom debates on the military draft.

Figure 34.   Civil debate ends in handshake.

When a class member encourages a debater to "pound his opponent," our guest offers a different strategy. Citing an ancient Chinese book on the philosophy of war, he encourages students to "always give your opponent a way out, a way to save face." While debating (or arguing a case in court, for that matter) he advises, "Never take it personal. Never make it personal. Stick with issues and stick with facts." Class ends, but two students, Kaia and Fareed, stay through recess for additional coaching on their upcoming debate.

Jena Six

The widely publicized case of the Jena Six captivates the two, and they prepare to debate whether justice was served. Familiar with the case, our guest admires the young debaters' dedication to preparing in-depth arguments on the charged topic. In a racially tense and predominantly white school in New Orleans in 2006, Black students had asked the principal for permission to sit under a tree that was the usual hang-out of White students. He gave his permission. However, when the Black students arrived in school the next day, nooses were hanging from the tree—a defiant act labeled by some as a threat by Whites to do physical harm to Black students, labeled by others as a school-yard prank. Taking the latter view, the school principal did not stem the rising tide of racial tension, and physical fighting eventually occurred. Finally, six Black teenagers were indicted by the district attorney for beating up one of the White students.

Kaia and Fareed ask the assistant district attorney to recommend strategies for arguing the debate proposition: "The Jena Six were justified in fighting to defend themselves." To Kaia, arguing for the affirmative, he recommends researching definitions and court rulings on ethnic intimidation. To Fareed, arguing for the negative, he suggests researching alternatives the Black students had instead of physical violence, such as engaging in civil disobedience. To both, interestingly, he suggests researching Gandhi's writings!

When they conduct their debate a week later, it is obvious Kaia and Fareed have spent much time out of class following these leads. Kaia cites cases in which courts have affirmed that the hanging of a noose is ethnic intimidation. Further, she argues, courts have affirmed the rights of individuals to defend themselves when threatened with ethnic or racial intimidation. Fareed counters that the hanging of nooses, while contemptible, did not amount to a physical threat. He cites numerous historical examples of the use of civil disobedience such as boycotts, marches, and petitions in cases in which people's civil rights were violated. The Black students should have used nonviolent protest, he contends.

Their debate-class peers—and we teachers—are mesmerized as the debaters cite judicial cases, offer counterarguments, and energetically but civilly cross-examine each other. Finally, we're intrigued when Kaia and Fareed both invoke contrasting statements from Gandhi to bolster their positions. While we can hear a pin drop during the debate, we all burst into deafening applause at the end as the talented debaters shake hands. We gather the chairs in a circle to begin the compromise phase of the discussion, entering the delicate realm of race relations in our own school.

Student Evaluations

After a contentious debate on the use of torture (with references ranging from the U.S. Constitution to the Geneva Conventions), we ask participants, "Did the debate affect your personal opinion?" One debater replies, "Actually it was interesting. Before this debate, I was against torture. Now, taking on the role of someone arguing for it, I can see why people say we should torture. I still don't like it, but I understand it."

We ask the class, "Should kids your age be talking about controversial topics like this?" One jumps up, "Yes! We should talk about everything!" His classmates rowdily agree.

Lickona and Davidson (2005) write that the ability to constructively and civilly consider and discuss controversies must be taught by schools so that students can effectively participate in democratic life. Young debaters given the further opportunity to compromise and act on these controversies gain additional skills needed to manage controversies nonviolently.

MODEL UN

Students in Model UN class also immerse themselves in controversy and cooperation as they spend a trimester preparing to participate in a middle-school Model UN conference at either the George Washington University in Washington, DC or the United Nations in New York. Students research such issues faced by the global community as child labor, global

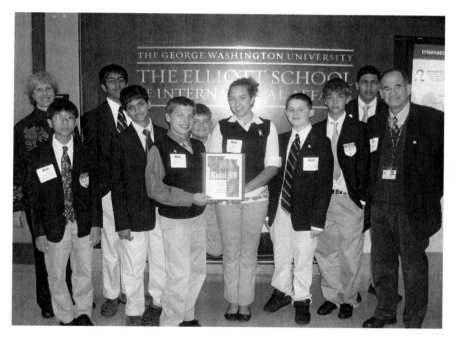

Figure 35. Model UN students at conference in Washington, DC.

warming, nuclear disarmament, and peace in the Middle East. Teaching collaboratively with our director of service learning or teacher Chip Hollinger, a scholar steeped in the history of developing nations, my colleagues and I model passionate engagement in the wider world as we involve student-diplomats in exploration of these essential questions:

1. What is the United Nations and what does it do?
2. How is diplomacy used to solve international problems?
3. Can there be positive outcomes to conflict?
4. What contribution can I make to solving international problems?

Course content includes an introduction to the history of the United Nations, diplomatic terms and procedures, and examples of international initiatives. We study the United Nations (UN) General Assembly's *Universal Declaration of Human Rights* (1948), and we investigate the structure of the UN, identifying member nations, committees, and the role of nongovernmental organizations (NGOs), as well. The world map is ever-present as we explore connections among global events and trace the historical, political, and geographical underpinnings of current-day dramas.

We employ teaching and learning materials from various sources, including those from the United Nations web pages, books, and videos on the issues. Materials from conference organizers point teachers and students to other sources of information—too numerous to absorb, but inviting to try. Depending on the country, we may even speak directly with embassies of the countries we represent, learning from first-person sources the perspectives of another global entity. We are grateful, for example, to the Russian and Saudi Arabian embassies, whose staff members patiently explain issues from their countries' perspectives via conference calls and e-mails. My colleagues and I supplement the information with current events articles, historical documents, and our own summaries.

No Empty Role Play

At the conferences in Washington and New York, students take on roles of representatives to the United Nations, conferring and debating with delegates from public and independent schools from across the country—and world. One year, waiting in line to enter the UN, for example, we meet a team from Mexico, another from Ghana, a third from San Francisco, and a fourth from Arkansas. Walking into a room full of high-energy, hopeful middle school diplomats, our students are soon swept into a role-play world of hand-shaking, conflict, caucusing, and alliance building. Here is an opportunity for them to experience the parliamentary procedure used in the United Nations and to learn methods of conflict resolution designed to promote global security.

In his letter to a middle school conference in 2009, UN Secretary-General Ban Ki-moon (2009) welcomed participants to the complex arena of international dialogue. "This exercise is no empty role play," he wrote, reminding delegates that they represent the half of the world's population that is under the age of 25! He challenged participants to eventually take on positions of leadership in the global community.

In Washington, the conference is run by students from the George Washington University International Affairs Society (n.d.). Sponsored by Global Classrooms and the United Nations Association for the United States of America [UNA-USA] (n.d.), the international middle school conference in New York is run by college students who—like their counterparts at G.W.—have engaged in Model UN since middle school. Thus, organizers become role models to our aspiring diplomats, providing information and coaching before and during the conferences.

Students represent such diverse entities as China, Niger, Palestine, Poland, Saudi Arabia, Sri Lanka, and Uganda, for example, and participate in such panels as the Security Council, World Health Organization, International Atomic Energy Agency, and the African Union. They must learn enough information—and understand multiple perspectives—about their roles and global crises so they can develop effective proposals for solving problems they will discuss. As we approach conference day, our students scramble to present their proposals to a challenging panel of our own Middle School history teachers, who grill them on their facts, practicality of their proposals, and clarity of their presentations. Despite sweaty palms, the student-diplomats impress their teachers with the scope of their knowledge and the creativity of their thinking.

Uganda's Perspective

Assigned to "the African Union," for example, Fareed and his fellow diplomats devote themselves to studying a 17-point peace proposal to end the crisis of the Acholi people, embroiled in civil war in Northern Uganda. As Ugandan representatives, they are intrigued with the power of Truth and Reconciliation Commissions in Africa and the force of societal forgiveness to heal wounds of war. They are further struck by the impact of poverty. Thus, Fareed selects these points for his peace proposal for Uganda. "We understand that the Lord's Resistance Army is our enemy, but we are willing to reconcile with them because of the African way … to forgive, not jail or punish them. We believe that this way will work because of how well it worked in Rwanda and South Africa." He goes on to cite economic statistics such as the gross domestic product of Uganda, and requests "food, clean water, clothing, irrigation, and waste systems" from developed nations to facilitate peacebuilding efforts in "his" country.

China/Taiwan

Organizers of George Washington University's conference have planned a crisis role play in which they escalate tensions between China and Taiwan through a series of communiqués, diplomatic blunders, and military advances. Thus, Gavin has a difficult task. He represents the government of the Peoples' Republic of China as "Propaganda Minister" as his "crisis group" meets to discuss Chinese claims to Taiwan versus the aims of the Taiwanese independence movement. Having deeply researched the tense relationship between China and Taiwan, Gavin takes on the hard-edged role, declaring the Party line in his opening communication.

> Even the corrupt spies of the American Central Intelligence Agency agree that ninety-eight percent of the inhabitants of the island of Taiwan are Han Chinese. Taiwan was even part of China until its unrecognized secession in 1946, and the UN does not recognize it as independent. If Taiwan continues to pursue a course towards independence, it will face the wrath of the Chinese military.

Yet, despite his initial harsh tone, in the course of crisis deliberations, Gavin is one of the staunchest defenders of creative diplomacy, offering proposal after proposal designed to allow both parties to save face and avoid military confrontation in this realistic crisis. He is commended with a best delegate award for his diplomatic persistence and ability to keep peace between China and Taiwan.

Niger and Access to Medications

Gabriel and Dean research access to medications in impoverished countries. Representing Niger at the "World Health Organization," they are initially overwhelmed meeting 80 other delegates in a conference room at United Nations in New York. Regardless, they begin building alliances with representatives of poor countries, incorporating weeks of research, creativity, cooperation, and risk to gain support for their win-win plan. "Niger proposes tax breaks for pharmaceutical companies so they can more easily provide affordable medications for developing countries such as Niger. If diseases are eradicated in developing countries, there is less chance of epidemics in first world countries."

Niger and Child Labor

Meanwhile, in another UN conference room, Lourdes and Jocelyn communicate via notes, speeches, and caucuses with fellow representatives on the "General Assembly" on the issue of child labor. Lourdes addresses her 80-member panel, presenting the "Joint Resolution" she and Jocelyn have crafted in UN format with colleagues representing Brazil, Democratic Republic of Congo, Iraq, Kazakhstan, Malawi, and Niger. They concur that child labor is the product of war, poverty, lack of education, demand from developed nations, and a disregard for human rights. Further, they emphasize that beginning work at a young age can deny child workers opportunities for advancement and education. Therefore, they write:

This resolution:

Calls upon employers to raise wages and decrease work hours for the crucial developing years of child workers.

Supports the establishment of compulsory educational facilities funded through willing countries and UN sources.

Requests that NGOs help fund stipends, allowing children and families to pull out of poverty, as has been used successfully in India.

Teachers' and Researchers' Evaluations

Teachers gather during Model UN conferences to share strategies and a commitment to help their students engage as global citizens. They agree that the benefits of research, speaking, and acting on the important issues encountered in Model UN activities spill over into students' lives— in school and out. Many teachers comment that students who were previously unengaged in learning have become motivated students after participating in Model UN.

Amy Ruggiero, UNA-USA's Director of Education Programs, cites preliminary research undertaken from 2001 through 2008 that indicates positive trends in Model UN participants' academics, testing, writing, reading, vocabulary, and ability to work cooperatively. In our conversations she emphasized that participating in Model UN helps teachers meet curricular requirements while actively engaging students and "can enhance the learning experience of almost any subject matter. We even have teachers using it to keep their GED students engaged because of the highly interactive experience." She notes that "students and teachers in underserved communities can benefit tremendously from the MUN

Figure 36.   Model UN students run practice session before conference.

experience." Indeed, Global Classrooms, a program of UNA-USA, introduces Model UN in disadvantaged public schools around the world.

Acknowledging that more long-term research needs doing, Ruggiero joined teachers at the 2010 conference in citing anecdotal evidence that keeps pointing to long-term positive effects. "I meet people in their 50s, 60s, even 80s who participated in Model UN conferences in their youth. They remember their country, committee, and issue they worked on. It definitely has impacted their lives." The positive effects are also evident in the 18- to 20-something political science, language, history, and economics majors organizing the conferences, who tell me they got their start in civic engagement in Model UN.

Avery, Johnson, Johnson, and Mitchell (1999) research the efficacy of activities in which students discuss controversies and solve conflicts diplomatically. They report that students understand and remember content, are able to undertake effective problem solving, are better able to understand the positions and feelings of others, forge better social relationships, and have improved self esteem after engaging in such activities. They conclude that students master the intellectual and social skills they will need to resolve conflicts constructively and further the pursuit of peace.

Fundraising

At conferences over the years, I have exchanged ideas with Nancy Schaefer, who teaches at Pulaski Academy in Little Rock, Arkansas. Nancy sees great value in bringing 20, 30, even 40 students to attend two conferences a year! She uses ingenious, low-overhead ways of raising money for conference fees and travel to Washington and New York. For example, she enlists the male and female faculty to play the boys' and girls' basketball teams in two 15-minute games. These popular contests, held during two recess/activity blocks in her school, draw hundreds of student observers willing to pay $3.00 to cheer the fun. She holds a 5K run and a faculty softball game as well, and has brought her athletic department colleagues with her on Model UN trips to give them a taste of what they are helping students experience.

Such strategies can be used in many school settings. Schools unable to bring their students to official conferences can hold simulations and conferences on their own, using strategies similar to those outlined in the *Debate* section of this chapter and information from websites such as the UNA-USA Global Classrooms website (www.unausa.org) to assist them with curriculum, training, and personnel.

Student Evaluations

What happens to students who become what one UNA-USA Model UN chair calls "diplomatic rock stars who learn to save the world in six hours or less?" They have the potential to see the underlying issues and root causes behind today's headlines and sound bites. They are among the few of their peers (and adults) able to appreciate the role of the United Nations and numerous governmental and NGOs engaged in global humanitarian efforts and peacekeeping. They understand that conflict and controversy are part of the human experience, as are cooperation and creative conflict resolution.

We observe many positive effects over the course of the trimester as quiet students become outspoken, opinions become fact-based, perspectives become empathetic, strangers become teammates, and seemingly disinterested youth become passionate about global issues.

Carlos states, "I learned about the nuclear problem in Iran, how to debate, how to ally, and rules and procedures of UN." (And we learn about Carlos's unique sense of humor on our 3-hour bus ride to DC) Numerous students are eager to address the school's Board of Trustees to build support for the Model UN program. They're hooked; with some, like Dean, attending multiple conferences: "Class was great! I learned a lot about child soldiers."

When I ask students what they have learned about diplomacy, negotiation, and peacemaking, there are eager responses. "It is hard to agree. Opinions often conflict. But it is fun to argue," reports one. Another asserts, "I learned a lot of diplomatic and compromising skills." Others say, "I learned to listen to other people and their opinions," or that one "must look at things from other people's viewpoints." A delegate learns that United Nations procedures are "really strenuous processes for creating peace." Another agrees that "peacemaking is a difficult process. It takes many people to make peace a reality." A student is humbled, "You have to compromise and accept that some ideas are better than yours." Another realizes how important it is to "make alliances; pay attention to everyone." A student learns that "it helps to have a third party in the room," appreciating the UN role of mediator in many global problems.

Jonas, a student who has attended numerous conferences, gets the final word:

> I LOVE Model UN! I learned to be a peaceful diplomat and have everyone's interests in mind. I also learned how the real UN performs. I learned more about causes and effects and to promote peaceful diplomacy. Awesome experience.

Follow-Up Action

Some choose to take subsequent action on behalf of the causes they research. Will the members of the World Health Organization panel present their recommendations to the student body? Do they want to do a fundraiser for tsunami relief? Do they want to circulate a petition about conflict minerals in Congo? We give them the option. Model UN gives students a unique opportunity to feel the power and responsibility of acting on the world stage. *PeaceJam* introduces them to leaders who do this daily.

PEACEJAM

In his book *I'd Rather Teach Peace* (2002), former *Washington Post* journalist Colman McCarthy details his fascinating journey from journalist to peace educator with high school and college students. He describes lively class discussions of topics including vegetarianism, capital punishment, abortion, and war. Especially meaningful to me is McCarthy's unyielding stand on the need to teach peace, as some of his colleagues

Figure 37.   Students create peacebuilding slogans for hallway bulletin boards.

suggest that he offer "balance" in his courses and teach his students "the other side" of various issues. Students have been immersed in a culture of violence over the courses of their lifetimes, he vigorously asserts. Indeed, by offering his course he provides the other side: the side of nonviolence and peace!

I have been carefully balanced over the course of twenty-five-plus-years in the classroom. But, like McCarthy (2002), I'd rather teach peace more overtly than I have before. The times demand it. Therefore, in addition to teaching the *Debate* and *Model UN* electives with colleagues, I designed an elective featuring the Nobel Peace laureates, agreeing with the thinking of Irwin Abrams on their importance.

Heroes to Emulate

A life-long peace activist and scholar, Abrams was appalled at a study that revealed young people's heroes were limited to pop-stars and sports-stars. Approached by a publisher to write a biography of the Peace Prize winners, Abrams (2001) wrote in the preface that he had noted that stories of individuals had always made an impact on his students in history classes. Thus his aim was to portray prize winners who would provide good role models for youth to emulate.

Eventually, I pitched the class, first alone, then in conjunction with the art teacher. Incorporating art, acting, and activism, I was sure the class would be stimulating and worthwhile. We would create a Nobel Peace laureate portrait gallery, and each student would take on the role of a laureate in videotaped "interviews." Calling the course *Nobel to Neighborhood*, I intended that our study of the laureates would culminate in action in our communities and awarding of our own "Neighborhood Nobels" to local activists who inspired us. But try as I might, few kids chose to enroll, and those who did couldn't fit the class into their schedules.

Disappointed, I bided my time. Then Irwin told me about *PeaceJam*, and I studied their dynamic website, www.peacejam.org. I showed the *PeaceJam* movie (2004) to some classes. Interspersing interviews of Columbine High School shooting-survivors-turned-activists with boisterous conferences featuring Nobel Peace laureates, the movie caught students' imaginations. Finally, I teamed up with our service learning coordinator to offer the *PeaceJam* elective. We would learn about the Nobel laureates and investigate how good leaders identify problems in their communities and take steps to solve them. Finally, we would take on local and global challenges ourselves.

We Have to Run This Class

Steve Morris, our Middle School head, is enthusiastic. "We have to run this class!" he exclaims, offering to personally invite students to join. Awarded a summer curriculum grant from the school, my colleague Susan Swanson and I use a variety of sources to design and develop the class. We begin with several essential questions:

1. How can students gain and inspire interest in the broader community?
2. How can they become aware of root causes of problems and injustices so they will not unconsciously perpetuate them?
3. How can students understand that they can change the world and that many people already have?
4. How can they know that all change starts somewhere?

Human Rights

In their work with Hague Appeal for Peace (www.hagueappeal.org), peace educators Betty Reardon and Alicia Cabezudo give theoretical and practical suggestions in their curriculum *Learning to Abolish War: Teaching*

Toward a Culture of Peace (2002). I take inspiration from them for activities involving human rights. After brainstorming our own list of human needs, for example, we examine the *Universal Declaration of Human Rights*. As we know, many students are unable to envision peace. This *Declaration* helps us understand the basic conditions to which each human is entitled. Thus, when we ask our inaugural *PeaceJammers* to draw pictures of peace, there are no blank stares. Instead, students get to work drawing images of clean skies and fruitful landscapes, teachers and students learning in well-supplied schools, and people helping and solving problems with local and global others.

Learning and Teaching About Peace Laureates

To bring the peacemaking heroes to life, we visit websites such as the Nobel Foundation's nobelprize.org, where we can read bios and view video interviews of laureates. Laureates and other activists are also featured in videos available via The Nobelity Project's (n.d.) nobelity.org. Very useful to us and ideally suited to the interests of middle school youth are the *PeaceJam Leaders* curriculum (PeaceJam Foundation, 2007) and *PeaceJam* books (Gifford, 2004 and Suvanjieff & Engle, 2008). Providing biographies detailing obstacles overcome by Nobel laureates as adolescents, the curriculum invites students to become actors for positive change, and the books describe youth who work with laureates to do so.

Hearing of our class, the Lower School chaplain invites our students to teach 500 Lower Schoolers about the meaning of peace and the work of the laureates. Our kids prepare a chapel program. First, they think about defining peace in kid-friendly language. "Peace is as simple as a smile equals another smile," says one. Another offers, "Peace is people working together for society and the environment." A third defines peace as "Putting others first. You help others, in anyway, anytime, anywhere." Then they select their favorite laureates, creating a slide-show connecting global peace concepts to the "Stripes," the school virtues the younger students know well.

After we sing a song about peace together, Gabriel reminds students about the nonviolent civil rights and peace work of Martin Luther King, Jr., the 1964 laureate. Then he introduces a peacemaker new to the audience, 2008 winner Marti Ahtisaari of Finland. "He helped people understand each other so that they can settle arguments peacefully and thoughtfully."

Jocelyn introduces another laureate:

> My favorite Nobel Peace Prize winner is Shirin Ebadi. She was the first
> female judge in her country, but when the laws changed in Iran, she wasn't

allowed to be a judge anymore because she is a woman. She was awarded her prize in 2003 for her efforts for human rights, especially the rights of women to have the same rights as men.

Lourdes chooses 2004 winner Wangari Maathai of Kenya, founder of the Greenbelt Movement:

> She wanted to help the people of her community so she decided that she would plant trees to provide shelter, firewood, and income for families. She gathered a group of people and they planted a few trees. Since then, the group has planted more than 45 million trees in Kenya!

Peacemakers are Flexible

Meanwhile, in class, we have been using agenda-setting and group cohesion activities adapted from *Writing for a Change* (Berdan et al., 2006). Our well-received chapel program behind us, we feel ready to use *PeaceJam's* (PeaceJam Foundation, 2007) model for assessing community needs, conducting interviews in our school, asking such questions as: "What does community mean to you? What is good/bad about our community?"

Instead, we take advantage of an unexpected opportunity to participate in the Model UN conference at the United Nations in New York. Regrouping our preconceived plans with the help of our kids (who are excited about the conference), Susan agrees to incorporate the community action components of the *PeaceJam* class into her service learning program, and I realize Student Council can take on community assessment as well.

Thus, the latest incarnations of the *PeaceJam* course include a Model UN component, and vice versa. A recent Model UN/PeaceJam class used knowledge of the Peace laureates, for example, to create a school-wide Peacemakers Scavenger Hunt prior to switching gears to prepare for the Model UN conference in New York. The fluid transition from learning about Peace Prize laureates to experiencing using diplomatic skills to solve global problems is an opportunity too good to pass up.

Student Evaluations

Does this curricular content relate to the needs of adolescents? "Yes!" Replies an eighth grade girl taking the course for the second time:

> This class makes students aware of what's going on in the world and what can be done to help. This class is oriented toward the future and preparing us for the "real world" by helping us form views about issues and thinking for ourselves. This class is appropriate for middle school students because

we know what our parents are talking about at dinner, and we know who and what we are praying for in chapel.

A seventh grade boy agrees,

This class is appropriate for my age group so we don't take things for granted. It helps us be kind and respectful toward other countries and in the way we talk about them. This class will help us in the future, but it's still something we need to study today.

Noddings (2005b, 2007) tells us such course content is crucial to students' development as human beings and global citizens, urging schools to commit significant portions of their curricula school wide to such issues. Gardner (2006) urges educators to expose students to local and global exemplars of excellence, ethics, and engagement in hopes of inspiring such qualities in our students. Lickona and Davidson (2005) highlight practices of schools that achieve education's "two great goals: to help students become smart ... and to help them become good" (p. xv). They discuss multiple strengths of character that are the hallmarks of a person with performance and moral character. I am certain that students in *PeaceJam* class (and *Model UN* and *Debate*) have these character strengths. They are becoming critical and ethical thinkers who are also able to act responsibly and respectfully as contributing members of societies in which they live.

When we ask our *PeaceJam* students why they chose this class, one answers, "I want to help everyone gain peace in our community, our state, our country, our world." Another replies,

I chose the *PeaceJam* elective so that I could be part of the millions of people who are striving for a more peaceful world. I also want to learn about world issues to broaden my awareness of events in the world so that I can work toward peace.

And when we ask what they know now that they didn't know before taking the class, Lourdes nails it for all of them, "Looking at the laureates and our Model UN research we saw how complicated it is to work for peace. Peace takes more work than I thought it would."

Transformative Optimism

Working with a commission to establish a National Peace Academy in the United States, sociologist Elise Boulding (1982/2004) states the goal is to train people to be able to enter into conflicts and negotiate solutions that benefit both sides. She urges us to visualize a world in which conflicts are handled peacefully and to further envision the practical steps needed to achieve such peace and justice.

Boulding combines pragmatism with vision—as do other giants among peacebuilding activists and scholars. Speaking of the struggle for a world of justice and peace, Martin Luther King, Jr. (1957/2004) warns us not to be "victims of a perilous optimism" (p. 183), noting that the process of change takes education, legislation, financial investment, leadership, nonviolent action, and sacrifice. Nonviolence expert Gene Sharp (1976/2004) also asks us to be both visionary and practical in our approach to peace, citing numerous cases in which nonviolent struggle has been used effectively in place of military conflict. Paulo Freire emphasizes the importance of hope combined with critical understanding of realities as well. Thus, Freierean scholar Cesar Rossatto calls for us to embrace *transformative* optimism: awareness of our potential for being effective actors in collective and critical efforts for transformation and change (Bajaj, 2008).

With knowledge and preparation gained from classes like these electives and the incorporation of peace education practices throughout our curricula and schools, my *transformative* optimism holds that students will be ready to undertake peacebuilding processes effectively, empathetically, and energetically. My practical hope is for all teachers to engage in work that enhances these capabilities in our students.

Teaching for the Peaceful Future

Education leaders such as Tony Wagner (2010) uphold the need for the types of strategies I have described in this book. He argues that students need critical and imaginative thinking skills; respectful and flexible collaborative and leadership skills: adaptability; initiative and entrepreneurship; and that they must be effective communicators and analyzers of information. I affirm these "seven survival skills" Wagner describes as not only serving the individual student, but the just, productive, and peaceful future of the human race as well.

We must practically *and* hopefully teach our students how to build a peaceful future. In doing so, we will bring into active practice the "five minds for the future" Howard Gardner (2006) calls for: we will help our students develop mastery of academic disciplines, help them analyze and synthesize the overwhelming quantities of information they face, give them opportunities to develop creative approaches to present and future problems, model the respect and empathy they need to be members of diverse communities, and support them in developing a strong set of ethical principles on which to act locally and globally.

Seven survival skills and five minds for the future boil down to three teaching imperatives. By teaching our students to think, care, and act, our teaching for the peaceful future starts today.

Questions to Consider

1. In your school or neighborhood, are there opportunities for students to act on their educational interests via electives and clubs? Will your school support a Model UN, *PeaceJam,* or debate club? Can you start such electives or clubs by meeting before or after school or at lunch? What fundraising would you have to do to bring your students to conferences? If you are already engaged, how can you bring colleagues on board? Will families help?

2. Would debating favorite pets, ice cream flavors, or music allow you to practice debating controversial issues civilly? Are you willing to watch courtroom dramas and political debates to get ideas of what works and what hurts in the civil debate process? Can you practice facilitating discussions with friends and colleagues until you feel comfortable and skilled enough to do so in the classroom with students?

3. In a 2007 radio interview with Krista Tippett, Dr. Rachel Naomi Remen posed the following question: "How would I live if I was exactly what's needed to heal the world?" What is your answer to this question?

4. Do you believe with Anne Kjelling that "anyone can be a Nobel Peace Prize winner?" Do you believe anyone can make a difference? Do you believe you make a difference in the lives of your students every day?

5. What is one new idea you are ready to try to help your students build a peaceful future?

AFTERWORD

Lessons From a
Global Peace Education Sabbatical

*"In our striving for a new word with which to express this new and
important sentiment, we are driven to the rather absurd phrase of
'cosmic patriotism.' Whatever it may be called, it may yet be strong enough to
move masses of men out of their narrow national considerations and cautions into
new reaches of human effort and affection."*

—Jane Addams (Newer Ideals of Peace, 1907/2002, p. 40)

*"We thought all Americans were arrogant and selfish, until we met you. We are so
happy to know there are lots of people like you in America!"*

—Japanese housewife, Toyohashi, Japan

*"You are like Confucius. He also traveled around during a time of war,
speaking of peace. I admire what you are doing."*

—Student, Kyoto-Seika University, Japan

Figure 38.   Author and participants in Toyohashi Station Peace Event (Japan).

After all the explanations of theory and practice in the foregoing chapters, what do I hope readers understand about peace education? Simply this: Teaching students to think critically and creatively, to care about classmates and global others, and to act honorably and effectively for the greater good are moral imperatives of peace education—and all education—that teachers must infuse into their practices daily. Why? Students who can think, care, and act are able and empowered to take on the challenging tasks that face them in school, at home, in the present, and in the future. Being able to think, care, and act enables students to become thoughtful, compassionate, and effective local and global citizens. Frankly, we can teach them all the content we want, but without teaching students to think, care, and act, we do not provide them with the tools to build a peaceful future.

To Think

What does it mean to *think* in an age in which citizens around the planet are distracted by media images from screens on our mobile devices to screens at school, work, and home? First, to be able to think means to be able to analyze the multiple messages surrounding us in the media bazaar. We must actively teach students how to do this. Students must be prepared to engage media with their critical thinking antennae up and working, when facing information in textbooks, primary sources, and newspapers (should they continue to exist); when evaluating information conveyed by teachers, parents, politicians, and others in authority; and when consuming messages conveyed in music, movies, TV, advertisements, online social networking venues, and YouTube videos (as well as multiple forms of new media to come).

Further, by encouraging imagination and the ability to *creatively* think about the past, present, and future, we provide students with the tools to envision and create the future in which they want to live. Creative thinking also allows students to imagine how others feel and helps them step into the metaphorical shoes of their classmates and international peers. Importantly, being able to think critically and creatively also invokes the ability to think with conscience. And conscience enables students to evaluate and uplift the moral worth of their thinking, caring, and acting by taking the perspectives and needs of others into account.

To Care

What does it mean to *care* for the local and global other in a society whose constant message is *it's all about me?* First, we must teach students to respect, care for, and appreciate the people around them, from family to peers and teachers. Knowing how to make others feel safe and welcome is a prerequisite for living and working effectively and collegially with others—in and out of the classroom. Second, we must help students widen their circles of care to include people in their neighborhood, country, and wider world. A story is told about a frog who lived in a small well. Looking up at its small circle of sky, it considered the world to be a tiny place that included it and it alone. We must encourage our students to jump out of their small wells into the larger world—virtually and in reality.

Lucky are the students and teachers who can travel and meet friends from afar. For those who cannot, however, there is virtual communication via Skype and Gmail video chats. If one has Internet connectivity and a video camera (and this is becoming a smaller "if" every day) one can meet friends from across the planet virtually. Social networking may have its dark sides in terms of online bullying and invasions of privacy, but such media also have the capacity to bring global others into a global neighborhood. We can utilize all these possibilities to help our students become caring and empathetic neighbors of all the communities in which they live. Our goal should be to teach them to love all lives as their own as they build an all-encompassing community of care.

To Act

Finally, what does it mean to *act* in a world whose problems seem overwhelming? It means to be able to use the powers of critical and creative thinking and compassionate and inclusive care to act effectively and conscientiously to solve those problems. Many schools have laudable service learning programs. However we do not want students to depend upon school-based initiatives in order to create a just and peaceful world. We want to help students see themselves as personally capable of making change—and responsible to do so—even when not earning credit through school programs designed by adults. Using the examples of activists in our neighborhoods and on the world stage, we can teach students to identify problems about which they care, examine the root causes at work, and design and implement actions to improve life for people, animals, and the environment. We must help them develop their own tools—as individuals and groups—to deal with the problems that face us all on an exploding and warming planet.

In addition, we must teach students to balance the multiple demands of their personal lives with an awakened attitude of action. Such tragedies as genocide, economic collapse, and environmental destruction occur when we citizens have fallen asleep. When we are preoccupied with the pressures or pleasures of daily life, we let such horrors happen step by step. If we can wake up as local and global citizens, if we can take preventative steps early—we can avoid resorting to wars, bailouts, and emergency clean-up to solve these problems. Students can preemptively begin to build a peaceful future one step at a time if we teach them how to do so.

Outcomes and Strategies

So, what are the outcomes of such teaching for peace? Students' fear of local and global violence is alleviated, and their prosocial behavior and academic progress enhanced, when we actively teach them about nonviolent solutions to local and global problems. They feel empowered to learn that people work for peace in countless ways, locally and globally, and that their own creative and compassionate energy is needed and powerful. They are able to take multiple perspectives and are empowered to empathetically engage in building a peaceful world.

As this text has shown, we can teach for peace vigorously, flexibly, and sensitively. Students can engage in effective peace education initiatives that are varied and suited to their settings. They may be stand-alone initiatives or integrated into the curriculum, and they should be part of the daily structure of the school and classroom environment. Peace education encompasses multiple educational aspirations, among them: global, character, multicultural, antibias, gender, moral, environmental, future, service learning, and social justice education. Every major component of good education is part of the peace education umbrella.

As we spread this umbrella, however, we must remember that teachers teach peace in our manner, classroom atmosphere, curriculum, and by personal example. An ill-informed, unkind, apathetic "peace educator" is an oxymoron. We teachers must ourselves be able to think, care, and act in order to teach our students to do so. Finally, teachers benefit from teaming with colleagues in peace education efforts. When such support is not available, pioneering peace teachers can "pilot" programs, create bulletin boards to inform the community, and interest families in peace education activities. Take the first step and keep walking.

Photo credit: J. Kadir Cannon

Figure 39.   Author interviews hibakusha, A-bomb survivor, in Hiroshima.

A Peace Education Sabbatical

I have been fortunate to teach in a school that values my teaching aspirations and have been able to take many steps on the path of peace education. During the 2005-2006 school year, for example, I was awarded a sabbatical to research and meet peace educators and peacebuilders. With my artist husband I embarked on a global adventure, learning and presenting peace education strategies in Japan, Denmark, Canada, and China. After meeting with educators, researchers, students, artists, and fellow global citizens around the world, I had thousands of insights. Here are 20:

1. Hiroshima, Japan, is a city with such a profound mood of tragedy underlying the modern surface, that for me as a visitor it was difficult to look at a river without imagining charred and blackened bodies or to walk on a path without feeling ash and bone. Yet, despite the eerie ghosts of those who were incinerated by the atomic bomb, I learned that in the modern, rebuilt city of Hiroshima with its parks, shops, and skyscrapers, life goes on. People work, shop, and picnic under cherry blossom trees; children play and laugh on their way to and from school. I was amazed at the resilience of the human spirit: our power to endure, change paths, forgive, and rebuild.

2. I met several hibakusha, A-bomb survivors, at Hiroshima's World Friendship Center. Every day they speak about the perils of nuclear weapons and the horrors of war to groups of school children from middle schools all over Japan. Hibakusha are aging, and the urgency with which they speak to the younger generation is palpable. Nuclear weapons must never be used again, they demand, and they offer themselves—with their deformities and losses—as proof. We cannot ignore them.

3. I learned from one hibakusha, Michiko Yamaoka-san, that she would continue speaking to group after group of children even though she is ill with radiation-related maladies. She has spent over 45 years speaking to school and civic groups about her experience and the evils of war. (It took the first 20 years after the bombing to get medical treatment—she was one of the Hiroshima maidens—and to get over her hatred toward the U.S. for dropping the bomb.) She recognizes Japan's militaristic past, even describing her work in junior high making fortifications, as she decries the stupidity of war and the horrors of nuclear weapons. She keeps speaking out, but it is clearly draining. She reasons, "If I speak to 100 children, and I reach just one … that one might make a differ-

ence." I learned that if I also speak out, and if even one student or teacher feels moved, that is a good outcome, and I must continue to do so.

4. I learned from college students in Kyoto that Japanese students feel pressured throughout their school careers. They take exam after exam and worry about getting into college, just like my U.S. students. And I learned that once they get there, they feel worried about getting jobs and good houses. They have no time to worry about issues such as human rights, the environment, and peace. From these students, and others in China, I learned that it is important to teach my students how to balance their lives so they can think about important issues, while doing the things they need to do to succeed personally. We teachers need to remember—and model—this balance as well.

5. I learned in Toyohashi, Japan, that students in Sakuragaoke Middle School can choose a global studies major that enables them to travel and learn about countries around the world for 6 years of their schooling. This is their school's answer to the horrors of Japanese military aggression during World War II. Interestingly, when we entered a high school history classroom, a student asked angrily, "What do you have to say about Okinawa in World War II?" Fortunately, I had also been reading about this question. I addressed the class, "My understanding is that the Okinawan people were a peaceful civilian farming population that got caught between two armies. The slaughter on Okinawa is an example of the huge human costs of war, in this case, one between the government of Japan and the government of the United States. We citizens must work to prohibit our governments from embarking on such war-making policies in the future." Students erupted in applause, and my confronter was first to take a photo with me, flashing the ubiquitous peace sign, of course. I learned that each culture tells its own stories of war, but at heart—we global citizens want to live in peace.

6. I learned that in Japan, the home of innovative peace education after 1954, nationalism is on the rise. Teachers who buck country-wide proposals to teach "patriotism" in Japanese schools often find their job security threatened. Teachers who refuse to rise for the singing of the national anthem, for example, have been fined, suspended, or sent by their school districts to distant schools as Japan begins to remilitarize, reported the *Japan Times* (Nakamura & Nakata, 2006).

7. Knowing how quickly patriotism turns to nationalism and then to militarism makes many educators—like me—apprehensive. I determined that I would teach teachers in the United States, and other countries I visit, about ways to teach for peace and an inclusive commitment to local, national, and global citizenship during our daily lessons, even at the risk of losing popularity or job security.

8. I learned in Toyohashi, Japan, that artists and educators can work together on peace projects—even when they cannot understand each others' languages—to create beautiful works of art and theater for peace. Artists from Toyohashi and Dayton, Ohio, cooperatively created banners, masks, and props for a dramatic anti-war street festival. I hung the peace poetry of my students, my husband hung his peace scrolls, and the area outside the Toyohashi train station, a beautiful plaza overlooking the city, became thought-provoking and colorful. Wearing signs in Japanese and English, masked actors (representing war, pollution, racism, famine, and unemployment) mimed taking control of citizens by using qualities of apathy, fear, and helplessness. However, in this play, there was a happy ending! The citizens woke up and regained control by cooperatively changing war to peace, pollution to clean environment, fear to confidence, racism to equality, famine to plenty, and unemployment to good jobs. The common people, now aware of their power to act on the world, unveiled a beautiful vision of Peace—a collaboratively created mural. Participants and audience members erupted into back-slapping, hugs, and cheers in Japanese and English! "*Ganbatte kudesai!* Go for it! Don't give up!"

9. I learned how inspiring the work of a small group can be to others. One Japanese artist wrote, "You taught us how to express our own opinion. You gave me energy. We have to start some action like you. The Toyohashi Peace Event was a great lesson for us."

10. I learned in Xinglong County, and in Beijing, Shanghai, and countless cities in China, how curious many Chinese people are about people in the United States, and that they will open their homes and schools to meet these visitors and make new friends. I learned how comforting it feels to be treated to wonderful food and caring guidance in a new country, and that hospitality is a gracious talent at which my Chinese hosts are experts. I vowed to be a better host when people visit my home, my school, and my country.

11. I learned that Chinese middle school students can be just as energetic, noisy, smart, kind, and impish as my U.S. middle school students, and I felt at home teaching them.

12. I learned how important it is for people in the United States to learn about Chinese culture, history, and development, and that the future peace of the world may well be found in the quality of the relationships involving these two peoples. It was a continuing thrill when classes of shy, yet curious students or teachers erupted into applause when their visitor from the U.S. simply walked into the room. I began presentations by expressing my hope that we common people can make lasting connections (*guanxi*) by learning about each other's cultures and languages. "Our governments may make policies that promote war," I told them, "yet we must remember the ties of humanity that bind us." I won their hearts by quoting Confucius: "How wonderful it is to greet friends from afar." Hearing this phrase, familiar to Chinese young and old, they applauded again. I saw over and over again the power of travelers—who take time to learn a bit of culture and language—to build cultural bridges.

13. I continue to learn to promote this connection. I created websites to help U.S. students learn about life in China, and to help Chinese learn about life in the United States. Many of my students are pictured on the website, and teachers and students all over the world have enjoyed their writing and art work about their hopes and dreams. Further, in 2010, two colleagues and I planned and chaperoned a student trip to China. The high school students we taught and escorted made friends and memories at our sister school in Shenyang that will last a lifetime. They have become global citizens who can promote understanding and friendship.

14. I also learned that many people who used to look at the United States with admiration have in more recent years looked at the U.S. with fear. "What is going on with your country?" was the most common question we were asked in Japan, China, Denmark, and Canada in 2006. (I heard it again in 2010.) Ordinary people we met had clear horror at the wars in Iraq and Afghanistan and concrete fears about possible U.S. actions in Iran, N. Korea, and elsewhere. However, another comment we heard often was, "We thought all Americans were arrogant and selfish—until we met you." I realized again the power of citizen-to-citizen diplomacy in a global society that helps remove barriers created by national governments.

15. I learned from one woman in Hiroshima that her post office was powered by rooftop solar panels. Throughout southern China I saw passive solar water heaters atop every roof. I learned from my Japanese and Danish hosts about water-conserving toilets. "Why can't

you Americans do things like this?" they asked. We can. Our new toilet works beautifully and saves water. There is much more to do.

16. I learned that my Chinese teacher friends walk, ride bikes, or take long bus rides to get to their schools each day, yet I know they wish they could drive to work as I usually do. Perhaps they are by now, adding to the thousands of new cars choking Chinese roads (and air) daily. I saw Chinese cities developing at a seemingly unsustainable pace and wondered how our two countries will solve problems of pollution and competition for resources in a peaceful and sustainable manner. Ironically, the Chinese, with their one-party system, may mandate climate-saving policies before gridlocked American legislators can stop bickering. The point is: we all must deal with environmental problems—effectively and immediately.

17. I learned in Canada, at the International Peace Research Association conference, that all over the world, in any country I could name, people are working on projects big and small to promote peace. There are hip-hop peace groups in South Africa and Israel-Palestine theater collaboratives in the Middle East. There are Argentinean peace musicians and diplomacy camps in Denmark and the United States. There are antibullying peer mediators on playgrounds at schools in Australia and environmental education programs online in Poland. And, there are researchers all over the world developing and studying the efficacy of such programs. I vowed to teach my students about these varied and unceasing initiatives to promote peace and justice. Reminding myself of the vast local and global network of peacebuilders reassures and inspires me.

18. I learned from Johan Galtung, Norwegian peace mediator, that many citizens of the world want Americans to walk humbly—to realize that we are a nation among nations and that we need to cooperate with the world community.

19. I learned that in a climate of distrust, in Denmark, reasoned, responsible free speech can promote understanding, while offensive, irresponsible free speech can destroy dialogue. In discussions about political cartoons I learned that ignorance of the culture of our neighbors can lead to violence with our neighbors.

20. I learned at the Norwegian Nobel Institute that everyone can be a peacebuilder. I interviewed Anne Kjelling, chief librarian, and asked her what my students most needed to know. "Tell them anyone can be a Nobel Peace Prize winner. They are just ordinary people, educated and uneducated, doctors, lawyers, housewives, volunteers. The thing is, they have done something for the cause of

peace. *Everyone can,*" she said. I vowed to tell my students her message, and I do—frequently.

For Fred

I also learned that in Danish, Swedish, and Norwegian *Fred* means *Peace*. I was visiting the *Nobel Fredcenter,* when I figured it out.

My father's name was Fred. A World War II combat infantry veteran, he did not have peace in his life. Yet, his name, his experiences, and his love for people propel me to work for Fred, for Paz, Heiwa, He Ping, Salaam, Shalom, Shanti, Peace.

I want my students to believe in the value of active peacebuilding: to understand that socially just policies and structures are more lastingly effective methods of solving global problems than violence and war. Finally, I want them to know that such pacifism is not passive. It is active, hard work, and it is not for the faint of heart.

I ask that my students be peacebuilders, encouraging them by saying,

Use your critical judgment when you watch TV, surf the web, or read the news. Take time to perceive what the other side thinks and feels about an issue. Have empathy for those you disagree with and work for just compromises. Walk, take the bus, carpool. Buy less stuff. Be good hosts. Do regular acts of kindness. Study about other cultures, religions, and countries. Make friends with people who are different from you. Care about your families and classmates and country, and also care about the billions of people who are your global neighbors. Learn how to select a cause worthy of your energy and work for it. Make time for peacebuilding. Think. Care. Act. "*Everyone can.*" Be one who does.

A Final Plea for Peace Education

During my year away from the classroom, historian Irwin Abrams shared with me his belief that peace education is effective—but long term—leading to an "unseen harvest." Encouraging me to believe that my labors as a teacher are meaningful and important even in a culture of war, he was emphatic that peace educators' big and small efforts yield fruits, whether or not we see them.

Yet, peace educator Ian Harris asks if I am so sure the harvest is unseen. Not totally. The small flowers that bloom, those changes that take place in the hearts and minds of the students I teach, are observable. I believe that harvest is growing increasingly abundant as I become a better peace teacher.

Figure 40.   Author leads Xinglong County (China) in-service teacher seminar.

Read the words of a parent, writing in gratitude to our head of school about her daughter's growth as a peacebuilder: "Sue helped Jenny and a friend start a petition and stay on task. She taught Jenny an ongoing lesson about being a peaceful agent of change." Another parent writes about her daughter's work preparing food for local homeless coalitions: "This CAP project truly brought out a caring side of Mackenzie. I was so proud how she took hold of this project and even insisted on paying for the ingredients out of her own money."

In an end-of-year evaluation, an English student recognizes the importance of care in the classroom:

> I think that our class has been a friendly, open, and caring community the whole year. You helped by encouraging us to go out on a limb. Also, you helped classmates be supportive of each other when we made presentations or shared ideas. If people laughed at others, you let them know that it was unacceptable.

In this end-of-year history evaluation, a student urges action:

I learned that it's important to not only learn about history, but to make history as well. Even if it's really simple, you're still helping to change the world. I think everyone should try to help make the world a better place.

Pondering the meaning of peace while taking my peace elective, an eighth grader creates her own morally sophisticated definition on which she can base her actions for peace:

Peace is a connection between people and things that creates a world in which everyone has everything they need to live a decent quality life. It is a connection that makes people understand what others need and others' views. Peace allows people to talk about those views without fighting and murdering in the process.

Sixth through eighth grade Student Council members evaluate their growth. "I understand the meaning of community better now." "I really feel part of something." "I was able to experience leadership." "I am not afraid to put my input on things."

Appreciating her new role as a global citizen, an eleventh grader writes of her trip to China:

I never expected to make friends at a school thousands of miles away and to meet so many genuinely nice people who were all excited to meet a foreigner. The connections I have made in China will last me a lifetime and will always be something I cherish.

A former student returns to teach my current class about her Peace Corps experience creating women's entrepreneurial initiatives in Morocco. Other students write, "You helped us so much and made us better people." "Now I know I can make a difference." "I like how you tried to spread peace and diversity throughout the class." "I am not sure if I have ever had a class that behaved as friendly to each other as I have had in here."

As I wrote some of these pages, the wind outside raged in icy blasts. Yet tiny yellow and purple crocuses and brilliant blue scilla flowers bloomed, in spite of the cold wind. These flowers are symbolic of our efforts to cultivate the beauty and sturdiness of a culture of peace able to grow and thrive in a chilling climate of war. I am sowing seeds and will work for a harvest. I think I see sprouts. Join me.

Photo credit: J. Kadir Cannon.

Figure 41.   Author with students in Toyohashi (Japan) high school.

APPENDIX

Annotated Bibliography of Resources for Teachers and Students

(Additional resources at www.teachforpeace.org include student handouts and recommended websites for teacher and student research and action.)

• Abrams, I. (2001). *The Nobel Peace Prize and the Laureates-An Illustrated Biographical History 1901-2001.* **Nantucket, MA: Science History Publications.** Life-long peace activist and scholar Irwin Abrams was appalled at a study that revealed the heroes of young people as pop-stars and sports-stars. Approached by a publisher to write a biography of the peace prize winners, Abrams said, "A chief motive for me was to portray the best of the prize winners as examples for the rest of us, especially young people, to try to emulate." See also **Ann Keene's *Peacemakers*** (below).

• Abrams, I. (1995). *The Words of Peace: Selections from the Speeches of the Winners of the Nobel Peace Prize.* **New York, NY: Newmarket Press.** Inspiring and thought-provoking, these selections are available in a small volume. Abrams begins with Bertha von Suttner speaking in 1905, "One of the eternal truths is that happiness is created and developed in peace, and one of the eternal rights is the individual's right to live. The strongest of all instincts, that of self-preservation, is an assertion of this right, affirmed and sanctified by the ancient commandment: Thou shalt not kill." Almost a century later, Yitzhak Rabin, a military commander, speaks of the somber moment after ordering a military operation, "That is the moment you grasp that as a result of the decision you just made, people will be going to their deaths. People from my nation. People from other nations. And they still don't know it.... Is there no other choice? No other way? And then the order is given and the inferno begins."

- **Ackerman, P., & Duvall, J. (2000).** *A Force More Powerful: A Century of Nonviolent Conflict.* **New York, NY: Palgrave.** This book takes strands of nonviolent action from around the world in the twentieth century and weaves a tapestry of individual and group stories of courage, imagination, and dedication to justice and peace. The film, directed by Steven York, contains six 30-minute episodes chronicling the nonviolent movements of South Africa, India, Poland, Denmark, Chile, and Nashville, Tennessee, and is available with teaching guide from York Zimmerman, Inc. (www.yorkzim.com). Breaking commonly-held stereotypes about nonviolent movements, York and Duvall assert, "Nonviolent resistance becomes a force more powerful than the hand of an oppressor to the extent that it takes away his capacity for control. Embracing nonviolence for its own sake does not produce this force. A strategy for action is needed, and that strategy has to involve attainable goals, movement unity, and robust sanctions that restrict the opponent." The DVD is an indispensable and inspiring resource for use in peace education classrooms, and the book provides the background information that will broaden and move the reader.

- **Barash, D. P. (2000).** *Approaches to Peace: A Reader in Peace Studies.* **New York, NY: Oxford University Press.** This book can be used for one's own background knowledge or with student groups. Barash introduces a diverse array of essays, poems, readings from world scriptures, and speeches with helpful insights and provides questions for discussion.

- **Barton, K. C., & Levstik, L. S. (2004).** *Teaching History for the Common Good.* **Mahwah, NJ: Lawrence Erlbaum Associates.** This college text looks at multiple perspectives of history teaching, but finally exhorts history teachers to foster caring and civic engagement in their students. The authors state, "Care-less history strikes us as a soulless enterprise.... Students will not bother making reasoned judgments, expanding their views of humanity, or deliberating over the common good if they don't care about those things."

- **Bajaj, M. (Ed.). 2008.** *Encyclopedia of Peace Education.* **Charlotte, NC: Information Age Publishing.** Slim but packed with foundational thinking in peace education, this multiarticle volume presents thinking by and about such seminal peace thinkers as Ian Harris, Johan Galtung, and Nel Noddings, as well as John Dewey, Maria Montessori, and Paulo Freire. Writing about the moral and spiritual foundations of peace, Dale Snauwaert asserts that "peace education is premised upon the cosmopolitan belief that the moral community includes all human beings, that all human beings have moral standing, and thus war and peace, justice and injustice, are global moral considerations." This is an essential book in a peace collection.

- **Berdan, K., Boulton, I., Eidman-Aadahl, E., Fleming, J., Gardner, L., Rogers, I., & Solomon, A. (Eds.) (2006).** *Writing for a Change: Boosting Literacy and Learning through Social Action.* **San Francisco, CA: Jossey-Bass.** Reflections from classroom teachers and Social Action practitioners, theoretical underpinnings, and suggestions for classroom activities provide readable and clear thinking on organizing for social change in the classroom. This National Writing Project book details the Social Action Process developed by The Centre for Social Action and influenced by Paulo Freire's educational philosophy (as articulated in his book *Pedagogy of the Oppressed*, 1970). As one teacher reflects, "I refuse to be labeled as powerless, and I do not want my students to view themselves in that manner, either."

- **Berger, R. (2003).** *An Ethic of Excellence: Building a Culture of Craftsmanship with Students.* **Portsmouth, NH: Heinemann.** While teaching in a small, public school Berger created a caring community that pursued excellence and ethics. Students built playhouses, mined for minerals, and made presentations to adult experts, demonstrating academic and character growth. Berger's engaging style and commitment are inspirations to teachers.

- **Berry, W. (2004).** *Hannah Coulter.* **San Francisco, CA: Counterpoint.** Berry's nonfiction writing about rural life and the environment gives food for thought about the true price of our material lifestyle. His novels about Port William give us a vision of life in community with people and nature. In *Hannah Coulter*, the chapter titled *Okinawa* gives a potent understanding of the incomprehensibility of war for the relatives of those who return from it.

- **Bigelow, B. (2008).** *A People's History for the Classroom.* **Milwaukee, WI: Rethinking Schools, Ltd.** The activities presented in this teaching guide are "a sampler" of lessons designed to compliment historian Howard Zinn's work. "Zinn begins from the premise that the lives of ordinary people matter … and also on how people's actions, individually and collectively, shaped our society." With lessons and role plays on defining terrorism, the U.S./Mexican War, and Vietnam War, among others, this book joins other valuable and inspiring teaching materials such as *Rethinking Columbus* (1991), *Rethinking our Classrooms: Teaching for Equity and Social Justice, Volume 1* (1994, 2007), and more from **Rethinking Schools** (www.rethinkingschools.org) and **Teaching for Change** (www.teachingforchange.org).

- **Boulding, E. (2000).** *Cultures of Peace: The Hidden Side of History.* **Syracuse, NY: Syracuse University Press.** "Put in the simplest possible terms, a peace culture is a culture that promotes peaceable diversity. Such a culture includes patterns of belief, values, and behavior, and accompanying institutions of behavior that promote mutual caring and well-being as well as an equality that includes appreciation of difference, stewardship, and equitable sharing of the earth's resources." From this introduction, Boulding (a sociologist and pioneering scholar of peace processes in civil societies) leads the reader through a scholarly discussion of historical and modern-day peace cultures as well as current conflict challenges.

- **Carlsson-Paige, N., & Levin, D. (1987).** *The War Play Dilemma: Balancing Needs and Values in the Early Childhood Classroom.* **New York, NY: Teachers College Press.** This volume details the developmental meaning of war play for children and various options for teachers and parents in dealing with such play.

- **Calkins, L., & Harwayne, S. (1991).** *Living Between the Lines.* **Portsmouth, NH: Heinemann Educational Books.** Calkins's landmark work helps teachers engage students in genuine writing that builds community and writing skills. Also see **Calkins, L. (1986).** *The Art of Teaching Writing.* **Portsmouth, NH: Heinemann Educational Books.** Calkins invites teachers to build writing-reading communities with their students and details effective methods.

- **Chomsky, N. (2005).** *Imperial Ambitions: Conversations on the Post-9-11 World.* **New York: Metropolitan Books.** In these interviews with David Barsamian, Noam Chomsky brings clarity, common sense, and an urgent call to action to combat the threat of American imperialist policies to global security. As to what citizens should do, he replies, "If you want to do something, you have to be dedicated and committed to it day after day. Educational programs, organizing, activism. That's the way things change. You want a magic key, so you can go back to watching television tomorrow? It doesn't exist." Also see **Chomsky, N. (2001)** *9-11* **New York: Seven Cities Press** among many others.

- **Cobban, H. (2000).** *The Moral Architecture of World Peace: Nobel Laureates Discuss our Global Future.* **Charlottesville, VA: University Press of Virginia.** "Destruction of your enemy is actually destruction of yourself!... So the concept of war, destruction of the other side, is not relevant in today's situation." These words of the Dalai Lama, spoken at a conference of nine Nobel Peace Prize laureates at the University of Virginia in 1998, are among the many portions of speeches and discussions included in Cobban's scholarly analysis of the conference. Another book on this conference listed below (*The Art of Peace* by **Jeffrey Hopkins**) is somewhat more readable and is based almost exclusively on the laureates' own words. Both books are inspiring lessons in world history and nonviolent social change in a wide variety of arenas, from indigenous people's rights, to the campaign to ban landmines.

- **Crawford, J. (2005).** *The Last True Story I'll Ever Tell: An Accidental Soldier's Account of the War in Iraq.* **New York, NY: Riverhead Books.** Crawford describes the plight of the returning war vet who has seen combat as "going to the bathroom during a party and returning 15 years later. Everyone has moved on." He also describes the daily sensations of danger and death with honesty and clarity. Like Tim O'Brien does with his account of Vietnam, this book provides a lens into the never-never land of war, and into Iraq in particular.

- **Damon, W. (2008).** *The Path to Purpose: Helping our Children Find Their Calling in Life.* **New York, NY: Free Press.** Damon urges teachers to share a sense of purpose with students as an integral part of the curriculum and daily teaching. Summarizing research and including writing by subjects of psychological studies, Damon's readable book reminds us that "Young people treasure guidance from experienced adults who care about them and know more about the world than they do.... Young people do not wish to be shielded from hard realities; they wish to learn how to accomplish their dreams in the face of such realities."

- **Dear, J. (Ed.) (2002)** *Mohandas Gandhi: Essential Writings.* **Maryknoll, NY: Orbis Books.** The editor writes, "Gandhi has helped me enormously in my work for peace, interreligious dialogue, civil disobedience, and opposition to nuclear weapons." Accordingly, chapters of excerpts of Gandhi's writings are selected on each of these topics. Dear concludes, "Gandhi's answer is always the same: steadfast, persistent, dedicated, committed, patient, relentless, truthful, prayerful, loving, active nonviolence."

- **Derman-Sparks, L., & Ramsey, P. (2006).** *What If All the Kids Are White? Anti-Bias Multicultural Education with Young Children and Families.* **New York, NY: Teachers College Press.** The authors write for teachers of White children who "have become aware of how discrimination affects everyone." With multiple examples of history, principles, and practice, they encourage teachers to enlist families, help students take multiple perspectives, and build empathy among all students for truly effective multicultural and antibias instruction. Geared for teachers of younger children, the ideas are easily transferrable.

- **Diamond, J. (2005).** *Guns, Germs, and Steel: The Fates of Human Societies.* **New York, NY: W.W. Norton.** Diamond uncovers the conditions of geography that led to European exploration and domination of the Americas, among other topics. The book is a must for teachers of early history of the Americas.

- **Diamond, L. (2001).** *The Peace Book: 108 Simple Ways to Create a More Peaceful World.* **Bristol: VT: The Peace Company.** This is a feel-good book, with practical advice for those seeking inner and outer peace. Encompassing themes of personal and spiritual renewal as well as neighborhood and global activism, the book is a useful "get-started" book for students and teachers alike.

- **Fischer, L. (Ed.) (2002)** *The Essential Gandhi: An Anthology of his Writings on his Life, Work, and Ideas.* **New York, NY: Vintage Books.** Taking the form of an abridged autobiography, Gandhi's words are used to detail his "experiments with truth" and his "experiments in the political field" throughout his life.

- **Forcey, L. R., & Harris, I. M. (Eds.) (1999).** *Peacebuilding for Adolescents: Strategies for Educators and Community Leaders.* **New York, NY: Peter Lang Publishing, Inc.** Divided into four sections: "Confronting Violence; Classroom Strategies for Peacebuilding; School Strategies for Peacebuilding; and School and Community," essays detail efforts in deterring school violence (peacekeeping), conflict resolution (peacemaking), and helping students actively value and work for social justice and peace (peacebuilding). Forcey and Harris explain, "The goal of Peace Studies education thus goes beyond merely stopping violence and reducing conflict in schools. The goal, to sum it all up, is to get young people to adopt a peaceful philosophy of life and way of living." Essays are readable and transferrable to a variety of venues and age groups.

- **Frankl, V. (1984).** *Man's Search for Meaning: An Introduction to Logotherapy.* **New York, NY: Touchstone Books.** Frankl describes his life as a prisoner in concentration camps during World War II and asks us to ponder individual choice in such a situation. "The experiences of camp life show that man does have a choice of action. There were enough examples, often of a heroic nature, which proved that apathy could be overcome, irritability suppressed.... They may have been few in number, but they offer sufficient proof that everything can be taken from a man but one thing: the last of the human freedoms—to choose one's attitude in any given set of circumstances, to choose one's own way."

- **Gardner, H. (2006).** *Five Minds for the Future.* **Boston, MA: Harvard Business School Press.** Renowned psychologist Howard Gardner, known for his theory of multiple intelligences, concisely argues for five kinds of minds necessary for the world of the future: the disciplined mind (developing expertise in a field), the synthesizing mind (organizing complex information), the creating mind (offering unexpected solutions), the respectful mind (exhibiting empathy and cooperation), and the ethical mind (enacting good citizenship and responsibility in local and global communities). He concludes, "As disciplined learners, it is our job to understand the world. But if we are to be ethical human beings, it is equally our job to use that understanding to improve the quality of life and to bear witness when that understanding (or misunderstanding) is being used in destructive ways."

- **Gifford, D. (2004).** *PeaceJam: How Young People Can Make Peace in Their Schools and Communities.* **San Francisco, CA: Wiley.** A welcome and readable book for middle school youth, the chapters detail initiatives conducted by youth groups in a variety of global settings under the guidance of Nobel Peace Prize laureates including Betty Williams, the Dalai Lama, Shirin Ibadeh, Rigoberto Menchu Tum, and Oscar Arias. See also **Suvanjieff & Engle (2008)** for updated book and DVD.

- **Goodman, J., & Balamore, U. (2003).** *Teaching Goodness: Engaging the Moral and Academic Promise of Young Children.* **New York, NY: Allyn & Bacon.** Character educator Usha Balamore maintains "Moral themes (such as respect, responsibility, honesty, and peace) form a canopy under which almost all prescribed curricular content can be studied and discussed." This book details specific, creative, and joyful approaches to working with young children with thematic teaching for moral and academic excellence.

- **Hamill, S. (Ed.) (2003).** *Poets Against the War.* **New York, NY: Nation Books.** When poet Sam Hamill was invited to the George W. Bush White House, he created this book and the website www.poetsagainstthewar.org instead. "Can 13,000 poems inhibit this or any administration planning a war?" Hamill asks. "It is only one step among many.... We join physicians against the war, teachers against the war, farmers against the war, and others." The collection contains almost 200 poems by known and unknown poets.

- **Hanh, T. N. (1992).** *Peace is Every Step: The Path of Mindfulness in Everyday Life.* **New York, NY: Bantam Books.** This book joins other such books of moral, religious, and spiritual guidance from many traditions in helping us find the inner peace that gives us the requisite qualities to work for peace in the world. Short passages of Thich Nhat Hanh's writings can be used for individual inspiration or with students for discussion. Another of his books is *Creating True Peace: Ending Violence in Yourself, your Family, your Community, and the World* (2003, New York, NY: Free Press) with strategies for creating inner and outer peace for children and ourselves in a conflict-filled world.

- **Harris, I. M., & Morrison, M. L. (2003).** *Peace Education* **(2nd ed.). Jefferson, NC: McFarland.** This book explains rationales and methodology for educating for peace. The authors write, " 'Peace,' a concept that motivates the imagination, connotes more than 'no violence.' It implies human beings working together to resolve conflicts, respect standards of justice, satisfy basic needs, and honor human rights. Peace involves a respect for life and for the dignity of each human being without discrimination or prejudice." From this definition, the authors progress through a series of chapters on theoretical, school, and family issues in peace education. This is an essential book in a peace collection.

- **Hedges, C. (2003).** *War is a Force that Gives us Meaning.* **New York, NY: Anchor Books.** Chris Hedges, a war correspondent for over twenty years, writes convincingly of the seductive nature of war on soldier and society alike. He warns, "We must guard against the myth of war and the drug of war that can, together, render us as blind and callous as some of those we battle." Also see **Hedges, C. (2003).** *What Every Person Should Know About War.* **New York, NY: Free Press.** This book makes us face the reality of war. Written in a question-and-answer format, Hedges acknowledges it is tough, but necessary, to read "in raw detail the effects of war, what it does to bodies, to minds and souls…. War, when we understand it, forces us to confront our own capacity for violence, indeed for atrocity."

- **Hershey, J. (1989).** *Hiroshima.* **New York, NY: Vintage Books.** Many of us are able to live in a dreamlike bubble, insulated from any thought about nuclear weapons and the threat they pose to humanity. This journalistic account, using interviews with hibakusha, atomic bomb survivors, is a powerful wake-up call. Hershey describes the experiences of six survivors on August 6, 1945, and in later years. **Laurence Yep** has written a novella, *Hiroshima*, more suitable for primary grade students to read.

- **Hopkins, J. (Ed.) (2000).** *The Art of Peace: Nobel Peace Laureates Discuss Human Rights, Conflict and Reconciliation.* **Ithaca, NY: Snow Lion Publications.** Imagine being privy to candid and informative conversations among nine inspiring Nobel Peace Prize laureates, and you have a feeling for the flavor of this book. Hopkins organized a conference at University of Virginia and recorded the words of the nine speakers, including Betty Williams, Desmond Tutu, Rigoberta Menchu Tum, and Oscar Arias Sanchez. Short biographies, speeches, and question-and-answer sessions provide understandable and moving lessons in world history and non-violent social change. This book is useful to teachers and students who might recreate a peace conference using this primary source book of the laureates' own words.

• **Jones, E., Haenfler, R., & Johnson, B. (2007).** *The Better World Handbook: Small Changes that Make a Big Difference.* **Gabriola Island, BC (Canada): New Society.** Exhorting readers to break the "Cycle of Cynicism" and embark on a "Cycle of Hope," the authors invite us to "think about the world that you would like to live in," and proceed to give steps to create that world. This book is a good classroom resource with information on shopping, food, building community, transportation, media, politics, and more.

• **Kincheloe, J., & Weil, D. (Eds.). (2004).** *Critical Thinking and Learning: An Encyclopedia for Parents and Teachers.* **Westport, CT: Greenwood Press.** In short articles on a wide variety of critical thinking topics (diversity, democracy, empowerment, literacy, media, teaching and learning, values, work, art, literacy, math, and science, and more), numerous researchers clearly articulate comprehensive views of critical thinking, enabling teachers to ground themselves in theory and access methods of engaging in critical thinking practice effectively.

• **King, M. L., Jr. (1981).** *Strength to Love.* **Philadelphia, PA: Fortress Press.** Dr. King writes on the power of love and the urgent need for our action: "The ultimate measure of a man is not where he stands in moments of comfort and convenience, but where he stands at moments of challenge and controversy." He notes further, "Our scientific power has outrun our spiritual power. We have guided missiles, but misguided men."

• **Knox, A., Wangaard, D. B., & Michaelson, S. R. (2003).** *Service-Learning: Planning and Reflection, a Step-by-Step Guide.* **Chapel Hill, NC: Character Development Group.** Like *PeaceJam's* Student Journal, this paperback workbook gives background information on planning service projects as well as worksheets to help students assess team cooperation, character traits, community needs, decision-making steps, and outcomes of action. Questions encourage students to break large projects down into achievable steps, to reflect on what they have learned in the process of serving their communities, and to plan future projects effectively.

- **Lewis, B. (2008).** *The Teen Guide to Global Action: How to Connect with Others (Near & Far) to Create Social Change.* **Minneapolis, MN: Free Spirit.** Lewis has gathered stories of youth activists, summaries of issues and statistics, and useful online resources to help young people start local and global social action projects that are meaningful and effective. This slim book is a readable resource for kids to use independently or with teacher guidance.

- **Libresco, A. S., & Balantic, J. (Eds.). (2005).** *Peace Lessons from Around the World.* **New York, NY: Hague Appeal for Peace** (www.haguepeace.org)**.** The editors have gathered lessons from international peace educators to present a wide variety of thought-provoking lessons, from analysis of laws, quotations, and TV violence; to case studies of nonviolent peace movements, to art projects. The editors explain, "First, we are aware of the difficulty for young people (and adults, for that matter) to imagine the unimaginable; that is, to think that the abolition of war is possible and not just some pie-in-the-sky idea. To that end, we present lessons that ask students to picture a world without war, and then systematically detail the preconditions and steps that can get us there." Good research and practical worksheets make this a crucial classroom resource.

- **Lickona, T. (1992).** *Educating for Character: How our School Can Teach Respect and Responsibility.* **New York, NY: Bantam Books.** This book has been a bible for me in my own work in the classroom. Built on theoretical underpinnings, it notes hundreds of classroom strategies to promote character in students. Lickona' 2004 book (*Character Matters: How to Help our Children Develop Good Judgment, Integrity, and Other Essential Virtues.* **New York, NY: Touchstone**) is also extremely useful to educators and parents. Lickona asserts, "Schools cannot be ethical bystanders at a time when our society is in deep moral trouble."

- **Lickona, T., & Davidson, M. (2005)** *Smart & Good High Schools: Integrating Excellence and Ethics for Success in School, Work, and Beyond.* **Cortland, NY: Center for the 4th and 5th Rs (Respect & Responsibility)/ Washington, D.C.: Character Education Partnership.** Lickona and Davidson conducted research in 24 exemplary high schools to illuminate practices that help students become smart and good. "Young people need *performance character*—diligence, a strong work ethic, a positive attitude, and perseverance—in order to realize their potential for excellence in … school, work, and beyond. They need *moral character*—integrity respect, cooperation, and justice—in order to be fulfilled in their relationships." Chock full of diverse practices, more information, a PDF version of the report, and updates can be found on their website www.cortland.edu/character/highschool .

- **Lin, J., Brantmeier, E., & Bruhn, C. (Eds.) (2008).** *Transforming Education for Peace.* **Charlotte, NC: Information Age Publishing.** The essays in this collection detail research and practice designed to "facilitate the formation of a compassionate and loving global community." Initiatives involving families, multicultural community groups, classrooms, colleges, and electronic communication tools are detailed with refreshingly positive outlooks. "Peacebuilding is possible," write the editors, "when we love one another, reach out and build connective relationships, and act both locally and globally toward social and environmental justice."

- **Loewen, J. W. (2007)** *Lies my Teacher Told Me: Everything your American History Textbook got Wrong.* **New York, NY: Touchstone.** "Not understanding their past renders many Americans incapable of thinking effectively about our present and future," states James Loewen in this critique of traditional history textbooks. Pointing to rampant nationalism, mindless parroting of "facts," and dumbing down of content, Loewen provides issues to debate and suggestions for better teaching materials for our students.

- **Lynd, S., & Lynd, A. (1995).** *Nonviolence in America: A Documentary History.* **Maryknoll, NY: Orbis Books.** Take an exhilarating ride through American history of nonviolence from William Penn's letter to the Delaware Indians in 1681 to Shoshone Nation's anti-nuclear protests in 1992. An excellent introduction leads the reader through the sequence of primary sources that tell the tale of alternatives to violence in American conflict resolution. Essays, letters, and speeches from Henry David Thoreau, Jane Addams, William James, Martin Luther King, Cesar Chavez, Howard Zinn and others are included.

- **Maathai, W. M. (2006).** *Unbowed: A Memoir.* **New York, NY: Alfred A. Knopf.** 2004 Nobel Peace Prize winner Wangari Maathai describes her childhood, education, and family, as well as the political, moral, and ecological awareness that inspired her to found Kenya's Greenbelt Movement. Recounting jailings, beatings, and ridicule, Maathai writes, "What I have learned over the years is that we must be patient, persistent, and committed." Comparing peace to a traditional African stool, whose three legs represent human and ecological rights, sustainable management of resources, and cultivation of cultures of peace, she reminds us that the trees we plant today benefit others in the future.

- **McCarthy, C. (2002).** *I'd Rather Teach Peace.* **Maryknoll, NY: Orbis Books.** *Washington Post* journalist McCarthy details his fascinating entry into educating high school and college students about peace. Especially meaningful to me, in addition to descriptions of energetic class discussions of topics ranging from war making to vegetarianism to capital punishment, is McCarthy's unyielding stand on the importance of teaching peace. Replying to colleagues who challenge him to teach "the other side," McCarthy replies, "What I have a surety about is that students come into my classes already well educated, often overeducated, in the ethic of violence.... I can't in conscience teach the other side." From McCarthy's Washington, DC Center for Teaching Peace, other books and supplementary materials are available, such as McCarthy's edited collections of essays on nonviolence by educators and others *Strength through Peace: The Ideas and People of Nonviolence* (**2004**) and *Solutions to Violence* (**2002**).

- **McKibben, B. (2007).** *Deep Economy: The Wealth of Communities and the Durable Future.* **New York, NY: Holt Paperbacks.** Bill McKibben's long line of books points in the same direction: we must abandon the addiction to global growth and begin building local—durable and sustainable—economies. For high school and college economics and environment students (and others), McKibben's concise, fact-filled, and moving prose will bring life and urgency to the reality of global warming. His 2008 retrospective: *The Bill McKibben Reader: Pieces from an Active Life* (**New York, NY: Holt Paperbacks),** revisits topics on which McKibben has written during a long career, including consumption and media, climate change, and peace heroes including Wendell Berry and Afghanistan's "Gandhi," Abdul Ghaffar Khan. See also McKibben's www.350.org for more information on environmental destruction and renewal.

- **Medina, J. (2008).** *Brain Rules: 12 Principles for Surviving and Thriving at Work, Home, and School* **Seattle, WA: Pear Press**. Fun to read and riddled with dramatic examples, Medina makes the case for connectedness between teacher and student to promote a caring and stress-free classroom. Small classrooms and teachers who can "read" their students and know them deeply help students learn.

- **Merton, T. (Ed.). (1965).** *Gandhi on Non-Violence: A Selection from the Writings of Mahatma Gandhi.* **New York, NY: New Directions.** Merton writes in his introduction, "Whether we may think he succeeded or failed, Gandhi never ceased to believe in the possibility of a love of truth so strong and so pure that it would leave an 'indelible impress' upon the most recalcitrant enemy, and awaken in him a response of love and truth." And in the selected passages, Gandhi's words inspire us: "Given the proper training and proper generalship, non-violence can be practiced by the masses of mankind."

- **Moix, B., Smith, D., & Staab, A. (2004).** *Peaceful Prevention of Deadly Conflict: If war is not the answer, what is?* **Washington, DC: Friends Committee on National Legislation.** This pamphlet, available in quantities from FCNL, deconstructs the doctrine of preemptive war and details policies for a more secure world without war.

- **Nieto, S. (2004).** *Affirming Diversity: The Sociopolitical Context of Multicultural Education* **(4th ed.). Boston, MA: Pearson Education.** Nieto writes, "I believe one of our primary roles as educators is to interrupt the cycle of inequality and oppression. We can do this best by teaching with heart and soul." Her book details the meaning, rationales, and practices of multicultural education and invites pre- and in-service teachers to think about their own and their students' various identities in ways that will lead to humane and inclusive education for all students.

- **Noddings, N. (2005a).** *The Challenge to Care in Schools: An Alternative Approach to Education* **(2nd ed.). New York, NY: Teachers College Press.** Noddings prods us to add care to our curriculum, and assures us (through research, anecdotes, and examples of good practice) that we can—and must—do so to "produce competent, caring, loving, and lovable people." In her 2007 book **Critical Lessons: What our Schools Should Teach (New York, NY: Cambridge University Press),** Noddings continues her arguments about care to include self-understanding, war and peace issues, home and parenting, nature, livelihood, gender, and religion, among other life issues at the heart of our education of our youth.

- **Noddings, N. (Ed.). (2005b).** *Educating Citizens for Global Awareness.* **New York, NY: Teachers College Press.** In a series of essays by prominent educators, Noddings and others argue forcefully for—and give examples of—internationalism in education. Peggy McIntosh, for example, asks, "Can U.S. educators muster the character needed to widen the sense of loyalty and care in themselves and in students beyond the units of family, team, class, school, town, city, state, and nation?" This book offers research and methods to do so.

- **O'Brien, T. (1991).** *The Things They Carried.* **New York, NY: Penguin Books.** Included in the English curricula of many American high schools, this book is a must-read for all. As John Crawford does for Iraq, Tim O'Brien writes a poetic, horrific historical fiction account of Vietnam, based on his experiences there as a foot soldier from 1969-70. He cautions us to evaluate war stories with care. "If a story seems moral, do not believe it. If at the end of a war story you feel uplifted, or if you feel that some small bit of rectitude has been salvaged from the larger waste, then you have been made the victim of a very old and terrible lie.... You can tell a true war story if it embarrasses you. If you don't care for obscenity, you don't care for the truth; if you don't care for the truth, watch how you vote. Send guys to war, they come home talking dirty."

• **Palmer, P. (2007).** *The Courage to Teach: Exploring the Inner Landscape of a Teacher's Life*. **San Francisco, CA: Jossey-Bass.** Palmer writes the way he urges us to teach: warmly and with empathy. He encourages connectedness in the face of divisiveness imposed by educational structures. Palmer remind us that if we "address our students' fears rather than exploit them—we would move toward better teaching."

• **PeaceJam Foundation. (2007).** *PeaceJam Leaders: Fostering Leadership & Positive Identity through the Study of 12 Nobel Peace Laureates.* Available to teachers after taking online training, the curriculum materials are valuable resources, providing teacher lesson plans and student journals. It is a "standards-based curriculum that explores the adolescent stories of 12 Nobel Peace Laureates and the strategies they used to overcome problems in their lives and their communities…. Youth also develop leadership and problem-solving skills while engaging in service-learning activities that address local needs." More information about curricula for elementary, middle, high school, college, and juvenile justice system students is available at the informative website www.peacejam.org .

• **Poliner, R., & Lieber, C. (2004).** *The Advisory Guide: Designing and Implementing Effective Advisory Programs in Secondary Schools*. **Cambridge, MA: Educators for Social Responsibility.** Based on the authors' extensive experience researching and developing advisory groups in various settings, this book contains rationales, examples, and strategies for implementing a variety of types of advisory programs in secondary settings.

• **Raviv, A., Oppenheimer, L., & Bar-Tal, D. (Eds.). (1999).** *How Children Understand War and Peace: A Call for International Peace Education*. **San Francisco, CA: Jossey-Bass.** In this collection of studies conducted globally, researchers contend, "Critical thought about war, peace, and other public issues may not occur unless it is enhanced through instruction, modeling, and practice." Developmental perspectives, socialization and experience, and school learning are considered by various authors, including Ian Harris and David and Roger Johnson. Such topics as perspective reversal during academic debates and children's understanding of war and peace at different ages and in different cultures are included in this wide-ranging and important volume.

• **Reardon, B., & Cabezudo, A., et al. (2002).** *Learning to Abolish War: Teaching toward a Culture of Peace* (Books 1, 2, & 3). **New York, NY:**

Hague Appeal for Peace. This three-volume downloadable instruction manual is one of the most comprehensive peace education teacher training tools I have found and is divided into three sections: Book 1 (*Rationale for and Approaches to Peace Education*), Book 2 (*Sample Learning Units*), and Book 3 (*Sustaining the Global Campaign for Peace Education*). The mission is clear, "In order to combat the culture of violence that pervades our society, the coming generation deserves a radically different education—one that does not glorify war but educates for peace, nonviolence and international cooperation." Visit www.hagueappeal.org.

- **Roy, A. (2003).** *War Talk* **Cambridge, MA: South End Press.** The author of *The God of Small Things* writes passionately in these political essays about global militarism, fascism, and racism. Writing "it's not enough to sing songs about giving peace a chance…. Are we ready to get off our starting blocks? Are we ready, many millions of us, to rally, not just on the streets, but at work and in schools and in our homes, in every decision we take, and every choice we make?" Roy gives the reader better understanding of long-simmering issues in India, Pakistan, Iraq, and the Middle East, as well as American involvement and war policy.

- **Seeley, R. A. (1981).** *Choosing Peace: A Handbook on War, Peace, and your Conscience.* **Washington, DC: Central Committee for Conscientious Objectors.** Seeley advises the reader, "to use this book to do two things: to learn about war and decide where you stand; and to decide how to act on your stand once you've made it." The handbook includes chapters on conscientious objectors, war, peace, American draft law and an annotated list of further reading: "A Short Course on War and Peace."

- **Suvanjieff, I., & Engle, D. G. (2008)** *PeaceJam: A Billion Simple Acts of Peace.* **New York, NY: Puffin Books.** This book provides a readable tour of teen activism combined with short biographies of *PeaceJam*-affiliated Nobel Peace Prize laureates. Each chapter details the efforts of a teen activist working on an issue such as racism, the environment, or poverty and is followed by steps the reader can take as follow-up. The 30-minute DVD is a useful introduction to students, and this book is a great classroom resource or independent read for adolescents.

- **Thompson, M., & Barker, T. (2004)** *The Pressured Child: Helping your Child Find Success in School and Life.* **New York, NY: Ballantine Books.** Thompson, a school psychologist, explains to parents and teachers their children's depth of feeling. Offering in-depth insights into students' lives and writing as well as explanations of psychological underpinnings, this readable book inspires those of us who parent or teach children to realize their depth of cognitive, emotional, moral, and spiritual development. "They are always searching for fairness and honesty and meaning. They are extraordinarily sensitive to adult hypocrisy and cruelty. Children are intensely curious about the major spiritual questions that confront all human beings."

- **Thoreau, H. D. (1993).** *Civil Disobedience and Other Essays.* **New York: Dover.** Getting a sense of history from this short collection of Thoreau's famous essays is a helpful way to interpret current events and our responses to them. This volume contains *Civil Disobedience* (1849), in which Thoreau details his objections to the Mexican War, *Slavery in Massachusetts* (1854), and other short essays such as *Life without Principle* (1863). "What is it to be free from King George and continue the slaves of King Prejudice?" Thoreau asks.

- **Tolstoy, L. (1968).** *The Wisdom of Leo Tolstoy.* **New York, NY: Citadel Press.** This volume contains excerpts from Tolstoy's *My Religion* and allows one to trace the thread of nonviolent thought uniting Tolstoy, Gandhi, and King. As did U.S. Air Force Catholic chaplain George Zabelka, who renounces his wartime invocation of Christianity to rationalize violence and war making (see Zabelka's 1985 speech on the 40th anniversary of the bombing of Hiroshima), Tolstoy comes to a post-military-service understanding of Christianity's foundations, "Thou shalt not kill," and "Turn the other cheek." He writes, "If there were a society of Christian men that did evil to none and gave of their labor for the good of others, such a society would have no enemies to kill or to torture them…. A Christian … must renounce war and do good to all men, whether they are foreigners or compatriots."

- **Totten, S., & Pedersen, J. (Eds.). (2009).** *Social Issues and Service at the Middle Level.* **Charlotte, NC: Information Age Publishing.** Detailed chapters written by teacher practitioners can be of great help for teachers who want to get started in social justice and service learning.

- **Turner, G., & Vincent, P. F. (Eds.) (2004).** *Promising Practices in Character Education* (Vol. 2): *12 More Success Stories from Around the Country.* **Chapel Hill, NC: Character Development Group.** Each of twelve chapters in the book details the effort of a different school district, school, teacher, or community to provide students with an education that is both "intellectual and moral."

- **United Nations Department of Public Information (Ed.). (2008).** *Everything You Always Wanted to Know About the United Nations.* **New York, NY: Department of Public Information.** This book is an excellent classroom resource to help intermediate and secondary students understand the work and organization of the United Nations. The book explains international treaties designed to protect human rights world-wide and the role of the United Nations in meeting such goals as allevi-ating poverty, protecting the environment, controlling weapons, and eradicating disease.

- **Vincent, P. F., Wangaard, D., & Weimer, P. (2005).** *Restoring School Civility: Creating a Caring, Responsible, and Productive School.* **Chapel Hill, NC: Character Development Group.** Building community, estab-lishing fair consequences, expecting common courtesy, and creating an atmosphere of consistency are elements that restore school civility, with-out which learning and moral behavior will not take place. Replete with quotations, research data, and examples from schools, the authors also include faculty worksheets for evaluating and improving classroom and school climates.

- **Viola, H. J., & Margolis, C. (Eds.) (1991).** *Seeds of Change.* **Washing-ton, DC: Smithsonian.** Useful for supplementing textbooks in the class-room, this is a companion book of research and primary source material related to the Columbian Exchange 500-year anniversary exhibit at the Smithsonian Institution in Washington, DC. The book describes crop exchanges among America, Africa, and Europe, and slave life on planta-tions in the West Indies.

- **Wade, R. C. (2007).** *Social Studies for Social Justice: Teaching Strategies for the Elementary Classroom.* **New York, NY: Teachers College Press.** "This book is about good teaching, but not just good for children. Teaching for social justice is also good for the planet," explains Rahima Wade. Going beyond theory, the author details practices of over 40 ele-mentary teachers in dealing with curriculum mandates, school culture, and classroom strategies for teaching social justice.

- **Walzer, M. (2006).** *Just and Unjust Wars: A Moral Argument with His-torical Illustrations.* **New York, NY: Basic Books.** "For as long as men and women have talked about war," Walzer writes, "they have talked about it in terms of right and wrong. And for almost as long, some among them have derided such talk, called it a charade, insisted that war lies beyond (or beneath) moral judgment.... But the truth is that one of the things most of us want, even in war, is to act or to seem to act morally." Walzer examines both rationales for beginning a war as well as rules of engagement during combat. Rife with historical references, this book provokes thinking about the nature of war and individual belief about war.

- **Westheimer, J. (Ed.). (2007).** *Pledging Allegiance: The Politics of Patrio-tism in America's Schools.* **New York, NY: Teachers College Press.** Using essays and political cartoons from various perspectives, Westheimer invites readers to abandon "authoritarian patriotism" and instead think critically about what he calls "democratic patriotism." One of my best classroom lessons in a middle school debate class was built on one of the essays in this book as students used critical thinking to analyze the role of their country in the world.

- **Wiggins, G., & McTighe, J. (2005).** *Understanding by Design* **(2nd ed.) Boston, MA: Prentice Hall.** Researchers Grant Wiggins and Jay McTighe encourage teachers to plan units and lessons by taking a big picture and a long view: focusing on desired long term understandings. Formulating "essential questions" helps students grasp "enduring understandings" about literature, science, math, and history concepts. Rather than focus on the tiny details students will soon forget, UbD asks teachers to provide curriculum planning and lesson structures that promote life-long critical thinking.

- **Wink, W. (Ed.). (2004).** *Peace is the Way: Writings on Nonviolence from the Fellowship of Reconciliation.* **Maryknoll, NY: Orbis Books.** Walter Wink has gathered short articles from the writings of such social change pioneers and scholars as Mahatma Gandhi, A. J. Muste, Martin Luther King, Dorothy Day, Gene Sharp, Elise Boulding, and others to provide a veritable primer on nonviolent social change. Wink comments on the importance of nonviolent theory, "It introduces to the world a new strategy for resisting evil without creating new evils and becoming evil ourselves. But more important, it articulates a new way of being that yields a vision of peace more powerful than all the armies of all the nations in the world."

- **Zinn, H. (2005).** *A People's History of the United States: 1492-Present.* **New York, NY: HarperCollins.** In this landmark resource, Zinn asks us to think differently and more critically about the story of the United States. He has also created a version of the book suitable for use with middle school students. Focusing on the lives and daily choices of everyday people, he calls attention to the unsung heroes of American history, people of color, women, and workers, among others. He muses, "What struck me as I began to study history was how nationalist fervor—inculcated from childhood on by pledges of allegiance, national anthems, flags waving and rhetoric blowing—permeated the educational systems of all countries, including our own. I wonder now how the foreign policies of the United States would look if we wiped out the national boundaries of the world, at least in our minds, and thought of all children everywhere as our own. Then we could never drop an atomic bomb on Hiroshima, or napalm on Vietnam, or wage war anywhere, because wars, especially in our time, are always wars against children, indeed our children." See also *A People's History of American Empire*, below.

• Zinn, H. (2002). *You Can't be Neutral on a Moving Train: A Personal History of Our Times*. **Boston, MA: Beacon Press.** Feeling defeated? Read Howard Zinn's account of his life and his long view of history to bolster your belief that people can change things for the better. **The Zinn Education Project** collaboration between **Rethinking Schools** and **Teaching for Change**) also provides curriculum materials to support teaching using Zinn's perspective. Such materials as Ellis and Mueller's documentary film narrated by actor Matt Damon, *Howard Zinn: You Can't Be Neutral on a Moving Train*, are available. See the websites www.rethinkingschool.org and www.teachingforchange.org and www.ZinnEdProject.org for more information.

• Zinn, H. (2010). *The Bomb*. **San Francisco, CA: City Lights Books.** Zinn finished the introduction to this book, containing two reissued essays, just weeks before his death in 2010. Drawing on his experience as a World War II bombardier and his research of the atomic bombings of Japan, Zinn concludes that there is no justification for war. "*Someone, no we, must stop that cycle now.*"

• Zinn, H. (Ed.) (2002). *The Power of Nonviolence: Writings by Advocates of Peace*. **Boston, MA: Beacon Press.** With an introduction by historian Howard Zinn, this collection of essays is global in scope and includes offerings by great thinkers including Jane Addams, Thomas Merton, Arundati Roy, Albert Camus, Daisaku Ikeda, and Buddha. Zinn writes in his introduction, "The cry for peace in these essays is not simply a protest against war. It also presents a vision of a different world, and suggests a way to fulfill that vision."

PICTURE BOOKS ON PEACE AND GLOBAL AWARENESS

• **Andreas, J. (2004).** *Addicted to War: Why the U.S. Can't Kick Militarism*. **Oakland, CA: AK Press.** This graphic-novel-format exploration of U.S. foreign policy and the backfiring nature of war will provoke conversation and debate. Book includes antimilitarism resources.

• **Barr, D., & Juffkins, M. (Eds.) (1995).** *Intermediate School Kit on the United Nations*. **New York, NY: United Nations.** Although statistics are dated, basic information and role play game cards are valuable resources for teaching about the role of the United Nations in building peace worldwide.

• **Dorling Kindersley. (2002).** *A Life Like Mine: How Children Live Around the World*. **New York, NY: DK Publishing.** This book, published in association with UNICEF (United Nations Children's Fund), brings

Figure 42.   Middle school students relax with peace picture books.

to vivid life the *Convention on the Rights of the Child*. With photographs
and text the book invites discussion of such rights as education, health
care, food, shelter, play, protection, and more.

- **Keene, A. (1998). *Peacemakers: Winners of the Nobel Peace Prize*. New
  York, NY: Oxford University Press.** Keene's two-page biographies of
  Nobel Peace laureates from Henri Dunant and Frederic Passy in 1901
  through Jody Williams and the International Campaign to Ban Landmines in 1997 is richly illustrated with photographs and is a quick introduction to the Prize and its winners. Irwin Abrams's scholarly
  biographies are more detailed (see above).

- **Kindersley, B. & A. (1995). *Children Just Like Me*. New York, NY: Dorling Kindersley.** In these pages rich with photographs and text, the
  Kindersleys introduce us to children from over 30 countries. "You'll
  learn about these children's daily lives, their hopes and fears, and their
  dreams. And you'll discover how much these children have in common
  with each other—and with you!" See also their book *Children Just Like
  Me: Celebrations*, which details festivals and holidays from around the
  world.

- **Lalli, J. (1996).** *Make Someone Smile ... and 40 More Ways to Be a Peaceful Person.* **Minneapolis, MN: Free Spirit.** "Accept other points of view.... Appreciate differences.... Practice solving problems." These are three of the 40 ways to peace in this simple picture book with lively black and white photographs of children working together.

- **Maruki, T. (1980).** *Hiroshima No Pika (The Flash of Hiroshima.* **New York, NY: HarperCollins.** This book expresses the experience of a hibakusha (atomic bomb survivor) in simple text and powerful, disturbing images. Preview before reading with young children.

- **Menzel, P. (1995).** *Material World: A Global Family Portrait.* **San Francisco, CA: Sierra Club Books.** Stunning photographs of families and their belongings make this book a terrific introduction to lifestyles and economic realities around the world. Images are also available in poster and CD-ROM formats. Images and statistics on families from 30 countries are in this book.

- **National Geographic Society. (2009).** *Every Human has Rights: A Photographic Declaration for Kids.* **Washington, DC: National Geographic Society.** "All humans are born FREE with the same dignity and rights." With these words, and with compelling photographs, poetry, and art work, the book brings to life the *Universal Declaration of Human Rights* for students.

- **Parr, T. (2004).** *The Peace Book.* **New York, NY: Little, Brown and Company.** Colorful images and simple text make this a good book for youngest children.

- **Radunsky, V. (2004).** *What Does Peace Feel Like?* **New York, NY: Atheneum Books for Young Readers**. "What does peace sound like? Like laughter and happiness, children on their birthday, and parents when their children get married ... like voices singing ... like no bad words." With beautiful illustrations and excerpts from the writing of children, Radunsky has provided a good introduction to a poetry lesson or discussion of peace.

- **Scholes, K. (1989).** *Peace Begins with You.* **San Francisco, CA: Sierra Club Books.** This deceptively simple book gives a crash course on the components of sustainable peace, the choices that lead to war, and the work of peacemakers. Colorful illustrations depict global settings. This book is a good conversation starter for a classroom discussion of war and peace for middle grades.

- **Smith, D. J. (2002).** *If the World Were a Village: A Book about the World's People.* **Toronto, ON: Kids Can Press.** Acknowledging the world population of 6 billion, Smith asks readers to imagine "the whole population of the world as a village of just 100 people … 61 are from Asia, 13 are from Africa, 12 are from Europe." Smith illuminates figures on nationalities, access to safe water, literacy, and more in this colorful and beautiful book.

- **Seuss, Dr. (1984).** *The Butter Battle Book.* **New York, NY: Random House, Inc.** "'I'll blow you,' he yelled, 'into pork and wee beans! I'll butter-side-up you to small smithereens!' " Dr. Seuss ridicules the concept of war and nuclear deterrence in this book, also available in video.

- **Thomas, S. M. (1998).** *Somewhere Today: A Book of Peace.* **Morton Grove, IL: Albert Whitman & Company.** This simple photograph book has few words, but is useful in working with young children on specific actions for peacemaking every day.

- **United Nations. (2008).** *Universal Declaration of Human Rights: Illustrations by Eric Puybaret.* **New York, NY: United Nations.** Beautiful illustrations illuminate the *Universal Declaration* for students.

- **Zalben, J. (2006).** *Paths to Peace: People who Changed the World.* **New York, NY: Dutton Children's Books.** Short biographies of peacemakers like Cesar Chaves, Eleanor Roosevelt, and Anne Frank are accessible to readers and accompanied by intriguing artwork.

- **Zinn, H, Konopacki, M., & Buhle, P. (2008).** *A People's History of American Empire.* **New York, NY: Metropolitan Books.** Suitable for teens and young adults, this graphic novel articulates arguments Howard Zinn has expressed in a lifetime of research and antiwar, anti-imperialism education. Speeches and passages from books will be familiar to followers of Zinn's work, and the detailed "comic-style" drawings strengthen Zinn's compelling words.

MORE SUGGESTIONS can be found at *Teaching Skills of Peace Through Juvenile Literature:* The Ohio Department of Education Conflict Resolution Commission's Annotated Booklist is available at http://www.disputeresolution.ohio.gov/pdfs/biblio.pdf .

REFERENCES

Abrams, I. (2001). *The Nobel Peace Prize and the laureates: An illustrated biographical history 1901-2001*. Nantucket, MA: Science History Publications.

Ackerman, P., & Duvall, J. (2000). *A force more powerful: A century of nonviolent conflict*. New York, NY: Palgrave.

Addams, J. (2002). Newer ideals of peace. In H. Zinn (Ed.), *The power of non-violence: Writings by advocates of peace* (pp. 39-41). Boston, MA: Beacon Press. (Original work published 1907)

Alliance for Climate Protection. (2010). Retrieved September 5, 2010, from http://www.climateprotect.org/

Asim, J. (2007). *The N word: Who can say it, who shouldn't, and why*. New York, NY: Houghton Mifflin.

Avery, P., Johnson, D., Johnson, R., & Mitchell, J. (1999). Teaching an understanding of war and peace through structured academic controversies. In A. Raviv, L. Oppenheimer, & D. Bar-Tal (Eds.), *How children understand war and peace: A call for international peace education* (pp. 260-280). San Francisco, CA: Jossey-Bass.

Baker, R. (2002). Want to be a patriot? Do your job. *Columbia Journalism Review, May/June*. Retrieved September 5, 2010, from http://www.russbaker.com/archives/CJR%20May-June%202002%20-%20Patriotic.htm

Bajaj, M. (2008). Introduction. In M. Bajaj (Ed.), *Encyclopedia of peace education* (pp. 1-11). Charlotte, NC: Information Age Publishing.

Berdan, K., Boulton, I., Eidman-Aadahl, E., Fleming, J., Gardner, L., Rogers, I., & Solomon, A. (Eds.). (2006). *Writing for a change: Boosting literacy and learning through social action*. San Francisco, CA: Jossey-Bass.

Bigelow, B. (2008). *A people's history for the classroom*. Milwaukee, WI: Rethinking Schools.

Bigelow, B., Miner, B., & Peterson, B. (Eds.). (1991). *Rethinking Columbus: Teaching about the 500th anniversary of Columbus's arrival in America: A special issue of Rethinking Schools*. Milwaukee, WI: Rethinking Schools.

Boulding, E. (2004). Envisioning the peaceable kingdom. In W. Wink (Ed.), *Peace is the way: Writings on nonviolence from the Fellowship of Reconciliation* (pp. 129-134). Maryknoll, NY: Orbis Books. (Original work published 1982)

Bronson, P., & Merryman, A. (2010, July 19). The creativity crisis. *Newsweek*, 3(CLVI), 44-50.

Calkins, L., & Harwayne, S. (1991). *Living between the lines*. Portsmouth, NH: Heinemann.

Calkins, L. M. (1986). *The art of teaching writing*. Portsmouth, NH: Heinemann.

Cannon, S. G. (2006). *Teach for peace*. Retrieved September 5, 2010, from http://www.teachforpeace.org

Carlsson-Paige, N., & Lantieri, L. (2005). A changing vision of education. In N. Noddings (Ed.), *Educating citizens for global awareness* (pp. 107-121). New York, NY: Teachers College Press.

Chomsky, N. (1989). *Necessary illusions: Thought control in democratic societies*. Cambridge, MA: South End Press.

Chomsky, N. (2005). *Imperial ambitions: Conversations on the post-9-11 world*. New York, NY: Metropolitan.

Collier, J., & Collier, C. (1974). *My brother Sam is dead*. New York, NY: Scholastic.

Covell, K. (1999). Cultural socialization and conceptions of war and peace: A cross-national comparison. In A. Raviv, L. Oppenheimer, & D. Bar-Tal (Eds.), *How children understand war and peace: A call for international peace education* (pp. 111-126). San Francisco, CA: Jossey-Bass.

Crawford, J. (2005). *The last true story I'll ever tell: An accidental soldier's account of the war in Iraq*. New York, NY: Riverhead Books.

Damon, W. (2008). *The path to purpose: Helping our children find their calling in life*. New York, NY: Free Press.

Deats, R. (2004). The global spread of active nonviolence. In W. Wink (Ed.), *Peace is the way: Writings on nonviolence from the Fellowship of Reconciliation* (pp. 283-295). Maryknoll, NY: Orbis Books.

Derman-Sparks, L., & Ramsey, P. (2006). *What if all the kids are white? Anti-bias multicultural education with young children and families*. New York, NY: Teachers College Press.

Diamond, J. (2005). *Guns, germs, and steel: The fates of human societies*. New York, NY: W. W. Norton.

Dieringer, L. (2004). Preface. In R. Poliner & C. Lieber, *The advisory guide: Designing and implementing effective advisory programs in secondary schools* (pp. 5-8). Cambridge, MA: Educators for Social Responsibility.

Duckworth, C. (2008). Maria Montessori and peace education. In M. Bajaj (Ed.), *Encyclopedia of peace education* (pp. 33-37). Charlotte, NC: Information Age Publishing.

Earth Force project. (n.d.). Retrieved September 5, 2010, from http://www.earthforce.org/

ECHOES Alliance. (n.d.). *Empowering cocoa households with opportunities and education solutions alliance*. Retrieved September 5, 2010, from World Cocoa Foun-

dation website: http://www.worldcocoafoundation.org/what-we-do
/current-programs/ECHOES_summary.asp

Elbow, P. (1981). *Writing with power*. New York, NY: Oxford University Press.

Ellerbee, L., & Lucky Duck Productions (Producers). (2005, February). *Nick News with Linda Ellerbee: The legacy of slavery* [Television broadcast]. New York, NY: Nickelodeon Channel. Retrieved September 5, 2010, from http://www.nick.com/videos/clip/legacy-slavery-full-episode.html

Ellis, D., & Mueller, D. (Directors). (2004). *You can't be neutral on a moving train* [Motion picture]. United States: First Run Features.

Fadden, R. (Producer). (1995). *They lied to you in school* [Motion picture]. United States: White Buffalo Multimedia.

Freire, P. (2000). *Pedagogy of the oppressed* (30th anniversary ed.). New York, NY: Continuum International. (Original work published 1970)

Gale. (n.d.). *Opposing viewpoints resource center*. Retrieved September 5, 2010, from Opposing viewpoints resource center database.

Gardner, H. (2006). *Five minds for the future*. Boston, MA: Harvard Business School Press.

Gifford, D. (2004). *PeaceJam: Nobel laureates and teens in action*. San Francisco, CA: Wiley.

Global Campaign for Peace Education [GCPE]. (1999). Campaign statement. Retrieved September 5, 2010, from http://www.haguepeace.org/index.php?action=pe#statement

Goodman, J., & Balamore, U. (2003). *Teaching goodness: Engaging the moral and academic promise of young children*. New York, NY: Allyn & Bacon.

George Washington University International Affairs Society. (n.d.). *Greater Washington Conference on International Affairs [GWCIA]*. Retrieved September 5, 2010, from http://gwias.com/GWCIA/

Guggenheim, D. (Director). (2006). *An inconvenient truth* [Motion picture]. United States: Paramount.

Gurwitch, R. (n.d.). *Building strength through knowledge*. Retrieved September 5, 2010, from www.dreamhistory.org/sitebuildercontent/sitebuilderfiles/lp_6-8_rg.doc

Hague Appeal for Peace. (2003-2005). *Hague appeal for peace*. Retrieved September 5, 2010, from http://www.haguepeace.org/

Hanh, T. N. (2003). *Creating true peace: Ending violence in yourself, your family, your community, and the world*. New York, NY: Free Press.

Harlan, J., & Crow, S. (n.d.). *The dream flag project*. Retrieved September 5, 2010, from http://www.dreamflags.org/

Harris, I. M. (1999). Types of peace education. In *How children understand war and peace: A call for international peace education* (pp. 299-317). San Francisco, CA: Jossey-Bass.

Harris, I. M., & Morrison, M. L. (2003). *Peace education* (2nd ed.). Jefferson, NC: McFarland.

Hedges, C. (2003a). *War is a force that gives us meaning*. New York, NY: Anchor Books.

Hedges, C. (2003b). *What every person should know about war*. New York, NY: Free Press.

Hedges, C. (2005, September 18). The myth and reality of war [Editorial]. *The Philadelphia Inquirer.* Retrieved September 5, 2010, http://www.cis.upenn.edu/grad/documents/ptsd-inq.pdf

Howlett, C. (2008). John Dewey and peace education. In M. Bajaj (Ed.), *Encyclopedia of peace education* (pp. 25-31). Charlotte, NC: Information Age Publishing.

Jacobs, H. H. (2006). *Active literacy across the curriculum: Strategies for reading, writing, speaking, and listening.* Larchmont, NY: Eye on Education.

Janeczka, P. B. (Ed.). (1990). *The place my words are looking for: What poets say about and through their work.* New York, NY: Simon & Shuster Books for Young Readers.

Jane Goodall Institute. (n.d.). *Roots & Shoots.* Retrieved September 5, 2010, from http://www.rootsandshoots.org/

Joint Committee on National Health Education Standards. (2007). *National health education standards: Achieving excellence* (2nd ed.). Retrieved September 5, 2010, from dpi.wi.gov/sspw/doc/natlhlthed.doc

Justice learning: Civic education in the real world. (2002-2010). Retrieved September 5, 2010, from Justice Talking and New York Times Learning Network website: http://www.justicelearning.org/

Kabat-Zinn, J. (1990). *Full catastrophe living.* New York, NY: Delta Trade Paperbacks.

Kealy, W. (2004). Media literacy. In J. Kincheloe & D. Weil (Eds.), *Critical thinking and learning: An encyclopedia for parents and teachers* (pp. 287-291). Westport, CT: Greenwood Press.

Ki-moon, B. (2009). Letter from UN Secretary-General Ban Ki-moon (United Nations Association for the United States of America [UNA-USA], Ed.). In *2009 UNA-USA middle school model United Nations conference booklet* (p. 2) [Brochure]. New York, NY: UNA-USA.

Kincheloe, J. (2004). Into the great wide open: Introducing critical thinking. In J. Kincheloe & D. Weil (Eds.), *Critical thinking and learning: An encyclopedia for parents and teachers* (pp. 1-52). Westport, CT: Greenwood Press.

Kincheloe, J., & Weil, D. (Eds.). (2004). *Critical thinking and learning: An encyclopedia for parents and teachers.* Westport, CT: Greenwood Press.

King, M. L., Jr. (2004). Facing the challenge of a new age. In W. Wink (Ed.), *Peace is the way: Writings on nonviolence from the Fellowship of Reconciliation* (pp. 178-186). Maryknoll, NY: Orbis Books. (Original work published 1957)

Knowledge Unlimited (Producer). (1994). *Pride and prejudice: A history of black culture in America* [Motion picture]. United States: Knowledge Unlimited.

Kraft, N. (2004). Students as scholar practitioners. In J. Kincheloe & D. Weil (Eds.), *Critical thinking and learning: An encyclopedia for parents and teachers* (pp. 358-362). Westport, CT: Greenwood Press.

Lewis, B. (2008). *The teen guide to global action: How to connect with others (near & far) to create social change.* Minneapolis, MN: Free Spirit.

Lickona, T. (1992). *Educating for character: How our schools can teach respect and responsibility.* New York, NY: Bantam Books.

Lickona, T. (2004). *Character matters: How to help our children develop good judgment, integrity, and other essential virtues.* New York, NY: Touchstone.

Lickona, T., & Davidson, M. (2005). *Smart & good high schools: Integrating excellence and ethics for success in school, work, and beyond.* Cortland, NY: Center for the 4th and 5th Rs (Respect & Responsibility) & Character Education Partnership.

Lin, J. (2008). Constructing a global ethic of universal love and reconciliation: Reenvisioning peace education. In J. Lin, E. J. Brantmeier, & C. Bruhn (Eds.), *Transforming education for peace.* (pp. 301-316). Charlotte, NC: Information Age Publishing.

Loewen, J. W. (2007). *Lies my teacher told me: Everything your American history textbook got wrong.* New York, NY: Touchstone.

Loris, M. (2007). Using the novel to teach multiculturalism. In C. Irvine (Ed.), *Teaching the novel across the curriculum: A handbook for educators.* (pp. 53-63). Westport, CT: Greenwood Press.

Lourenço, O. (1999). Toward a positive conception of peace. In A. Raviv, L. Oppenheimer, & D. Bar-Tal (Eds.), *How children understand war and peace: A call for international peace education* (pp. 91-108). San Francisco, CA: Jossey-Bass.

Lowry, L. (1993). *The giver.* New York, NY: Random House Children's Books.

Maguire, M. C. (2004). Gandhi and the ancient wisdom of nonviolence. In W. Wink (Ed.), *Peace is the way: Writings on nonviolence from the Fellowship of Reconciliation* (pp. 159-162). Maryknoll, NY: Orbis Books.

McCarthy, C. (2002). *I'd rather teach peace.* Maryknoll, NY: Orbis Books.

McIntosh, P. (2006). White privilege: Unpacking the invisible knapsack. In E. Lee, D. Menkart, & M. Okazawa-Rey (Eds.), *Beyond heroes and holidays: A practical guide to k-12 anti-racist, multicultural education and staff development* (pp. 83-86). Washington, D.C.: Teaching for Change. (Original work published 1988)

McKibben, B., & 350.org. (n.d.). *350.org.* Retrieved September 5, 2010, from http://www.350.org/

Medina, J. (2008). *Brain rules:12 principles for surviving and thriving at work, home, and school.* Seattle, WA: Pear Press.

Merriam, E. (1968). *It doesn't always have to rhyme.* New York, NY: Atheneum.

Mortenson, G., & Relin, D. (2007). *Three cups of tea: One man's mission to promote peace … one school at a time.* New York, NY: Penguin Books.

Mullen, C. (2004). Scholar practitioners as classroom teachers. In J. Kincheloe & D. Weil (Eds.), *Critical thinking and learning: An encyclopedia for parents and teachers* (pp. 353-358). Westport, CT: Greenwood Press.

Nakamura, A., & Nakata, H. (2006, April 29). Diet handed "patriotic" education bill: Proposed change of '47 law has foes, including teachers, fearing Big Brother. *Japan Times.* Retrieved September 5, 2010, from http://search.japantimes.co.jp/cgi-bin/nn20060429a1.html

Naseem, M. A. (2008). Peace-education value of the world wide web: Dialogue and confidence building in cyberspace—An analysis of Chowk.com. In J. Lin, E. Brantmeier, & C. Bruhn (Eds.), *Transforming education for peace* (pp. 185-202). Charlotte, NC: Information Age Publishing.

National Association of Independent Schools [NAIS]. (2008, January 31). Middle school educators. In *Principles of good practice* [Brochure]. Retrieved August 10,

2010, from http://www.nais.org/about/seriesdoc.cfm?
ItemNumber=150586&sn.ItemNumber=146810

National Council for the Social Studies [NCSS]. (1994). Thematic strands. In *Expectations of excellence: Curriculum standards for social studies*. Retrieved September 5, 2010, from http://www.socialstudies.org/standards/strands

National Middle School Association [NMSA]. (2009, November 5). Executive summary. In *This we believe: Keys to educating young adolescents: Position paper of National Middle School Association*. Retrieved September 5, 2010, from http://http://www.nmsa.org/portals/0/pdf/about/twb/This_We_Believe_Exec_Summary.pdf

Nieto, S. (2004). *Affirming diversity: The sociopolitical context of multicultural education* (4th ed.). Boston, MA: Pearson Education.

Nobelity Project. (n.d.). *Nobelity project*. Retrieved September 5, 2010, from http://nobelity.org/

Nobel Prize.org. (n.d.). *Nobel Prize.org: The official site of the Nobel Prize*. Retrieved from http://nobelprize.org/

Noddings, N. (2005a). *The challenge to care in schools: An alternative approach to education*. New York, NY: Teachers College Press.

Noddings, N. (Ed.). (2005b). *Educating citizens for global awareness*. New York, NY: Teachers College Press.

Noddings, N. (2007). *Critical lessons: What our schools should teach*. New York, NY: Cambridge University Press.

Noguera, P., & Cohen, R. (2007). Educators in the war on terrorism. In J. Westheimer (Ed.), *Pledging allegiance: The politics of patriotism in America's schools* (pp. 25-34). New York, NY: Teachers College Press.

Nussbaum, M. (2002, October 25). *Liberal education and global responsibility: A talk for a symposium at Carleton College, in honor of the inauguration of Robert A. Oden, Jr. as president* [Speech]. Retrieved September 5, 2010, from http://www.ditext.com/nussbaum/carleton.html

Palmer, P. (2007). *The courage to teach: Exploring the inner landscape of a teacher's life*. San Francisco, CA: Jossey-Bass.

Peace and Justice Studies Association. (n.d.). Building cultures of peace. In *Peace and Justice Studies Association* [2008 PJSA conference: Call for proposals]. Retrieved September 5, 2010, from http://www.peacejusticestudies.org/conference/2008/call.php

PeaceJam. (2004) *Nobel Prize winners work with youth* [DVD].

PeaceJam Foundation. (n.d.). *PeaceJam: Change starts here*. Retrieved September 5, 2010, from http://www.peacejam.org

PeaceJam Foundation. (2007). *PeaceJam leaders: Designed for youth ages 11-14: Fostering leadership & positive identity through the study of 12 Nobel Peace laureates*. Arvada: CO: Author.

Peace One Day Ltd. (n.d.). *Peace one day*. Retrieved September 5, 2010, from http://www.peaceoneday.org/en/welcome

Pennies for Peace. (2009). *Pennies for peace*. Retrieved September 5, 2010, from http://www.penniesforpeace.org/

Peterson, B. (1994). The complexities of encouraging social action. In B. Bigelow, L. Christensen, S. Karp, B. Miner, & B. Peterson (Eds.), *Rethinking our class-*

rooms: Teaching for equity and justice (pp. 40-42). Milwaukee, WI: Rethinking Schools.

Poliner, R., & Lieber, C. (2004). *The advisory guide: Designing and implementing effective advisory programs in secondary schools.* Cambridge, MA: Educators for Social Responsibility.

Raviv, A., Oppenheimer, L., & Bar-Tal, D. (Eds.). (1999). *How children understand war and peace: A call for international peace education.* San Francisco, CA: Jossey-Bass.

Reardon, B., Cabezudo, A., & Teachers College, Columbia University Peace Education Team. (2002). *Learning to abolish war: Teaching toward a culture of peace: Vol. 1. Rationales for and approaches to peace education.* Retrieved September 5, 2010, from http://www.haguepeace.org/index.php?action=resources

Rodriguez, L. (1995). *The concrete river.* Willimantic, CT: Curbstone Press.

Rosenberg, L. (Ed.). (1999). *The invisible ladder: An anthology of contemporary American poems for young readers.* New York, NY: Henry Holt.

Ryan, M. (2006). My favorite poet: Emily Dickinson. In *Poets.org: Poetry, poems, bios, & more.* Retrieved September 5, 2010, from http://www.poets.org/viewmedia.php/prmMID/19269

Rylant, C. (1990). Comment. In P. Janeczko (Ed.), *The place my words are looking for: What poets say about and through their work* (pp. 109-110). New York, NY: Macmillan Books for Young Readers.

Seligman, M. (2002). *Authentic happiness: Using the new positive psychology to realize your potential for lasting fulfillment.* New York, NY: Free Press.

Semali, L. (2004). Indigenous ways of knowing and critical thinking. In J. Kincheloe & D. Weil (Eds.), *Critical thinking and learning: An encyclopedia for parents and teachers* (pp. 167-171). Westport, CT: Greenwood Press.

Serra, M. (2006). Social action and parent involvement. In K. Berdan, I. Boulton, E. Eidman-Aadahl, J. Fleming, L. Gardner, I. Rogers, & A. Solomon (Eds.), *Writing for a change: Boosting literacy and learning through social action.* (pp. 73-78). San Francisco, CA: Jossey-Bass.

Shaping America: U.S. history to 1877: The slave South [Motion picture]. (2004). United States: Dallas Telelearning.

Sharp, G. (2004). Disregarded history: The power of nonviolent action. In W. Wink (Ed.), *Peace is the way: Writings on nonviolence from the Fellowship of Reconciliation* (pp. 231-235). Maryknoll, NY: Orbis Books. (Original work published 1976)

Sharp, G. (2010). Disregarded history: The power of nonviolent action. In *Fragments* (nonviolence) [Original work published in 1976]. Retrieved September 5, 2010, from James VanHise website: http://www.fragmentsweb.org/fourtx/dishistx.html

Suvanjieff, I., & Engle, D. G. (2008). *PeaceJam: A billion simple acts of peace.* New York, NY: Puffin Books.

Swofford, A. (2004, May 31). My turn: The homecoming, and then the hard part [Editorial]. *Newsweek.* Retrieved September 5, 2010, from http://www.msnbc.msn.com/id/5031075/site/newsweek/

Taylor, M. D. (1976). *Roll of thunder, hear my cry.* New York, NY: Puffin Books.

Teaching Tolerance. (n.d.). *Mix it up at lunch day.* Retrieved September 5, 2010, from Teaching Tolerance: A Project of the Southern Poverty Law Center website: http://www.tolerance.org/mix-it-up

Thompson, M., & Barker, T. (2004). *The pressured child: Helping your child find success in school and life.* New York, NY: Ballantine Books.

Tippett, K. (Director). (2007). Listening generously: The medicine of Rachel Naomi Remen [Radio series episode]. In K. Tippett & K. Moos (Producer), *Speaking of faith.* Saint Paul, MN: American Public Radio. Retrieved September 5, 2010, from http://speakingoffaith.publicradio.org/programs/listeninggenerously/

United Nations Association of the United States of America [UNA-USA]. (n.d.). Retrieved September 5, 2010, from http://www.unausa.org/

United Nations cyber schoolbus. (n.d.). Retrieved September 5, 2010, from http://cyberschoolbus.un.org/

United Nations General Assembly. (1948, December 10). *Universal declaration of human rights.* Retrieved September 5, 2010, from http://www.un.org/en/documents/udhr/

Utopia. (n.d.). *Encarta world English dictionary (North American edition).* Retrieved September 5, 2010, from Microsoft Corporation website: http://encarta.msn.com/encnet/features/dictionary/DictionaryResults.aspx?lextype=3&search=utopia

Villaverde, L. (2004). Developing curriculum and critical pedagogy. In J. Kincheloe & D. Weil (Eds.), *Critical thinking and learning: An encyclopedia for parents and teachers* (pp. 131-135). Westport, CT: Greenwood Press.

Vincent, P. F. (2004). Introduction. In G. Turner & P. F. Vincent (Eds.), *Promising practices in character education:12 more success stories from around the country* (Vol. 2, pp. vii-xii) [Introduction]. Chapel Hill, NC: Character Development Group.

Vincent, P. F. (2006). Considerations of civility. In P. F. Vincent, D. Wangaard, & P. Weimer, *Restoring school civility: Creating a caring, responsible, and productive school* (pp. 7-31). Chapel Hill, NC: Character Development Group.

Viola, H. J., & Margolis, C. (Eds.). (1991). *Seeds of change.* Washington, DC: Smithsonian.

Wade, R. C. (2007). *Social studies for social justice: Teaching strategies for the elementary classroom.* New York, NY: Teachers College Press.

Wagner, T. (2010). *The global achievement gap: Why even our best schools don't teach the new survival skills our children need—And what we can do about it.* New York, NY: Basic Books.

Weil, D. (2004). Values and dispositions of critical thinking: Developing habits of mind as moral commitments to thought. In J. Kincheloe & D. Weil (Eds.), *Critical thinking and learning: An encyclopedia for parents and teachers* (pp. 484-490). Westport, CT: Greenwood Press.

West, C. (2004). *Democracy matters: Winning the fight against imperialism.* New York, NY: Penguin Press.

Whelan, G. (2000). *Homeless bird.* New York, NY: HarperCollins.

Whitman, W. (1867). Song of myself (verse 2). In *Poetry Foundation* [Poem]. Retrieved September 5, 2010, from http://www.poetryfoundation.org/archive/ poem.html?id=174745

Wiggins, G., & McTighe, M. (2005). *Understanding by design.* Boston, MA: Prentice Hall.

Williams-Boyd, P. (2004). Middle schools: Curiosity and critical thinking. In J. Kincheloe & D. Weil (Eds.), *Critical thinking and learning: An encyclopedia for parents and teachers* (pp. 92-96). Westport, CT: Greenwood Press.

Winfield, B. (1999). Community-based service: Re-creating the beloved community. In L. R. Forcey & I. M. Harris (Eds.), *Peacebuilding for adolescents: Strategies for educators and community leaders* (pp. 290-307). New York, NY: Peter Lang.

York, S. (Director). (2000). *A force more powerful* [Motion picture]. United States: York Zimmerman.

Zinn, H. (1995). Just and unjust wars. In S. Lynd & A. Lynd (Eds.), *Nonviolence in America: A documentary history* (pp. 492-503). Maryknoll, NY: Orbis Books.

Zinn, H. (2002). *You can't be neutral on a moving train: A personal history for our times.* Boston, MA: Beacon Press.

Zinn, H. (2005). *A people's history of the United States: 1492-present* (Zinn Education Project Edition ed.). New York, NY: Harper Perennial Modern Classics. (Original work published 1980)

INDEX

ABOUT THE AUTHOR

Susan Gelber Cannon is a peace and character educator with 25 years of classroom experience. She has also taught middle school students and trained preservice and in-service teachers in China, Japan, and the United States. Her special fields of interest are character, global, multicultural, and peace education: developing teaching methods to help students think, care, and act honorably, locally and globally. Trained in moral development at Harvard Graduate School of Education, Cannon teaches history and English, as well as Model UN, peacemaking, and debate at The Episcopal Academy, near Philadelphia, Pennsylvania, United States.

CPSIA information can be obtained at www.ICGtesting.com
Printed in the USA
BVOW030355171111

276203BV00004B/1/P